D1461755

# Guilty Until
## YOU PROVE YOURSELF INNOCENT

## Welcome to America

**Ricky Dale**

ACORN BOOKS
www.acornbooks.co.uk

First published worldwide by
Acorn Books
*www.acornbooks.co.uk*

Acorn Books is an imprint of
Andrews UK Limited
The Hat Factory
Bute Street
Luton, LU1 2EY
*www.andrewsuk.com*

# Contents

# Guilty-Until
## YOU PROVE YOURSELF INNOCENT

### Welcome to America

*This book is based on a true story.*

*Dedicated to Cheryle & Brandon*

Chapter 1

# Welcome to Hell

*God has mercifully ordered that the human brain works slowly; first the blow, hours afterwards the bruise.*

Walter De La Mare

I was sitting on the floor with my back to the wall, the floor and wall of a jail cell. I was suffering from concussion and having dizzy spells. I had a very severe migraine, a cut down my face, a graze on my right cheek and the inside of my lip was bust. Before I sat down on the floor and as I was being lead into the jail cell I was limping quite badly. The only clothes I had on were a small pair of shorts and a very thin T-shirt, well more of a white vest really. It was freezing cold. The air con must have been on full.

A Rastafarian gentleman had his head resting on my legs, just above my knees. His dreadlocks were matted with thick grease and dirt. The smell from this guy was beyond words. It was very obvious that this gentleman had shit himself. He smelt like a cesspit on legs.

It was a small cell holding about 15 guys including myself. You could not swing a cat in this hellhole. Some of these guys you would not want to meet in a dark alley even armed with a machine gun of the heavy-duty type. They looked very evil and dangerous to say the least. Some of the guys in there looked very drugged up and others just very drunk. Some of them had obviously been in a fight. They were bruised and wearing blood stained clothes. At one point one of the guys stood and had a piss. I could not move out of his way and his piss splashed my feet. He did this despite the fact that there was a toilet in this cell. I asked the raster man to move.

"Fuck you! Mother fucking white piece of shit," he replied.

When a police officer passed by I asked when it would be possible to talk to someone about what had happened that night but I was just ignored and told by another officer to shut the fuck up.

This night was to become one of the longest of my life; well that's what I thought at the time. Little was I to know that this was only the beginning of what was to turn out to be one of many long nights. A real nightmare was about to start.

I could not believe what had happened to me or how I had come to be arrested without being given the chance to tell my side of events. No one to this day ever asked me for a written statement as to what actually happened and worse still no one even seemed interested. I cannot believe, even now, that me and Lily (my wife) never sat down and discussed what had happened. Surely if this had happened they would have seen through Lily and seen who was telling the truth? But no. I thought it was only a matter of time for this to happen and for all this to be sorted out. Lily must surely be in trouble for wasting police time. Our marriage was definitely over.

Throughout this night I had to sit with this vile smell in my nostrils. Every 5 minutes seemed to last an eternity. No one was talking to anyone in this cell. The hatred I felt was mind blowing. The light in the cell is now dimmed.

Everyone now seemed to be asleep. I heard the odd groan and I stared at the ceiling. I had tears running down my face. If my family had known of this and they could have seen the situation I was in they would have been horrified. My brother John was a police officer back in England and he would also have been horrified and angry.

2

Before moving to America I was married back in England and had a lovely son called Craig, he had Downs Syndrome. As I thought about my wonderful family, five sisters and two brothers, my wonderful son and my beautiful house I left behind my tears continued to flow.

The only crime, if I had committed one, was that I stood firmly by my beliefs. My marriage vows meant everything to me "for better or for worse, in sickness and in health, for richer or for poorer, as long as you both shall live."

I knew now my wife Lily was ill in the mind and I really believed that I needed to be strong and to stand by her, to make her happy. To show her what love really was all about. I really did think things would work out for us in the end.

I knew Lily had had a terrible time in the past and I wanted to prove to her that we could be very happy together. I needed us to be happy. I felt a real failure. I wanted all of Lily's horrors of the past to be gone forever but sadly for me Lily could not take this step. It was impossible for her to believe in herself. I was due to pay a very heavy price for what some people might say was my blind stupidity. But even then I still believed that I had done the right thing.

You do not cut and run because things become difficult. I was now really, really thirsty and I needed a drink of water badly. My mouth was very dry and my head was hurting. I thought I needed to see a doctor.

As daylight came there had been a shift change and a lot of different officers were now here. Time itself seemed to not move at all and appeared to be standing still.

I was now really desperate for a drink of anything, water, anything. A lady police officer passed by and I asked her if it was possible for me to have a drink of water. I told her that I was in a lot of pain and felt quite ill. She looked straight through me and said nothing.

This stinking rotten Raster man now had his head on my stomach. I had to move him or I was going to be violently sick

3

all over him. I slowly and firmly pushes him off and he turned and looked at me.

"If we weren't in this cell, you white piece of chicken shit, I would kill you mother fucker."

I tried to tell him I was sorry and that my legs were going numb with his weight and that I felt really sick and I need to get up and stretch my legs. When I did try to stand I felt very, very dizzy. I thought I was also suffering vertigo from my concussion.

Another police officer passed by and as politely as I could manage I askes him if I could please have a drink of water. He just said yes in a while after I had been processed. What did he mean?

I told him I desperately needed to speak to someone about what had happened that night. He simply replied that I had to wait until I had my photo taken and had been processed.

"Wait a minute officer."

But he just walked away ignoring me.

"You dumb shit," said the Raster man, "you're wasting your time talking to these assholes, stupid mother fucker!!!"

The others started to wake up but no one was talking. It was as if it wasn't the done thing. Everyone just seemed to stare at each other but when you looked into their eyes they would just look away or stare right at you with a chilling cold gaze till you looked away again.

Slowly the police started to take us out of the cell one at a time to another room. When I was taken I was handcuffed to an officer and stood against a wall. Then my photo was taken and I was processed. I asked again if I could speak to someone, anyone but I was told no and that I would be moved very soon. I was by now in a lot of pain begging to have a drink of water and an aspirin. All these people were very cold and indifferent to me. One officer, a very mean looking man, coldly looked through me and said

"You're not in a fucking hotel. You're here because you've committed a serious crime."

I tried to tell him that I had not committed any crime at all that I had done nothing and was innocent of any crime. If only I could talk to someone this whole affair could be quickly sorted out. He then replied

"Listen to me asshole, in here; you're guilty until you prove your innocence!!"

"You are English is that correct?"

"Yes," I replied.

"Then welcome to America sir."

I then said to him if I couldn't speak to someone, how could I possibly prove my innocence. Was he not interested that I was innocent? He just stared and said nothing. I then asked him if I could please have something to wear as I was very cold and my feet were also bare. He laughed at me and said I would be given a nice new suit later. I felt really angry at this and thought quietly to myself.

"Fuck you!!"

I thought he could see this in my face but I had said nothing out loud. I just felt a terrible fear over what would happen to me next and what if anything I could do about it.

I was next taken out to a police van with very small windows. We were all handcuffed to each other. One or two of the inmates were having a conversation. I felt totally bewildered by it all. This was not a bad dream, this was definitely happening to me. Soon after, we reversed to a ramp and were quickly taken out, lead into a large room and as the doors to this room opened I heard a horrible whacking noise. This sound made me shudder. The noise was to become very familiar to me. Overlooking this room was a control centre with large windows so that the police could view all of the inmates. As we entered this room one at a time the police did a roll call and checked that everyone was accounted for. Once in the room I could see that it had at floor level small rooms with bunk beds and steps leading to more small rooms again with more bunk beds.

I was not given one of these rooms. I was made to sleep on the floor on a thin mattress with no pillow. I was still limping, still felt dizzy and was very unsteady on my feet. My head was really hurting. People seemed to be looking at me. Possibly this was because I was still only wearing shorts and a thin T shirt with nothing on my feet. I was very cold and thought that if I was not careful I could end up with pneumonia. I was now starting to get a bad cough and horrified does not cover how I feel about my situation.

I kept myself to myself and I was being given some very nasty looks from the other guys in the room. Some of the inmates were having a conversation so to be friendly I tried to speak to them but they just looked at me as if I was a piece of shit then turned away. I heard a voice behind me saying

"Are you English?"

"Yes," I replied.

The voice then said,

"English be careful who you speak to. You could get beaten up in here, and no one will help you".

"English" was soon to become my regular name. At least someone had spoken to me without turning nasty. I turned to ask his name and to my surprise he told me it was none of my fucking business and just walked away. I just could not relate to any of these guys I felt that they didn't like me being in their space.

Food was now being brought into the room on a trolley with plastic trays covered with plastic tops so they were stackable on top of each other.

I was hungry but more so incredibly thirsty. When I was given my tray I took the top off, looked at my food and felt really sick. I drank a carton of orange juice but couldn't eat any of the food, it didn't look very good at all. I was happy I at least had a drink. They had also given me a large container of water from which I continued to quench my thirst.

The guy that had spoken to me earlier now said

" Hey English are you not going to eat your food?"

"No."

" Can I have it then English?"

"Yes if you want it."

He took it without a word of thanks and walked away.

I was to quickly learn that I could get a response from these inmates through food. When I was given anything I didn't want I would simply speak out loud

"Does someone want this?"

More than one guy would say "I'll have it!"

I simply put it on a table and said here guys and walked away from it.

They would race each other to get my food, but strangely they didn't look at me in a menacing way anymore and some gave me a very slight nod. Oh, I thought I was making progress.

Whenever I saw an officer leaving the control room I would limp across and ask very politely if it was possible for me to have an interview with someone about my arrest. They told me that someone soon would be in touch when the time was right.

I told them that I wasn't very well and also very cold. I had nothing except the thinnest of mats to sleep on. No pillow or blanket.

They told me I would be given a blanket later. And that tomorrow I would be given a medical and moved on in the next day or so to a stockade.

"What do you mean by a stockade I need to speak to someone, anyone".

I had done nothing wrong and when was I getting out of here!!!! The police officer just walked away.

One guy nearby said to me "We're all innocent in here English".

I was eventually given a blanket of sorts, very thin but no pillow. I just lay down on my mat and curled up in a ball, freezing cold with nothing on my feet, which were turning a pinkie blue colour. On the cold floor I noticed the soles of my feet seemed to be getting hard.

During the night I just couldn't get comfortable at all. My head was still hurting and my cough was getting worse and I felt my situation was becoming surreal, unbelievable and that the rest of the world had forgotten me.

I kept saying to myself that Chuck and Wendy would surely find out what has happened and come to my rescue. But I was now getting worried that in here I would get beaten up. How could Lily have done such a thing to me? I had tried so hard to make her happy. At this point I had no idea what Lily had told the authorities. I feared the worse. This was going to be an incredibly long cold night.

## Chapter 2

# This Isn't Happening To Me

*Isn't it nice to think that tomorrow is a new day with no mistakes in it yet?*

LM Montgomery

The next morning they came for me early around 7.30 or 8.00 and gave out razor blades of the Bic type.

If you wanted a razor they took your name and then later at a certain time collected back all the blades ticking your name off a list. My stubble was by now quite bad and the razor I'd been given was blunt, used no doubt many times before. When I did use it it cut my face. It was difficult to shave because of the dried cuts and grazes on my face. My lip was busted and cut inside. It was very painful to shave completely but I did my best.

I looked around the room and carefully listened to the murmur of conversation going on around me. Listening, I soon picked up the fact that a lot of these guys appeared to be experts in the law and they were speaking to each other about their arrests, the crimes they'd been arrested for and what advice they could give each other even to the extent of which lawyer or attorney would be best.

Breakfast arrived. The food was still horrendously bad.

I ate some of the bread and again offered the rest of my food to whoever wanted it. I knew I had to eat something.

The atmosphere you could have cut with a knife. The characters in here were ruthless, hard and dangerous. It seemed like I had been here forever already.

Suddenly, two male police officers and a female police officer arrived. It was difficult to tell at first sight, which one of them in actual fact was the female. She was extremely butch, more like a Russian soldier. I wouldn't have wanted to meet her in a dark alley. We were taken away, handcuffed again to each other in pairs, told to take a shower and to put over each other a quantity of white delousing powder. Whilst showering I overheard a couple of the guys saying that the white Englishman would make a nice bitch for someone. What could I say except that the mere thought of such a fate made me shudder? After the shower I was given an orange suit to wear. The police officers always seemed to be shouting.

What a sad sight, me in an orange jail bird outfit. I just hit another low!

How could this be possible? What would my family and friends think if they saw me now? There I was again, handcuffed to some idiot that didn't want to be handcuffed to me. The black lads didn't take kindly to being cuffed to me. It didn't bother me what colour the guy was. I found it very unpleasant just being handcuffed to anyone. I was then taken for a medical where I sat at a desk. My doctor turned out to be a female doctor and when she started to speak I was pleasantly surprised. She was polite and seemed very nice. After recent events this came as a relief.

She asked me lots of questions and did a thorough check up on me. I told her the pain I still had and about my dizzy spells. She was very concerned. I asked her if she would take a note of my injuries. She asked if I'd been in a fight and I replied yes and no. I told her about hurting my leg when I had slipped on the stairs but that my wife had caused the rest of my injuries.

A bunch of names were called out and my name was amongst them. I asked her again not to forget to write down my cuts and scrapes including the graze on my face and my cut inside my lip. I told her that I had committed no crime, that my wife had a serious drug problem and that no one had yet interviewed me or asked me about the events leading to my arrest. I asked her if she could possibly ask around for someone to come and talk to me so that I could give my version of what had happened. The doctor told me she would have a word with someone but really she was only there to do the medical.

I asked again about the dizzy spells and she told me I had a slight concussion.

By now I was feeling quite emotional, embarrassed and sorry for being upset at my horrifying situation. I still couldn't believe what my wife had done to me. The doctor was very nice to me but she said she had to carry on with her next interviewee. I thanked her for her help and understanding but had to go. At least I had met someone human. All these events took up most of the day and by the time I returned to the hellhole it was early evening.

After arriving back at the jail, dinner was brought to us. All the others had already eaten. We were late back anyway. I just picked at my food then gave the rest of it away. As I looked around me I felt it was impossible for anyone to understand the total and utter helplessness and despair I found myself in. When I looked at this ridiculous outfit I was being made to wear I thought what a dickhead I looked. I felt outraged at what was happening to me and anger at the lack of human rights. What happened to innocent until proven guilty? I felt like I'd been sentenced after having been to court which so far I hadn't. As the officer had previously told me "Guilty until you prove yourself innocent" and then when he had added, "welcome to America," I felt like I was going mad my on-going concussion not helping. I felt that I had missed part of what had happened to me then I realised that nothing was missing it was all real, a bad dream and one that it didn't look like I

was going to wake up from. Statue of Liberty.....Bullshit!!!
Then I thought to myself perhaps they'd made a mistake and
processed the wrong guy. Yes a mistake with the paperwork!!
No, No I was loosing it. I could only sit and pray to God...
where was he now when I needed him????

Aahh!! Right! He was out to lunch. He wasn't here, this was
hell.

I just had to sit tight and wait, surely it was only going to be
a matter of time before I had a proper interview with someone
from the legal establishment. Only then would I feel I had
been given assistance and help.

What was Lily trying to do to me?

All I had ever done was try to love her, help her to be happy.
This was really awful and I felt very emotional. I felt that I
could not allow these cretins inside to see me upset otherwise
they would think I was a right pussy and that image would not
have helped me in here.

Then it was time for sleep. The lights dimmed and all I
could think about were pleasant things such as my mother,
brother, sister, my son Craig and my home. Also some of the
shows I had appeared in as I was an entertainer, a damn good
one.

The other thing that struck me was the colour prejudice
that still exists in America.

Back home in England, I had some really good friends who
were black and wonderful neighbours to me. Friends who
came into my home, put the kettle on and asked me if I wanted
a cup of tea as they were making themselves one and then
asked where are the biscuits? They then sat and had a chat to
me. I didn't think any of these fuckers in here were going to
make me a cup of tea.

I had no doubt that I was hated by some here in my new
home simply because I was white. In this hellhole there were

many different races but not that many whites as yet. The other thing in here was when they asked each other, "What are you in here for bro?" The answer was "I'm innocent, I've done nothing wrong, they have the wrong guy." They laughed. It was usually the black guys that talked to each other like this. When they did, they said, "Yo bro, big five, how ya doin nigger"? I can only imagine what would happen to me if I said that to one of these guys. This was only said between one black guy to another.

The lights went out. Another long night ahead. Yes, the shit was slowly but surely hitting the fan.

# Chapter 3

# A Brief History and Betrayal

*I hope you feel better about yourself. I hope you feel alive. I hope that good things happen to you, and I hope that when the inevitable bad things happen you can handle them and learn a lesson and move on.*
Stephen Bowe

I was married in England with a son Craig who had Down Syndrome. He was now ten years old, a beautiful little boy and I love him dearly. Sadly his mom, my wife, had an affair for 5 maybe 6 years. When I found out I divorced her. My home was very near to where Craig and his mum lived. She met a guy in the RAF and moved to Wales. I had a good relationship with him and he was very good to my son and my son liked him but because of the 200 mile distance between there and Wales, I didn't really get to see much of my son. This was one of the reasons I ended up moving to America.

I had been in the states for approximately two and a half years and I had, again, already been married before I met Lily. No, I didn't like bloody wedding cake!! Sadly that hadn't turned out well either, but that was another horror: Her name was Donna, another American.

Donna played a very serious part in my story and this mess, I will not discuss Donna now, I will come back to her... go on I hear you say, but no I will have to come back to Donna later, you'll have to wait.

Now, before I start to tell you about my final day of freedom, I need to say my relationship with my now wife Lily had been an extremely difficult one and very traumatic one to say the least. The events in the evening of our final day were to be the final straw, as the saying goes, the straw that breaks the camel's back. I knew in my heart that things were coming to an end, unless Lily could change her ways. I wanted so desperately for us to be happy and even on the last day I still loved my wife Lily. There's a saying "You can lead a horse to water but you can't make it drink." Sadly in Lily's case this was a very true one. I was told by my close friends and by some of Lily's close friends that I should have left her long before. I had known Lily for only one year or so and we had been married just over six months. It was only two weeks ago that we had our marital fraud interview. I married both Lily and Donna for all the right reasons, I loved them both very much, I did not marry either of them for a bloody green card. I actually had other opportunities where I could have very easily dated and married and had wealthy partners but I ended up with two who were not well off at all and both extremely difficult women, both of which carried an awful lot of baggage. I really did believe in both cases that we would be happy. You always start out happy, but I knew very soon into my marriage with Donna that it wasn't going to work out, because of the politics of Donna's life. We didn't make it to the Marital Fraud Interview and despite the fact that we were not together she wanted us to attend the interview as she said it would help me.

"No," I said, "Unless we are to be a happily married couple, I'm not going to any interview."

Donna had a lot of financial difficulties, I know she was going back to her ex, he still loved her and she had a son to him: Eric. Her ex had a very good job and he wasn't short of money. I told her I loved her and that we could work things out. Donna married me for all the wrong reasons, then simply dumped me when she realised I wasn't going to become a star as quickly as she thought I would. I actually gave a loan of 1300 dollars after we split up, she never paid me back.

I struggled to understand why people destroyed people's lives when all I had done was my best to make us happy. I actually thought Donna might have thought that if she went to the Marital Fraud Interview, in some way she would think she was helping me and that if I ever was to be successful that she'd possibly come back at me for money. I just wanted us to be happy and sort out any money problems she might have had.

As I had said before I came to America I was a professional entertainer. I wrote my own songs and I walked away from everything. I was a well-established entertainer with an agent and plenty of work. On the night I met Lily, I was attending the grand opening of a new club in Fort Lauderdale called the Village Zoo. I had met with the owner a few days earlier and we got on very well. He said he didn't know if they were going to have cabaret but gave me a VIP entry and said I could bring a partner if I wished. When I arrived at the club, there was a long cue to get in so I walked to the front to give the doorman my ticket. I was alone, no wife or girlfriend as I was now divorced from Donna. Lily took my arm and said,

"I'm with you sweetie."

Lily was wearing a really nice red dress, quite short and she looked a really fit woman psychically with a very cheeky smile. I thought "What the hell, I like people with that tenacity."

I told her my name was Ricky, which was my stage name, and she said "Hi, I'm Lily."

We went in together. I thought once we were inside that she would go off and do her own thing, but she stayed with me. When she hit the dance floor, she didn't stop. She was incredibly fit with a very strong grip, she told me she'd been a trapeze artist in a circus and more recently a jockey.

"Well," I said, "what a coincidence, when I first left school I was an apprentice jockey."

We both laughed and I took a liking to her. Lily was very forward and at the end of the night she said, "We'll meet again Ricky, I'll phone you sometime next week but there will be no sex."

What a thing to say I thought.

Well that's how we met. I dearly wish I had stayed at home that night. At the time I was living with a dear friend Doug. Doug was like a brother to me, I will tell you more about Doug as time passes by.

My final day of freedom, on the night of my arrest we had invited Chuck and Wendy to go out with us, but first they came to our home. I had a long phone call from my mother and some of my sisters. I spoke with them for around 45/50 minutes. Lily chatted to my family for a while but she seemed on edge. I also introduced Chuck and Wendy to my family. We then watched a video of me singing a song I had wrote myself about a puppet with children that neither Lily or Chuck and Wendy had seen before. I love kids! Lily was not bothered. We then left to go to a pub restaurant where I was to do an audition for the owner.

We were to have a meal before I sang. I didn't really like to eat before doing a show and Lily kept pushing me to get up and sing. I hadn't even finished my meal and I told her to calm down. I would get up and sing when the time was right. She didn't like this and seemed a little agitated. Lily was also complaining about how cold it was when we were having dinner, so we moved tables. She was now starting to act more and more strange. Lily went to the toilet, Chuck and Wendy mentioned how Lily seemed in a strange mood. When Lily returned from the toilet she started to get a little loud, insisting I go to sing now.

"I'll go when I'm ready!" I said.

Chuck and Wendy noticed how she was getting more agitated. I didn't notice as much as I had my mind firmly on the show I was about to do. My show went really well and the owner was really happy.

"I'll call you soon Ricky." He said. Lily was very happy with me again.

We all left to go to the Mark 21000 Club. People got up to sing and a lady called Maria played the piano. I was very popular here. People used to take the tab for my table as a thank you for me singing. I was very happy and Chuck and Wendy loved every minute of it. Lily also seemed very happy. Lily was now getting quite tipsy to say the least, not really drunk but on her way and I'd noticed she'd been to the toilet a few times. She was being quite affectionate to me and even hinted to me that I was going to get lucky tonight.

Well what a really wonderful night. It was time to leave and we said goodnight to Chuck and Wendy outside. They then went to their car.

Chuck and Wendy were dear friends to me. I loved them very much and they were like family to me. They were in their later fifty's, very caring, loving, family people. Two of the most honest people you could wish to meet. I met them through my singing. I did singing telegrams for a company in Fort Lauderdale called Captain Telegrams. Chuck had phoned this company to ask if they had something different, a little special and they told him about me. It was Chuck and Wendy's anniversary, Chuck was told I did specialised Romantic singing telegrams and that if Chuck wished he could give me champagne, flowers, chocolates and a balloon with a message from him. Chuck was very, very interested and asked for my phone number as he wished to speak to me first. When Chuck phoned me, I sang Three Times a Lady and Lady in Red over the phone.

"Definitely," Chuck said.

Chuck was a very professional person, a computer expert, very thorough in his work, a very respected man. I went to a tax office where Wendy worked and I sang to her in front of the other staff and whoever was in the office at the time. Chuck stayed in touch and we became very good friends. Chuck and Wendy, by this final night were already aware of my problems with Lily. I'd told them that Lily had a problem with drugs and that Lily had mood swings during the course of the day. One moment she could be very loving, the next a very hard and aggressive person. Lily had very little time for Chuck and Wendy. I think she was a little jealous of the love and support they showed me which was very sad really as they tried to be friends to Lily and they were the type of friends Lily did need in her life. I must be honest; I really didn't think much of Lily's friends at all. They all seemed really dubious. I now know where she got the drugs from, well some of them anyway. When we visited some of her friends I'd be left outside in the car for quite some time. This I didn't like but she told me they were very unclean people and it was dirty inside. I did my best to draw her away from these folks but she said they were like family to her as Chuck and Wendy and Doug were to me so I respected that and kept my distance. Not at all correct.

The area where Lily lived was a very bad area and known for drugs and a red light zone. I was never allowed to just turn up at Lily's home. I had to beep her first. When we decided to be together we found an apartment that was larger than Lily's house and in a bit better area but still a little dangerous to be out at night alone. It wasn't far from the 1.95. Lots of down and outs slept near to our home which was very near to a black area not far from The Fort Lauderdale Airport.

In our relationship sometimes Lily would be romantic and loving. But as time passed she became less and less romantic and more and more unpleasant. It was just sex in the end and I would often say I didn't just want sex; I wanted to light candles, have romantic music and then at some point make love to my wife and relax with a glass of wine. It became so bad that when I complained, she jumped on the bed pulled her panties to one side, and say. "Here sweetie. Here's some romance, stick the fucker in and get it over with."

This was when her mood swings were unbearable. I'd just go for a walk, realising what a serious problem I now had. This I know was the drugs but other times she could be a really sweet and a funny person to be around and that was the person I fell in love with. It was clear to me, she must be doing more drugs. When I was out working in the day, Lily would often drink cheap Champaign and I'd come home and she'd often be in bed, very tired. One of Lily's party tricks, which became very annoying to me and very embarrassing, was that she was very proud of her breast implants. Three thousand dollars they had cost and she'd pull her top down and show people especially when she'd being doing drugs and drink. Before our final night out, Chuck and Wendy had told me a few weeks earlier that Lily had turned up at their house in the day. This was totally out of character for Lily to do this as she had very little to do with them. She thought they didn't really like her. That was not true. They thought she could be very nice, but it was clear for them to see that Lily had problems and they were very concerned and didn't think she was right for me. Lily had a cup of tea with them and suddenly said,

"I'm glad Ricky has got you, as he's going to need you soon."

Shortly after Lily left. They told me what she had said and I simply had no idea what was going on in Lily's head. I told Chuck and Wendy that if Lily didn't stop the drink and drugs and show me more respect and more love I would leave her and go back to Doug's house at West Palm Beach.

I asked Lily about her visit to Chuck and Wendy's and she just said she wanted to visit them and gave me no other explanation as to why I would be needing them very soon. I thought she was now playing mind games. I had to tell you about all of this as it was very relevant. When Lily gave me no explanation about what she meant about me needing Chuck and Wendy very soon, I told her that I had told them if she didn't stop the drugs and drink and show me more love and respect and if we didn't start being happy, that I was going to leave her and go back to Doug's in West Palm Beach. She was horrified!! She told me very angrily,

"If you ever do leave me, you fucking arsehole, you won't go to live with Doug, you'll go back to fucking England with all your family you talk about! You're a threat to my lawsuit and two million dollars!"

I told her I wasn't interested in her lawsuit that I'd leave and divorce her and get on with my life.

"No," she said, "you'll go back to fucking England."

I have to say my relationship with Lily was now more difficult than ever before and things were to get far more traumatic for me very soon.

So now, back to the Mark 21000 club. Chuck and Wendy had now said goodbye and left in their car. Lily was being very nice to me now and as we walked to our car she was laughing. As we get near the car she pulled her dress down, flashing her tits and said, "Look at me," licking her lips. I told her to stop being silly and get in the car before someone saw her.

She was laughing in the car, telling me how much she loved me and how proud she was when she saw me singing in to the club that night. She said, "When we get home, I'm going to light some candles, put some romantic music on and make love to you." She was smiling, looking at me in a really loving way, stroking the side of my face. I put some music on the radio and Lily fell asleep. Apart from Lily being a little strange at times, tonight was actually a really nice evening with friends, Lily really captured me, I had a desperate need to be loved, to feel loved. I was unfortunately still in love with this idiot. My emotions were totally messed up.

At the moment, this seemed to be the woman I fell in love with and I felt a kind of false sense of security, thinking maybe she could possibly pull through. I felt confused, happy, but sad at the same time. There are still many things I haven't told you that had happened with Lily. At this moment I was supposed to believe she wasn't not doing drugs, but in my heart I believed that even tonight with Chuck and Wendy that Lily had done some drugs. I did say, for better or for worse, in sickness and in health, but how far could I possibly run with this? I reminded myself what my dear friend Doug told me,

"Ricky, leave Lily, I know you love her, but she's a dangerous woman. She somehow, one day, will get you in a lot of trouble; you may even end up in jail if you're not careful."

I could never say I wasn't warned could I? Doug said Lily was terribly damaged. He said I had been a very good husband, hard working and that I'd already taken more than anyone he knew could possibly take, but Lily was totally incapable of trusting anyone. All Lily's life had been tragic. She'd been abused by other partners and Lily's family were a waste of time. Her mom was an alcoholic. Lily's two daughters only wanted their mum when they wanted something or if they thought she had some money. One of Lily's daughters knew that Lily had a cocaine problem, but despite the fact that both daughters couldn't understand why I was with their mum as I was so different to their mum. They knew she had a lot of problems and could be very difficult and as they loved their mum, one of the daughters actually asked me not to give up on her and that she could be a very good person and become a good wife. They feared that if Lily lost me, that I was probably her last chance and that there mum would possibly end up dead with cocaine and drink.

Talk about blowing me away. Lily was still asleep in the car. She looked so peaceful, like butter wouldn't melt in her mouth as the saying goes. My mind was all over the place. I started to remind myself of a very horrific thing Lily had done to me not so long before, something I could never forget but could try to forgive her for although I was finding it very hard. One day we'd been on the beach, we were having a lovely day, but what was to happen next no one could have possibly thought possible.

We went to a bar close to the beach and we were having a drink. It was a very nice bar and we were getting along very well with the bar staff. Lily told them I was a singer and she then asked me to sing to them with no music, a song called Annie's Song, a John Denver classic. So I did and everyone clapped except one guy who was trying to take the piss out of me. He was very drunk, an arrogant man, no one liked him and everybody said not to take any notice of him that he was a fucking arsehole. He then gave me a dollar bill, saying that was all I was worth and that that was too much. I gave him the money back. Lily to my surprise became very angry with me. She took back the dollar bill and I then took it back off her and gave it back to this guy.

"We don't need the money from the likes of him." I said. She stormed off and left me in the bar. The guy left laughing at me. All the people in the bar said he was a complete dickhead. "Ignore him Ricky!" they all said.

Lily did not return to the bar and her car had gone. I waited a few hours but then took a taxi home. Lily was not at home and I was locked out. I'd left my key in the house. I had to contact the landlord through a neighbour so he could let me in. Lily didn't come home and I was out of my mind with worry. I phoned everybody later that night. Lily left me not knowing where she was and didn't phone for two days. When she did finally phone she was uncontrollably emotional.

"I've done something very bad Rick, very, very bad, some very bad things, I'm so sorry, you don't deserve this shit, you are a very good person, you'll not be able to forgive me it's so bad, keep my dog, everything in the house, I'm never coming back."

She then put the phone down. I just sat in total silence, wondering what the hell to do. What had she gone and done now? I felt really sick. But I had to try and pull myself together. I had a very important show to do that night. I just had to believe she'd come home at some point. The show I was doing was for Rob Freeman. Rob and I were at that time in the process of putting a new production company together. We were to be partners, both on salaries I was to be the only artist on our label at first. A banker from Brickal Ave Miami was putting up the money, 350000 dollars. Michael Bordarsky and Alan Chacoby, music attorneys to the Bee Gees were to handle all our legal affairs. I had to attend a wedding where I was to sing only one song, Bryan Adams, *Everything I Do, I Do It For You*, from the film Robin Hood Prince of Thieves. Rob had been Number 1 billboard producer with eight platinum albums.

Before I left the house to go to Miami for this wedding, Lily still hadn't phoned me, I was worried sick.

When I arrived at the wedding, Rob asked where Lily was and I said I didn't know. Rob knew I had problems with her. He never really got to know her, but said I was far better off without her.

I had met Rob a month or so before I married Lily. Rob came to our wedding with his wife to be and his two daughters. He played the organ, the wedding march. We married at the Calder Race Track Chappell. I will tell you more about the wedding later. The run up to our wedding and the wedding itself was very eventful, nothing normal happens around me, that's for sure.

I arrived home from Rob's wedding very late. It was a fair drive but when I got home there were no messages on the phone from Lily. The next day I just sat and waited then at 3pm she finally phoned me. She was in a really bad way, far worse than before and she told me again what a terrible, terrible thing she had done and that she was a bad, bad person. I told her to come home and that she was not a bad person. I told her she had been let down by so many people, deeply hurt and whatever she had done we would work it out somehow.

She said she wanted to die and that she would lose me for sure when I found out what had happened.

"No, come home," I said.

Then she put the phone down. It was a wonder I hadn't had a heart attack. I felt really ill and sick. Two hours later the door bell rang. I opened the door and it was Lily, but to my absolute horror it was very obvious to anyone that she was totally messed up with drugs and in a real bad way, she could barely stand up. I have never in my whole life seen anything like it. I wanted to take her to the hospital but even though she was struggling to hold a conversation she said no. I laid her on the sofa, got a bowl of warm water and cleaned her up. I was really emotional not really knowing how to deal with this situation. I could smell she'd been drinking also. She was talking in riddles, not making any sense at all. I held her in my arms to comfort her.

"I'm a bad girl," she said, "you'll never forgive me, you'll never forgive me, I'm so sorry."

I whispered in her ear, "We'll work it out. You must stop the drugs and I will help you."

There was a silence for a moment, then in a whispered voice she said, "Ricky, I went to a hotel with a guy, he had a lot of cocaine. He was a horribly, perverted man, but he had lots of cocaine. I've never seen so much cocaine in my life. I had to have sex with him or he wouldn't give me any."

I just sat in silence, simply bewildered and completely distraught. She then carried on in graphic detail, telling me how he made her let him fuck her in the arse with a double headed dildo and with that she went to sleep in my arms, I was devastated. I wanted to kill myself, I sat with her a while then put her to bed. I was crying and I gently tucked her in with tears streaming down my face, her nose had a little trickle of blood, so I wiped it clean. I was in a real bad way, snot running from my nose, I couldn't control my anguish. I slept on the sofa. It was very late the next day before Lily came round from a deep sleep. I hated her for what she'd done, a big part of me wanted to leave, I felt an absolute failure, if I did leave now she was as good as dead but was it conceivably possible that any human being could somehow overcome such betrayal and be realistically capable of forgiving someone, after all that she'd done?

# Chapter 4

# Arrested

*Love never dies a natural death. It dies because we don't know how to replenish its source. It dies of blindness and errors and betrayals. It dies of illness and wounds; it dies of weariness, of witherings, of tarnishings.*

Anais Nin

I had a beautiful house in England, for eighteen months the girl who had rented my beautiful home had not been paying the money she got from social security into my back account. My brother hadn't told me about this because of all the problems I'd been having. My brother went through a very stressful time, but she finally left. The damage to my house was severe. My beautiful gardens were now three feet high in grass and it took my brother and various other members of my family a few months to put it back to how it been but the bank was threatening to take my house because of the back payments for the mortgage that were still outstanding. I knew I could find some way around that. I was so pleased that through the very hard work of members of my family that I still had my home. I thought at least if anything went wrong, I'd still have a home to live in. However it wasn't to be.

Whilst Lily was sleeping it off, I had a phone call from my niece, my brother's daughter. She was very upset because of all the problems with my house causing her dad a lot of stress. Speaking in a very firm voice, she told me she was very worried for her dad's health and that something serious might happen to him because of all this with my house. That I should stop being so selfish and thinking about myself, I should think about her dad, my brother, before something terrible happened to him and that I should sell the house for whatever I could get for it and get rid of it. When she finished and ended the call, I sat on the floor breathless. I loved and adored my brother, I couldn't possibly live with myself if anything had of happened to him because of my house. So I picked myself up and phoned my brother.

"John, sell the house. Get rid of it."

"Hold on," he said, "after all the heart ache of getting her out of your house and the hard work in putting it back as it was, you now want to sell it?

"The building society will take it off me and I can't pay the back money. It's nothing but problems, sell it for what you can get."

John was really upset, all the hard work.

"We should keep it if we can, it's your home."

"No John, it's just not worth the hassle."

I didn't tell him about the phone call from his daughter, it was beyond words and I told him nothing about my current problems with Lily, and yes, I gave Lily another chance, but I knew it would be very difficult to deal with the fact of knowing what she had done.

Day in and day out, I couldn't stop thinking about what she's told me, sometimes I actually thought I was starting to deal with it, but very soon Lily started with the mood swings again. I knew things were getting worse and that she must be doing some drugs again. I sat Lily down.

"You're not doing as you said. If you continue to be like this I will leave and go back to stay with Doug."

She became really nasty.

"I've told you before, if you ever leave me, you'll go back to England!"

28

We were back in the car and Lily was still asleep. We were nearly home after being out with Chuck and Wendy. Well my good friends, if you think it's been bad so far and that things haven't gone too well up to now, you've got a bloody shock coming as things haven't even started yet.

I felt like I had driven my car through a factory full of mirrors and I hadn't just break one mirror, I must have broken thousands.

Back in the car, were nearly home. I felt quite relaxed. We were just around the corner from our apartment when Lily woke up. I just glanced at her and suddenly without any warning, really, really nasty and agitated she said, "Don't even think about sex." She actually shocked me, shook me up. I just didn't expect her to wake up in such a vile mood, it was a bit similar to when jet plane flies low over your head, it shocks and frightens you at the same time and you feel like shouting at it. The effect Lily waking up, in the way she did, had a similar effect. I was really angry with her. I told her that I didn't just want to have sex. I wanted to make love to my wife as she said before she went to sleep. She told me in a very nasty manor to forget it. I was now really angry, here we go again something really nice had happened and she had to destroy it, giving me the come on even telling Chuck earlier that I was going to get laid that night (something I forgot to mention earlier). I said if I were Mick, her ex, or one of her other boyfriends she would want to. I was now really starting to open up verbally, it was as if I had to get it out and tell her what I thought, I was on a run now. We were at the back of the car. I needed to get my cassette recorder. I continue to tell her that maybe if I was perverted, did cocaine, robbed her and set fire to her bus she once lived in (something which she told me one of her ex's had done to her in the past). Or maybe held a gun to her head like one of her other ex's had done in the past (something which I also didn't mention earlier).

I told her that not even her own family phoned or visited her, I told her everyone she had ever loved had treat her like dirt, maybe that was because she was a piece of dirt. As I opened the hatch back door to her car to retrieve my cassette player and black bag, I called her a fucking hoar. I know none of these things were very nice to say, but I couldn't help myself, after all it was the truth. I was saying this as I was lifting the player out of the car. Lily took hold of my cassette player and threw it to the ground. As I tried to catch it before it hit the ground, she started to come down on me and hit me. As I told you, Lily was very strong from being a trapeze artist. In my defence I slapped her across the face and told her to back off. She hit me in the mouth and it bloody hurt. I was now bleeding. I could taste blood in my mouth. This was all very nasty now. I had my cassette player under my arm and black bag in my other hand as I walked from the car to the apartment Lily continued to hit me. I managed to duck out of the way of most of it, but she was picking me off as I walked alone.

The meal we had had was spaghetti. She hit me over the back of my head with the doggy bag with the remaining spaghetti in it. She then took some and was throwing it at me as I went up the steps. The spaghetti was all over the steps. Lily now had nothing on her feet as she'd also been kicking at me and lost both her shoes whilst doing so. When I got to the top of the stairs, put the cassette player and black bag down and picked some of the spaghetti up went down a couple of steps to her and rubbed it in her face, I know a very childish thing to do, but it's the kind of stupid thing people do, when they're upset. I then turn around to go back up the stairs, Lily shouting and swearing at me. If it wasn't so serious it would have been sheer comedy. Before I got back to the top of the stairs, I slipped on the spaghetti. Falling onto my right thigh, I was able to grab the railing with my right hand, which stopped me from falling down the stairs. Lily came up the stairs to my left, a couple of steps behind me. She also slipped on some spaghetti and as she had nothing on her feet it was even more slippery. There was no rail up the left side of our stairs and Lily slipped down the stairs and hit the rail at the bottom. I thought "ouch", but she jumped straight up and continued shouting... can you possibly imagine the scene? I told her again to go back to her cocaine sniffing ex husband, so she could stuff her nose full of cocaine with him and that they belonged together. Lily then walked off down the street.

I took my cassette recorder and black bag into the small bedroom and then went to our bedroom that over looked the street to see if she was outside. I was a little calmer now. When I looked out of our bedroom window, I could see Lily walking down the street. She had no shoes on her feet and was only wearing a sundress with no bra. I felt that she should not be walking down the street late at night, especially dressed like that. I knew now it was over, but despite what had happened, I still had love for her, so I went down the street to her. I told her to come home, that she wasn't safe to walk the street at that time of night, but she refused. I took her arm and started to pull her home. As I've said before Lily was very strong and she started to hit me again. I tried to put her over my shoulder, like a fireman's lift but I could not hold her, she was too strong for me and she was shouting and trying to hit me. I told her to stop being stupid and come home for her own safety but she carried on hitting me. I took hold of her hair and held her at arms length so that she couldn't hit me. I then led her home slowly. We were about one hundred yards from our home and she was jumping around trying to hit me. I told her again, stop being silly, that she was going home to bed. When I got her home I told her to go to bed and sleep it off. I told her that she could do whatever she wanted in the morning and that we were finished. I couldn't stand the way she was any longer.

As I walked to the bedroom door, I told her I was going to sleep in the other bedroom. She came at me shouting that she was going to kill me. I put one hand on her shoulder pushing her back onto the bed, telling her to sleep it off. I then left the bedroom closing the door, thinking well that's that. Then I heard her on the phone, so I went back into the bedroom, as I walked towards her, she jumped on the bed shouting at me to stay away and leave her alone, even though I was nowhere near her at the time. She went to the back of our bed with her back to the headboard. I didn't realise that she'd put the record button on the phone. I then took the phone into the kitchen, I could hear her on the phone again, I didn't want her bothering people at this time of night with our problems, but I'd forgotten that even if you take the handset away from the phone, you can still use the base like an intercom. I went back into the bedroom to take the base of the phone away. When I entered the bedroom, Lily was talking to the police to my fucking horror, pardon the French. I then realised she'd actually phoned them earlier and pushed the record button on the base of the phone. That was why she was shouting, get away from me, so it would be recorded and she was making a real big thing of it. I just stood in sheer horror. I now knew that this was very serious indeed, it was as if everything went really slow for a moment in time, I had to think. What do I do now? I calmly said in a loud voice that Lily could leave if she wanted and take a taxi wherever. Lily told them she was leaving the apartment. She then left and walked down the street. I went outside and I could still see her walking down the street, still with no shoes on her feet. I saw her shoes and picked them up and brought them inside. On my way back inside I picked up some of the spaghetti with my fingers. I was now very fearful as to what could happen next.

Within a very short time the police arrived and asked me what had happened. I told them that we'd had a bust up and they then asked where she was, I told them she had left the house and walked off down the street. They then left and I went into the house and changed my clothes into a pair of shorts and a tank top style t- shirt. I then phoned Chuck and Wendy and I told them we'd had a bust up and that the police had been involved. I told them that I thought the police might come back to discuss our situation. I told Chuck some of what had happened and that it had got very heated.

The police returned and I was very gentlemen like but the police officer told me that if he were plain clothed, he would have beat the shit out of me. As he was saying this to me, they threw me up against the wall, pushing my arms up my back and then handcuffed me. I thought they were going to break my arms. When I asked the officer why he wanted to beat the shit out of me, he told me that my wife had bruises on her. At that point I couldn't understand why. I had forgotten that we had slipped on the stairs, with Lily jumping straight back up like she did I hadn't realised she was hurt. Even when I had brought her home Lily was still jumping about shouting and trying to hit me, so I had no reason to thing she was injured. The police officer put me in the car without even letting me get dressed and put some shoes on. I was thrown into the back of a police car with a thick mesh between me and the two police officers.

At first I just sat in silence and was now way, way beyond horrified. At one point I told them I hadn't beaten her up or anything. I didn't know why but I just started to tell them as we drove to the police station that Lily had a drink and drugs problem and that I'd had lots of problems with her, that she'd even been unfaithful to me for drugs and that I took her back, cherished her, looked after her, tried to forgive her hoping that she would change. The police officer said, if that's true then your better off getting rid of her anyway. The other officer said I'd been a real dumb shit...what could I say to that, under my circumstances now?

Before I continue, during the course of writing this, I had at times found it impossible to sit and continue to put pen to paper, the emotional rollercoaster was utterly, utterly devastating. At times when sitting over what I was writing I had been a total mental wreck, often having to walk away, thinking there was no way I could bring myself to carry on writing this. At times I just left everything on the table for two or three days before finding the strength to carry on. At certain stages of writing this, I started from the beginning and read through to the end trying to get the balance right. So many things happened, so many ridiculous situations I didn't now how to even start? Some of what was to come will blow your mind as to how in this modern day and age any of this could even possibly begin to happen if there was a simple legal procedure. A phone call to the police, the police arrived, at that point at least to try to establish what might have happened, then if necessary arrest on suspicion and depending on how the person reacted when being arrested was reacting. There was no need in my case for any heavy handedness. I should have been given the opportunity to tell my version of events. Then if they wished I go to the station for further questioning which I would of been more than happy to do so thinking they would of interviewed me and my wife at some point together, I should never have been treated the way I was. I should have been allowed to at least put some clothes on. If they had interviewed us together, it would have been totally obvious for any officer to see that Lily was lying through her teeth. However that didn't happen.

When we arrived at the police station, I was simply thrown into a cell, nobody even attempted to ask me what had happened, no one would even spoke to me. So I was just sitting on the floor of the cell with my back to the wall, this was where my story began. So I was now back from the medical, I had eaten dinner and there was another long night ahead.

The next morning at 7.30am, they came with razors for whoever wanted one. I signed for my blunt bloody razor and by the time I finished my attempt at shaving my face it was a right mess, really painful and stinging. I noticed that there were some newly arrested people. I stood near a guy who was talking to someone else. He was a white American and he actually seemed ok. He was talking quietly saying he had been pulled for a drink driving offence. Then to my surprise he said he was a vet for the Calder Race Track. With that I thought what a huge coincidence. I thought he must know some of the trainers at the track so I turned to him.

"I'm sorry, did I just hear you say that you were a vet at the Calder Race Track?"

"Yes, why?"

I told him that my wife used to be a jockey and that I had been to the racetrack many times with Lily and actually done some hot walking. Hot walking is where you lead a horse out for exercise and you walk along side the horse very fast but trying not to let the horse trot. I told him that I was once an apprentice jockey in England. For the first time I shared real laughter and we shook hands. I thought, oh at last, someone I can relate to. He told me he wouldn't be there too long as he had bail. I told him about Lily and he told me he knew of her. I asked him if he knew Shaun Musgrave and Brian Smeak and he said he knew them both and that he would be seeing them the next morning. When he got out he said he would say hi from me and would also phone Lily and tell her how bad it was in the jail and tell her to get me out of this hellhole. When I asked him his name you would never believe this but his name was also Rick...what an incredible situation. He seemed like a really nice guy and this was a comfort to me. When I told him all that had happened he said "How sad, she sounds like a bit of a nutter Rick."

Rick had the opportunity to make some phone calls so I gave him Lily's phone number and instead of phoning her when he got out he phoned her while I was there. When she answered he told her where he was calling from and did she wish to speak to me. She said yes. He then asked if I wanted to speak to her and I also said yes.

It was then that Lily told me she was hurt. I assumed it was from her falling down the stairs. Incredibly she then told me that she loved me and at that point I felt really emotional. I told her that it was over between us and that I couldn't take anymore but I still loved her. She then told me that we could still be friends. She then asked if I could phone her back as she had a call coming through. I asked Rick if that was possible as I couldn't, I had no money. I thought what a bewildering set of events. Rick said that was ok. He said she seemed ok, very relaxed. He said that when he asked her if she wanted to speak to me that you wouldn't have thought anything bad had happened, he said what a strange woman. I told him about her lawsuit, which he thought was all very sad.

Rick then phoned Lily back and handed me the phone. Lily was now joking about what a great spaghetti fight we'd had. She was laughing. I told her it wasn't funny, I was in jail! I told her it was a hellhole and to get me out of there! She then said she was taking out an order for me to stay away from her. I told her that there was no need to do that, that I never wanted to see her ever again. I told her I'd go back to Doug's. She then told me she was going to send all of my things back to England. I asked her not to do that as I was going to stay in Florida and to not touch my belongings, I would arrange someone to collect them.

I found out sometime later from Wendy that Lily had phoned her asking what I was doing talking to Calder Race Track. As promised Rick must have spoken to Shaun Musgrave who she knew very well. Shaun must have spoke to Lily and possibly said that Rick had mentioned her lawsuit. Lily somehow thought that I had phoned the racetrack but I hadn't.

Anyway after my last conversation to Lily on the prison phone Rick was released. I felt very depressed. I was alone again. It was very helpful meeting Rick as I had in the jail.

I'm thinking now, it must only be a matter of time before I was leaving these (pardon my French)...fucking pricks.

I thought just sit tight, keep myself to myself; avoid talking to anyone so nobody could find reason to punch me. So I was waiting. About three hours later an officer came across to me and said, "James Edward Dunphy, known to some as English?"

"Yes that's me".

He gave me some papers. I was a little confused at first and I must have looked really puzzled, to such a degree that one of the guys said, "What's wrong English, you look really confused?"

I said I didn't understand what these papers were for. It was not that long ago I was talking to my wife. She said she was going to drop the charges, not that I'd done anything wrong. By now a couple more of these guys were standing close by listening to our conversation. One of them said,

"Can I have a look?"

I said "Yes of course."

After a short while of him reading he said,

"Ooohh unbelievable, fucking hell, what a bitch!"

"What? What is it?"

He said she had put a restraining order on me. Then he said there was a statement as to what she said I had done to her the other night. "Oohh you're in serious fucking shit bro, you really are in a lot of trouble!" I ask him what she had said? The statement said that I had slapped her more than once, that I had kicked her in the ribs twice, shaken her violently, dragged her down the stairs, dragged her back up the stairs then threw her down again and that I had told her that I was going to kill her when I got out of jail. She also said that I had dragged her a full city block by her hair. As this guy was reading this, he became louder and louder. Now everyone was laughing at me, some of them even shouting.

"They'll throw away the key, mother fucker. You're in serious trouble bro."

He gave me back my papers. I just sat totally dejected in silence as I looked at the statement. It actually hadn't stopped where he had finished reading it and to my horror it went on to say that I was a British Citizen and that I had beaten her three times whilst we were married. She also said that I'd hit my first wife's father. In addition, Lily accused me of hitting an ex girlfriend. I was very frightened as this statement was a total lie. How could this be possible? Lily had phoned the police from our bedside shouting get away from me. She went off down the street and the police came to our home asking where she was. They must have found her and she must have told them I had beaten her. I was arrested and she must have given them this statement at the police station, but no one, no one from the police that arrested me interviewed me or took a statement from me. No one from the police to this very day has ever asked me my version of events. How could that be legally possible? How could they possibly know if she was telling the truth just because she had bruises or just because she said so.

When I had spoken with Lily earlier some other things were said. At one point she said I bet you're really pissed off with me for having you arrested and that I would want revenge. I told her no, not at all and to just get me out of there. She then said she didn't deserve what I'd done to her. I said I hadn't done anything and she replied that she didn't deserve being slapped in the face. I just desperately wanted to get out so I said to her "No you didn't dear, now drop the charges and get me out of here." I now thought she might have been recording the conversation. How stupid of me but I knew I had to give her something or she would never drop the charges. I was desperate. The only time I slapped her was in my own defence was when I was picking up my cassette recorder as she

38

was hitting me. I only slapped her once and told her to back off. She must have known the restraining order along with her police statement were on the way to me as she was talking to me. How evil is that? What could I say? I just sat trembling with my head in my hands.

Chapter 5

# An Oasis of Kindness in a Desert of Hostility

*THE EDGE, there is no honest way to explain it because the only people who really know where it is are the ones who have gone over*

Hunter S Thompson

Something which I found out later from my friends was that Lily had apparently told the court, in the first few days, that if they deported me she would drop the charges. She just wanted me out of the country. I now know that she thought I would testify against her in her law suit against the Calder Race Track. There was nothing wrong with Lily. She was trying to sue the racetrack for two million dollars. One year earlier we went white water rafting in West Virginia and she actually complained that the water wasn't rough enough. We went

horseback riding in the mountains of Pennsylvania and jet skiing in Key Largo. I did mention that she would go to jail for fraudulent claims against the race track. I just wanted out of this mess. There was nothing wrong with Lily. She was trying to get me out of the country to keep me quiet.

Where would I go with this now? How could I defend myself when no one would even listen to what I have to say?

What next? I suppose the day was still relatively young, it was mid afternoon. After two hours, two officers entered the room calling my name out loud. Some of the other guys were now shouting.

"English is over here!"

Well I didn't have to wait too long did I? I was then handcuffed to one of the officers and led out of the room.

"What is happening to me now sir?" I asked.

He replied, "You'll see and speak when you're asked to speak!"

Another happy camper I thought. He wouldn't win any prizes for his personality that was for sure. I was taken to a holding cell and put in with another bunch of inmates. We just sat saying nothing at all to each other. At one point I couldn't stand it any longer so I said,

"Hi guys, my name is Ricky how's everybody doing?

Not one of them replied. Some of them just looked at me as if I was crazy. The others just looked at the floor of the cell. This carried on for a good hour. Then they came to take us all out, hand cuffed in pairs, very nice. We were taken outside and loaded into one of the prison buses and off we went.

Maybe ten minutes later we entered another prison facility and were led out two by two, like Noah's Ark, after all we were just a bunch of animals now. We were then put into another holding cell. Same thing, freezing cold and nobody spoke. It seemed like we were in there a long time before we were then moved a short distance to another room. The room had rows of chairs all facing the same way towards the front. Mounted on a wall was a very large television. No one was saying a word. Eventually the TV came on and it was a judge sat at a desk, I was near the back of this room. One by one, each name was called out. An officer would handcuff whoever's name was called and lead them to the TV where they would stand in front of it. Each person was then asked if it was their name that was called out, then a list of charges were read out relating to that person. An amount of money was stated to them which turned out to be the amount of money needed to bail each individual. This seemed to take forever, most of the charges seemed to be drugs, drink driving, and theft. The amount of bail set was between five and ten thousand dollars. The next guy had drugs and weapon charges his bail was thirty thousand dollars. Well now it was my turn, asking my name and then reading out the charges. I was on a battery charge and he then set my bail at twenty five thousand dollars

"What? Twenty five thousand dollars?"

It really shook me. I then asked if I could please let him know my version of events as no one had given me the opportunity to say a word in my defence and that I was completely innocent and had done nothing wrong. With that some of the others started to laugh, even some of the officers were having a chuckle.

The judge told everyone to calm down and asked if I had anyone to represent me? I said no. No one had even come to talk to me in days. He asked if I had the money for the bail set. I said no again. He asked if there anyone who could pay the bail for you? I said I hadn't been able to speak to my friends yet. He then told me he couldn't discuss my case anymore and that I would be given some numbers of attorneys/public defenders if I didn't have an attorney or couldn't afford one. He then said bail was Twenty Five Thousand Dollars and I was led away back to a holding cell. It appears that there was a holding cell for people before you went in front of the TV judge and a holding cell for those after they had been before this TV judge. At some point again some of us were handcuffed in pairs and led to the prison van. This time we were taken to a different place. When we arrived again we were put into another holding cell. I was the first name to be read out this time and handcuffed to an officer and taken to some kind of stores where I was given a blanket and a pillow. I was then asked my name and details again then I asked,

"Where am I now?"

They told me I was in a stockade, I was told I would be here till my day of arraignment, then put before a judge and sentenced.

"Sentenced?"

I had done nothing wrong! The officer just smiled. I was then taken to a really large room, all on one floor with bunk beds round the outside and tables in the middle. I was given a towel and a very small bar of soap, a tiny toothbrush and a small tube of toothpaste. I said that I hadn't eaten since breakfast and it was now 8pm at night.

"Haven't you been given anything to eat or drink? Have you not at least been offered it?"

"No," I replied.

They then brought me a sandwich and a carton of fruit juice and I thanked them.

When you entered this room, first you entered a square cage with an open hatch over- looking the room and there was a door to the side. You then entered this cage, closed the door behind you, then another metal gate was opened after the one behind you was locked, then you entered the room. I was led to a bunk and I had the bottom bunk. I was given my blanket and pillow as well as my sandwich and a drink and was left. It wasn't as cold in here, but it wasn't warm either. I had my drink and ate my sandwich which wasn't bad. Then I made my bed but I was still in a lot of pain. I was in a real mess and a few of the guys were looking at me. There were more white guys here but different nationalities. The guy next to me seemed to be of Mexican type origin. He had a very sad look about him but not an aggressive looking man.

I lay on my bunk unable to believe what had happened and what was happening to me. All because of Lily's Two Million Dollar Law suit, but how could this have been possible? How could she get away with what she had done so far?

I was very tired, but this was the first bed I've been given since I was arrested. That now seems like an eternity. As I lay on my bunk I started to think about other things that had happened with Lily.

I'd forgotten to tell you about a situation that happened with Lily some time after we were married. When I look back, I really had had many warnings as to what my dear wife was capable of.

One night we were watching TV together after having our dinner. We were sat on the sofa together and all was well. It had been a nice evening in. Lily decided to phone one of her old friends while I was watching a film. Lily turned the TV off and very nicely asked me if I would sing to her friend over the phone.

"Do I have to Lily?" I said in a whispered voice.

"Please," she said in a pitiful way, so I did.

Both Lily and I had a nice talk and there was now more than one person we were talking to. I had no idea who they were; we were told that a lot of their friends were now married. I asked Lily quietly,

"Does your friend know we are married?"

Lily said not to tell her, that her friend had lots of problems and she would fill me in after the call. I heard Lily's friend ask her how she was doing with the drugs. After the call, Lily refused to tell me why we couldn't tell her friend that we were married. I was very upset by that and we started to have words. Lily used to tell me she didn't have a problem with drugs, so why did I hear her friend as her about it?

I sat down and started to watch TV again. Lily then stood up, unplugged the TV with a smile on her face and said

"I'm going to show you something Ricky."

She took the TV into the bedroom and locked the door, I asked her repeatedly to open the door and stop being silly as I wanted to see the film. She just laughed. I told her if she didn't open the door that I would count to three and kick the door open, so I did. The door flew open as she walked past me with the TV.

We had a boom box which I used for my singing telegrams and we often used the boom box to prop the door open to the box room. I bent down to pick it up and by accident I turned it on. It came on full blast and she was then shouting.

"Turn the fucker off, you idiot!"

As I panicked trying to turn it off I dropped it and it smashed on the floor. She carried on shouting

"Look what you've done!"

She then said she was taking the dog for a walk. When she came back she had a police officer with her. He asked what had happened and I told him. He looked at me and rolled his eyes to the ceiling with a sympathetic look and asked if we needed him any further and was everything okay? We both said yes and with a smile he left. I told Lily I could not believe what she had done. She thought it was funny and laughed. She told me that she just wanted to frighten me. This was when I first started to learn what Lily was capable of. I told her it was a sick thing to do. I was horrified. She then sat on the sofa and continued to watch TV as if nothing had happened. Whenever I looked at her, she said

"What's up sweetie? Are you alright?"

This is how hot and cold Lily could run.

Back to my bunk bed at the stockade, it was a long night but I slept better than the previous nights. I was a bit tearful and wondered what the next day would bring. The next day I decided I had to really try to work out a way of contacting Chuck and Wendy. Some of these officers didn't seem as aggressive and I was hoping I would be given the chance to make a phone call, after all in films and detective programmes on the TV, prisoners are always allowed to make a phone call. The only chance I'd had to talk to anyone was when Rick the vet phoned Lily. Other than that I'd had no chance to phone anyone. You think that you only find these types of situations in films or books or TV programmes, but I was living proof that these things happen in real life. It was happening to me!

The next morning, again early, they came with razors so you could shave but I couldn't. My face was too sore and I thought it was best to leave it a while. Later breakfast arrived again. Trays stacked on a trolley. The same routine as before but here you stood in a queue. Everyone raced across the room, some really hard nuts simply walked to the front. A lot more men were in the room than before, maybe 65 in total. I told you before about the Mexican guy in the next bunk, well the guy on the other side of me was the most ugly, weirdest looking man I had ever come across in my life. A black man of about six feet four inches tall, as thin as a rake, with very, very large eyes which were set back in his head, frizzy hair standing up four inches high all the way around his head. A very long neck with a hawk like nose and he didn't speak to anyone. A complete loner. At first you could be forgiven for thinking he might be insane. No one seemed to like this guy at all but he was not aggressive. He spent a lot of his time underneath his bed sheets, using them like a tent.

It was a large room; you could walk about with tables central to the room. Many inmates sat at the tables when eating and it was obvious that most of the black lads kept themselves to themselves. There were some really big men in here and we had quite a large TV, but I soon learned that it was the black guys who had most of the say in what we all watched.

At the far side of the room, there was a large shower area and I felt the need to take a shower. The water was constantly hot, so I had a really nice shower and I felt a lot fresher. I had slept the night before but I was still mentally and physically exhausted. At some point in the morning a nurse arrived and stood in the cage I told you about. The men all lined up and they were given medication. Some of these guys, I was to find out, had been here some time. The floor was concrete, very smooth and very cold. I was still not well at all and looked a real mess. My cough was now a lot worse and it sounded more like a dog barking. I had noticed as I was walking around that some of these guys were looking at me because my cough was so bad.

As the line of men came to an end waiting to see the nurse for medication, I add myself to it. Soon I was faced with the nurse.

"Ok," she said, "What can I do for you?"

I told the nurse that I had just arrived last night and that I desperately needed to speak to someone and that I'd been arrested for a crime I hadn't commit. That my wife had a drugs problem and that she had lied to the police saying that I'd beaten her and that she needed to get me out of the country as she feared I would put a stop to her fraudulent law suit against Calder Race Track for two million dollars and she had nothing wrong with her. Again I said she was possibly trying to get me out of the country and sent back to England because of that. I told the nurse that the mess on my face had been done by my wife and also said I was in a lot of pain. The nurse and the assistant just looked at me. I could see a really vacant look on their faces and they didn't seem to know what to say. I was also a little breathless as I was desperate to tell them as much as I possibly could before someone told me to shut the fuck up. I thought if I could say as much as possible, something might stick with them.

I started to cough really badly and they looked concerned and asked me to sit down, asking me to calm myself down before I had a heart attack. The nurse was very kind to me and said,

"We need to ask the doctor to take a look at you, you don't look very good and we need to do something about that cough."

I was shaking a little and I was feeling very emotional and I was obviously suffering with my nerves now. She took a hold of my hand in a kind and comforting way and put her other hand on my forehead. I carried on talking in a very shaky voice telling them that no one, not one single person had even bothered to ask me what had happened. I hadn't been allowed to speak to any of my friends, Chuck and Wendy, so someone

47

could let my brother know what was happening to me. I explained that my brother was a police officer in England. I was told by a judge on a TV screen that I should be allowed to speak to the public defender's office as I had no money and no one as yet to defend me.

I told the nurse I had the most incredible headache and they gave me some painkillers with a drink of water. They said they would talk and tell the doctor to see me the next day and would tell someone in the office to arrange for me to phone and speak to my friends Chuck and Wendy. The nurse told me that they had to allow me to phone a friend or relative and that by law they had to provide me with a public defender from the public defender's office and that it was a human right that they provided me with the opportunity to defend myself. They asked me when was a good time for me to phone my friends, I told them between seven and eight pm. I was then told to go to my bunk and rest, so I did. As I was walking back to my bunk, I could see guys playing cards and some writing letters and as I walked past the guys playing cards I was being given some real dirty looks by some of the black lads standing together. I felt like saying,

"Who are you looking at?"

But I just went back to my bunk. The weird looking guy who was under the sheets actually sat up and whispered to himself. The Mexican lad gave me a nod so I said hi to him. I had a sleep but before I knew it, I was woken by a lot of commotion. It was feeding time at the zoo. I waited until the end and went to get my tray. I sat at a table, everything was metal, the table top and bench like seating was also metal and bolted to the floor. The tables were quite long, ten people could sit opposite each other, I left most of my food and I then said out loud,

"I don't want all this food, would anyone like my sweet?"
All of a sudden I had four or five guys stood around me whilst I was sat at the table. I gave it to a black guy and said,

"Don't worry there's always tomorrow for someone else to have what I don't want."

A voice came from behind me.

"You're not as stupid as you look English!"

I thought here we go again, bloody English. I said

"My name was Ricky to most people."

He then says, "then why did I hear them call you James or something?"

"Because that's my real name."

"What do you mean you're real name English?" I said "Ricky is a stage name, most people know me as Ricky, so it's what I call myself."

"Ok English, if that's what you say."

"Ignore him," said another guy, "he's a dickhead."

He told me his name was Bob.

"Hello Bob, how ya doin? I'd offer you a drink..." I said.

With that he started to laugh.

"I like that English; you'll need a sense of humour here."

He told me while I was asleep they had been outside in the yard and that by law they had to let us go outside for an hour or so and that there were a lot of weights and benches. He then told me not to get in the way of the black guys, to wait until they had done and then use the weights and benches.

I decided to have a little walk around, some men were lying in their bunks either asleep or reading, some sat watching TV, others sat at the tables playing cards. Some lads were playing dominoes; the black lads liked watching the soaps.

The news came on, Fox News. There was a lot of interest especially by the black lads as it was during the O J Simpson trial. I heard one black lad say,

"There'll be some serious shit in here if they find OJ guilty. These white motherfuckers won't know what's hit them; there'll be riots in all the jails and the streets."

I thought wonderful, just what I needed on top of everything else. I heard a white guy say,

"All hell will break loose if OJ gets it, God help all the whites."

There was still a lot of evidence to go through with the OJ case so I thought I'll be out of here soon before the end of the trial.

Along one side of this room was a walkway where the officers did their paper work. It was getting late, so I went to the cage. I thought I would wait until someone came out of the office. When an officer came out, I said, "Excuse me sir, excuse me sir," but I was just ignored, so I waited.

When another officer came out I said the same and this time the officer answered. I explained that I'd been told I could have a phone call to the public defenders office as I had no one to represent me.

"Who is your case worker?" He said.

I said I didn't know I had a case worker. He said I would have one but I would have to speak to someone tomorrow as no one was here now that could help me. Was I ever going to get to speak to someone?

## Chapter 6

# Madness Lurks Around Every Corner

*You must not lose faith in humanity. Humanity is like an ocean; if a few drops of the ocean are dirty, the ocean does not become dirty.*

Mahatma Gandhi

By now my cough was getting even worse. I was still getting dizzy and had numbness in my arms. My neck also now ached. Lily had hit me hard over the head with the doggy bag.

A little later a snack was brought out and a larger container of water. This time it was flavoured water. A mad dash happened with lots of pushing and shoving. The officer just left the container and some of the really big black lads just walked to the front and everyone was told just one plastic cup each. Some of the hard cases just stood and drank as many cups as they wanted. No one said anything and sometimes the container was empty before everyone had had a drink. There was one black lad in particular that was feared. He often looked at me and I knew he really didn't like me. I was standing watching some guys playing cards when there was a lot of shouting down by the showers. The black lads were shouting.

"You disgusting mother fucker."

I looked across to the mayhem. The guy called Bob says "It's the weird looking bastard English."

"What's going on?"

I was told the weirdo always took a shower when no one else was using the showers and he always masturbated.

The black guys would often stand and watch him but he just carried on with all the black lads shouting at him. That was what all the noise was about. The weirdo just carried on until he came and licked his own sperm off his fingers while looking across at the black guys and giving them a smile. Another thing the weirdo did when he was under his blanket was to write letters on the base sheet in pencil until the whole sheet was covered. Many of the inmates complained that the guy was mad and that he shouldn't be in this cell and that he should be in the mental ward in the next building. Bob just laughed and said many of the inmates refused to bunk next to him and the two Mexicans. I asked what was wrong with the Mexicans and Bob told me that the American blacks and whites regarded Mexicans as scum. I thought he seemed ok, harmless and friendly and that I'd much rather speak to him than most of these other arseholes.

It was lights out. I was lying in the dark and I simply had no words. I was also told that there were often fights in here and the officers would take out the offenders into a solitary cell for a few days until they cooled off and that they wouldn't be allowed to go into the yard.

The next morning was much the same, razors, breakfast and people playing cards or dominos. Some would simply walk round the tables as it was a big room. Mid morning my name is called out, so I went to the cage. There was an officer, he handcuffed me and told me I was to see a doctor.

I told the doctor about the loss of feeling in my arms, the numbness and headaches. I still had a limp and I now had a bad bruise on my right thigh. He said I must have fallen hard for that bruise to have come up like it had. He said I was still suffering a little concussion then he checked my chest and wasn't happy with my cough. He asked if I suffered with coughs often and I told him yes, I did. He asked if I had sweats and I also replied yes. I had been having really bad sweats before my arrest. He said he wanted a blood test.

I asked the doctor if he would help me. I still hadn't had the chance to speak to my friends and still hadn't heard from a public defender or my so called case worker. He told the officer to get me a request form. I was told to put in writing a request for a phone call to speak to a public defender and my friends. Then I was given more painkillers.

When I returned to the cell, I heard some of the guys talking about their arrests and discussing their paper work and the amount of bond they had. No one had anywhere near the bond I did.

"My bond is Twenty Five Thousand Dollars."

"For what? said one of the guys.

I gave him my papers and my bond information.

"Holy shit they've got you down as aggravated assault."

I was on a misdemeanour charge and that bond was far to high. He told me to ask for a request slip and for a bond hearing to reduce the bond. He said they would have to reduce my bond as it was far too high. He thought that maybe between five and eight thousand would be about normal. He asked if I had representation and I said no one had been to see me yet. He said that it was far too long and that someone should have been to see me way before now. Apparently this guy was well informed when it came to law. I let him read all my papers. He was very concerned and said because of the O J Simpson case I was being dealt with very severely. He said it wasn't correct at all. I sat with him a while and spoke of Lily. I was told that I could ask for a phone call to England as long as the people in England would accept the call charges.

So I put in a request asking if I could call my brother telling them he was a police officer. This guys name was Tom. My case and situation was becoming a bit of a soap opera. Some of the guys would sometimes say to me,

"Hey English, sounds like your wife's a real bitch, someone should sort that mother out."

Later after dinner, my name was called out. I was taken to an office where I was told I could make a phone call. I said I wanted to call my brother in England but I was told no and asked who I wanted to phone here? They let me phone Chuck and Wendy. When I phoned Chuck and Wendy it was a very emotional call. They were horrified at the way I had been treated. I told them what had happened and that my bond was Twenty Five Thousand Dollars and that I had put in a request for a bond reduction. They said that if they were to reduce the bond to a reasonable level that they would pay it and get me out to prepare my case. They told me not to worry and that this whole thing was crazy and that I would soon be out. I had never been arrested for anything in my life and this was totally unbelievable.

While I was going through all this I found out later that Lily had phoned my brother John in England. She told John that she was having me deported and that she was now pressing for a felony charge. She told him that because of me, one of her breast implants was leaking. She also told him that she had a broken collarbone and a broken rib. John didn't know this was a pack of lies. All Lily had was a black and blue breast, a small graze on the side of her head and a small bruise on her shoulder. After all she had slipped down a flight of stairs. My brother apparently told Lily that he was very sympathetic towards her but was still very worried about me. She told him that she was also worried about me. She told John she was sending my clothes to England and she also told him not to give me my stuff until I promised to get help.

I needed help? What do you think to this woman?

It was hard to believe that someone could actually invent such a tale, but to be actually getting away with it just made the American legal judicial system look very stupid and incompetent but this was nothing yet. If someone had only just given me the chance to say what had happened. You have to remember Lily told them in her written statement that I was supposed to have dragged her up a flight of concrete stairs then thrown her down, remember THROWN her down them, dragged her back up the stairs and then again thrown her down a flight of concrete stairs. I'll say that again a flight of concrete stairs!! She had nothing on her feet, wearing only a sun dress with straps over her shoulders and no bra, no stockings or tights, it would not take an idiot to work out the very serious injuries she would have sustained to her feet, legs and arms. When she was at the police station and gave this statement they only had to take one look at this idiot to see that she would have sustained far more injuries than she had if I'd done half of what she said I had. If only they had given me the chance, just once. I told them that she had slipped on spaghetti, any halfwit police officer could have gone back to the scene and they still would have seen the traces of spaghetti on the steps. They would have known immediately that she was telling lies and that it would have been impossible to only have the injuries she had. Apparently Lily's eyes were all swollen, but when Lily got upset, that's what happened, her eyes go really puffy, but again the police officer, a halfwit, along with a halfwit doctor, could have written a report saying it was impossible, what she had said had happened. They should have then cross examined her. Lily made complete idiots out of all of them and they didn't even know it.

Lily continued to phone John, my ex wife Sharon and my sister Maggie and was always phoning in the middle of the night. I found out later from one of Lily's best friends, a guy called Randy who she introduced me to and became a dear friend to me, that she was also phoning him and telling lies. Randy ended up being a witness against Lily on some very serious charges, but I will come back to Randy later as he also becomes important.

Lily also told my brother John that I had no friends what so ever and that even my best friend from West Palm Beach wanted nothing to do with me. John knew Doug from Palm Beach. John and my son Craig who has Down Syndrome actually stayed at Doug's house with me because they attended our wedding

John had tried to phone Doug after everything Lily had told him but Doug was out of town. John ended up leaving messages for Doug to phone him back. When there was no response, John started to think that there might be some truth in what Lily had said. When I had my first conversation with Chuck and Wendy, I asked them to phone my brother. John didn't know Chuck and Wendy at this point, so Lily by now had already told John all this incredible story.

When Chuck and Wendy phoned John and told him that they were dear friends of mine, imagine what John must have thought of Lily. After John told them what Lily had told him they were absolutely horrified. Chuck and Wendy told John not to believe a word and that Lily had told him a complete pack of lies. Wendy went on to tell John that she thought Lily had set me up, that she had been waiting for an opportunity to have me arrested for something to get me out of the country because of Lily's pending law suit. Wendy told John about when Lily visited them at their home and said that she was pleased Ricky has such good friends, as he would need them very soon. Wendy said she thought this was very strange but now knows why she said it.

My brother John finally made contact with Doug. Doug told John not to believe a word Lily had told him and that he was my best friend. He also told John than he did not trust Lily.

My brother then contacted the British Consulate in Orlando but they told him that they could do little to help. He also phoned Broward Jail, which was where I was being held, but they wouldn't even confirm whether they had me or not. As a police officer John was staggered by this because in England if a relative or personal friend phones a jail to make an inquiry as to whether someone is there or not, by law they have to acknowledge that they have you in custody. They don't have to give out any information but they do have to tell them if you are there or not.

You couldn't possibly make all this shit up. It was simply incredible what Lily had been allowed to get away with. I was totally innocent and Lily was in the process of breaking just about every law known to man.

So back to the jail. I was now allowed to phone the Public Defender's Office. I left many messages on the answer machine and the answer machine told you that someone would contact you from our office as soon as someone had the information.

Some of the people that came into our room in the stockade were quite fascinating. People came from the church and they sat around the table and all held hands. It was all blacks. Not one white man ever joined in while I was there until, yes, I decided one day to join them.

As I walked across, Bob asks, "What are you doing English?"

"I'm going to church."

"Your fucking losing the plot, don't be stupid!"

I walked across and calmly sat down. You should have seen the faces. The Chaplain was also black and he looked at me and gave me a smile. He asked the others, "Well, aren't you going to introduce me to this gentleman then?" No actor could have possibly captured this scene.

"It's English," someone said.

"That's ok sir, that's what everyone round here seems to want to call me and I'm happy with that."

I then ask if I might make a little speech.

"Yes you may English."

I stood up at the table and said I found it very sad that they felt such hatred towards me simply because I was white.

In England I had some very wonderful and good friends who were black and I know that they would be very upset to see what I had seen in here. I had no problem what so ever with any man because of the colour of their skin. All I ask is that they showed me the same respect that I would show to anyone sat at this table. The Chaplain then said, "Let's all sit and hold hands." You should have seen the faces of the guys sat either side of me.

Later on that day, the nurse arrived from the cage and called my name. When I went to speak to her she told me that she had the results from my blood tests. She said this was very serious and my tests had come back showing positive for TB. I could not believe my luck. I then went with her to see the doctor. I was told that I would have to take medication for six months because of the TB. He then told me that I had been in contact with an infected person and that my immune system was very low. I was also told that I was not a danger to anyone but anyone with an illness of virus was a danger to me because of my immune system being so low.

I was still waiting to hear about my bond hearing reduction, but nothing yet. To my horror, I had a paper given to me from when I had requested to make a phone call to my brother. My brother was to pay the cost of the call however written on this paper it just said the word "denied". Surely that was a human right violation?

One good thing was that Chuck and Wendy accepted reversing the charges to them whenever I was given the opportunity to phone them. The next day I was given a paper notifying me that after a total of fifteen days I would go to court for a continuation of Lily's restraining order. The guys thought this was hilarious. As if anyone would even consider wanting to see her again after what she'd done. I was visibly struggling with all this. I actually thought I was starting to loose the plot a little. I put in another request to see my caseworker so I could talk with him about my bond hearing reduction. He never came near me. Many said that he was a very arrogant man, an utter arsehole and worse. All he did was send me a paper with an officer telling me on the fifteenth day I would be in court at 10am. There was no mention what so ever about the public defender coming to see me to discuss my case and prepare my defence. I had been told by everyone that this was against the law. I was legally entitled to be defended. This was my human right. While all this was going on Lily had a three way conversation with Chuck, Wendy and Doug.

She actually said that she had slipped down the stairs. She also phoned Doug on his own to ask if he would testify on her behalf and said that I had admitted to what she had claimed I had done. He told her that what she was asking him to do was against the law and that he was not prepared to tell lies in court. He was my friend and told her where to go. I was later told by my friends what Lily had said to Chuck, Wendy and Doug in the three way call plus what Lily had asked Doug to do. They all said that they were coming to court to testify against Lily.

Doug told me that once the judge had heard all the witness testimony against Lily, he would very quickly realise Lily's case was based on a complete pack of lies. Also he would see for himself that she was doing all of this to protect her lawsuit and then the case would be thrown out of court and I would be free. Surely it was just a matter of time?

# Chapter 7

# Divorce

*Nice people don't necessarily fall in love with nice people.*

Jonathan Ranzen

A few days later I was given a letter from Lily's attorney telling me that Lily was divorcing me. This still hurt as I did have some love for her but I also hated her for what she was putting me through. I could only imagine what my family and friends were going through.

By now more of the inmates were interested in what was happening to me even more than they were interested in the O J Simpson case. They kept saying that none of them had ever heard or seen anything like it before and they were apparently even talking to their families about my case and my really evil wife. I really never wanted to see Lily again!

I still hadn't heard about my bond hearing reduction. The days are dragging by and I was not well at all. I thought I was loosing my mind.

Another thing that was on the TV an awful lot was the Cubans and the Haitians coming across to America on rafts and being arrested and taken to an immigration hold. We watched them climbing off their rafts and in some cases crawling onto the beaches exhausted after being at sea for long periods of time with very little food or drink. Now there's a joke, coming to start a new life in America, the land of equal rights and liberty and human rights. I believed some of these people were in for a real shock. As I wrote this many years later in my life, Haiti had just had the worst ever earth quake in two hundred years. The utter devastation was coming out on a minute by minute basis. It was absolutely horrific what these people were suffering. I will come back to these people as I, myself encountered some of these desperate people at first hand.

What would these people think if they found out that in this country you could be arrested for a very serious crime, locked up, never given the opportunity to defend yourself and not given the chance of an interview at least to discuss what had happened. What would they think of this?

Try to imagine yourself having been put through what I have suffered.

Not given the opportunity to at least be told immediately what you had been charged with and asked if you wished to be given the opportunity to give your version about what had happened and still, after all this time being held, not had a public defender or a phone call to your family.

Soon I am going to court before a judge called Mr Rothschild. When I told some of the guys in the stockade that I was going before him, they told me he was not a good judge at all. He was very firm and very strict. If he didn't like you he could be very hard when giving a sentence. They said it would be better if I had one of the other judges, although I was told of another judge who was the worst out of the lot, at least I was lucky enough not to have had him. Lucky. How could I possibly say that with my sets of circumstances? They said "Believe us English, it's good you didn't get the old bastard, as he's known, especially with your charge, aggravated battery.

"Rothschild is bad enough by the sound of things," I said.

Before we continue, I must speak more about Lily, it will help you understand even more how outrageous Lily's case was and why she had gone to all the extremes to have me arrested and deported. As I've said, I met Lily at the Village Zoo Club

VIP night. Lily sadly kept her word when she said we would meet again and that she'd phone me within a week. Lily did phone me, so we met up at the Hollywood beach where we went for a walk and to a bar. Lily was quick to tell me of her ex partner Mick; she told me that she and Mick lived on a bus, a really nice bus, top of the range. It had everything and she told me that she really loved living on this bus. Apparently, she told me when they first split up that Mick had a guy steal the bus, take all their belongings off and then set fire to the lot. Lily told me she lost everything. She told me that she ended up living in a garage next door to a friend's house who was called Randy. Randy became a dear friend and boss to me later in this saga. Lily had a terrible hatred for Mick and also his friend John. She told me that someone called Jimmy, a friend of Mick and Johns drove the bus for them. Lily was desperately trying to get her money back, on the phone on many occasions to detectives in Texas, so badly wanting to get back at this Mick and John. This John character was sent to jail on some other charges and Lily had a Forty Thousand Dollar lawsuit against this John and was pressing charges against him. Lily told me that Mick had told her if she pressed charges against him, he would kill her. This is when she first told me that she had done cocaine. She said that her and Mick did cocaine together and that it had become far more of a problem for Mick than her. Lily then told me she didn't do cocaine anymore and that it was only because of her husband Mick that she had used it. I told her I'd never, ever done any type of drugs, that I'd never smoked a joint in my life and that I was very anti drugs.

She gave me a big kiss when I told her this and said she was very happy about that. She then sadly went on to tell me that Mick was sexually perverted. On his birthday she told me that she had sex with a call girl to show him how much she loved him but she said she didn't enjoy any of it, she did it simply to prove that she loved him....yeah, yeah....yeah, I can hear you all saying, and you really believed her! Well ok folks, maybe I didn't, but maybe I thought she might be making it all up. I must admit it was not what I was used to listening to in Doncaster.

I was very concerned about her hatred towards Mick. It certainly wasn't healthy at all. Lily would often sit up till late at night, rocking in her chair, no jokes about the film psycho if you please, none of this was at all funny. I often told Lily to drop the whole thing; I thought it would make her very ill.

What I'm about to tell you, I wasn't going to mention as I didn't believe it at the time, but now after all I've witnessed with Lily, I did now.

She told me that on the night of their wedding Mick took her to a sex motel with blue movies, drugs and changing partners. Lily said she was very upset but said nothing as they had just literally been married. She also told me that Mick was gay and that he watched gay videos with a male friend, this I simply didn't believe at the time. Another guy called Brian Smeak, a trainer at the Calder Race Track became a friend to me. He told me that Lily was known to drink a little too much at times. Lily was a really rough and tumble kind of girl and she would often thump me on the arm in jest. I told her not to do this as it hurt and often had large bruises on my arm, but she just said I was a wuss and to have a laugh. Lily was always very private. I could never just turn up at her house. I always had to beep her first. She didn't give me her phone number for some time and when she did, I always had to phone her before setting off from Doug's house in West Palm Beach. It was a bit of a drive to Lily's house in Fort Lauderdale. I had to drive down the 195 which was a very busy highway or motorway as we in England would say.

I just couldn't stop myself falling in love with her. I felt really sorry for her as well and thought that she had just never had the opportunity to be shown some real love and affection, even then she could be moody, but I just thought, bloody female. Besides all of this we became very close.

Lily was the first to start and talk about marriage. I thought woah, but constantly she went on about it. I never did propose to her in the end, she said we were going to be together so I may as well let her get on with it. Lily always found it difficult to actually tell me that she loved me. She'd say you know I do Ricky or why would I want to marry you? I'd already been married in England for fourteen nearly fifteen years and recently had what you could call a bad experience with Donna. I was a bit hesitant when I said this to Lily as she would get really pissed off with me and say, "I'm not that fucking bitch, don't talk to me about her."

Donna still owed me money One Thousand Four Hundred Dollars and Lily would often say, "When is that bitch going to pay you back? We need that money for ourselves now."

I told Lily that I would phone to Donna's office in West Palm Beach and ask if I could go to talk with her. The sooner the better Lily would say. Unfortunately I have to tell you about Donna, how we met and how we ended up divorced.

You have to understand that Lily and I really did have a lot of fun together, it was really sad for me when she would suddenly have her mood swings when we seemed to be doing so well. I thought Lily was slowly moving on, that she could see for herself that her life was changing for the better; however her continuing hatred for Mick and this John character would keep raising its ugly head. We'd go many days sometimes maybe a week, then she would always be on the phone to someone in Texas, a friend who was a private detective. Whenever she'd been around George the private detective she was always wound up. Lily used to do private detective work with him and she would be paid by George to follow people or to go with him and witness him serving papers to people. Lily really enjoyed doing this. I think she would have liked to have been a private detective. I didn't like this man. Lily said he was just a friend, a fatherly figure. I told her he was jealous of me and that I could tell by the way he looked at her that he had some kind of feelings for her.

He was a really ugly man. I felt no threat from him, but knew I couldn't trust him, personally I didn't like him but Lily had known him for many years and it was good money when she did work for him, so I thought, OK. We never socialised with him, ever and that was fine by me.

As I've said before, Lily used to be a jockey and worked for many years at the Calder Race Track. Very shortly after meeting Lily I was invited to drive down from West Palm Beach and we'd go into the park to hot walk. Sometimes it was as early as 7am, Lily could hot walk so fast, I simply couldn't keep up with her, I sometimes had to jog and Lily found this really funny.

It was maybe a couple of weeks into our relationship when she told me about her lawsuit against the Calder Race Track. She'd never said anything previously, only about Mick, John and her lawsuit against him.

She told me that the day after Hurricane Andrew she was exercising a horse on the track and that her horse was spooked by something that had blown over and should have been moved. She was air lifted to hospital by helicopter. She had now been told by her lawyer not to hot walk, dance in public or do anything stressful, as the Calder Race Track lawyers would probably have her followed and filmed. I told her I would prefer it if she kept me out of anything to do with any of her lawsuits. She said that she was suing the racetrack for Two Million Dollars. I told her she was nuts and that if she wasn't careful she would end up in trouble. Lily did suffer a little pain, but I knew it wasn't a serious problem to her, she was told to stop any of her work as it would affect her case. This really did frustrate Lily and I think she found it to be a problem to do nothing.

I think this possibly had something to do with her taking cocaine more and more and sometimes drinking cheap

Champaign in the house. Lily often did a lot of sniffing and spitting, sometimes making a horrible noise. I didn't know at the time that this was often associated with a person that took cocaine. I would sometimes feel a little queasy when she did it but she told me that she couldn't help it.

Lily used to really love gardening but after her lawyer told her to stop anything strenuous she stopped. I then did all the gardening and this would make Lily very depressed, often making my situation even worse. She seemed totally possessed by this lawsuit.

Chapter 8

# Mind Games

*There are wounds that never show on the body that are deeper and more hurtful than anything that bleeds*

LK Hamilton

It feels like I'd been in here forever. A lot of my time had been spent in my bunk as I'd been constantly not well and having to visit the nurse a lot. I did actually get the chance to speak to the doctor about what Lily was trying to do to me, about the lawsuit and that it was really to do with Calder Race Track and that no one had given me the chance to discuss what had happened and the failure of the legal procedure to get me a public defender. I asked this doctor to talk to the sergeant and the public defender's office. He said he would but I don't really know if he did or he didn't.

I was way passed depressed and I didn't have much contact with the other inmates. I knew some of them have grown to like me in a way and realized my situation was a very bad one. But a lot of these guys just simply hated me. I was very much in a permanent state of nearly bursting into tears. You have to understand I used to talk to my mother every other day and my son Craig. We were a very close family. My mother and son must have wondered what had happened to me. The constant emotions of this and the sheer horror and disbelief that this was even possibly happening was way off the scale. The uncertainty of what to expect next was way beyond words.

Even some of the inmates here were wondering what was going to happen. I even started to watch them play dominos and cards and they asked me if I wanted to play a couple of times. That was some of the nicer guys. I didn't know how to play. I'd never really been a card player before. They had boards and match sticks for keeping scores and they even said that they would teach me but I told them thank you and declined their offer.

I'd grown a little bit friendlier with the Mexican. He was harmless. The really weird guy in the other bunk still just kept himself to himself.

I must admit I felt really afraid of what would happen in the morning. It was the continuance of Lily's restraining order and I wondered if she would be in court. I didn't know how I would feel if she was in court. How awful! In all, what a sad, silly woman she was.

It was now early in the morning. I had had a shave and I was waiting to be collected by some officers and taken to the court. The stress and pressure I felt now was enormous and I was really afraid. Yet again I was led out to the prison bus, handcuffed, where again we were all handcuffed together. The guy next to me was a black guy. I'd never seen most of this lot on the bus, but there are two black lads from our unit. They keep looking at me and asked me, "What do you think will happen now English?" I simply replied, "I haven't a clue guys, but I'm worried"

Once at the court we were again put into a holding cell. It was always cold, but this one was really bad, even the others made a comment. We all just sat quietly, apart from the odd comment about the cold. You could cut the atmosphere with a blunt knife. Eventually I was led with some of the others into court. The two black lads from my unit were also in the same court. I noticed a clock on a wall. It wasn't even 9am. The deputies were really nasty arrogant bastards. You could have been forgiven if you'd thought they were herding rats from one cage to another, so unnecessary, the emptiness of it all. I had no words.

This was a very large courtroom and we were put into a section. Over the other side of the room was where the public sat. A session was in process at the time but it was coming to an end. I felt shudders through my body, an experience impossible to explain, very daunting, harrowing and a feeling of helplessness. To help myself, I was just thinking that I might get some kind of opportunity to at least say something here, surely?

I was terrified. We were all now cuffed to the benches we were sat on. All of this in front of the public. No dignity at all and I could feel people looking through me.

I heard one black guy say to another as they gave each other a high five, "Here we go mother fucker!"

They seemed to be enjoying it now, as if it was a day out. I was looking around the room slowly, having a little trouble with blurred vision at times, which I think was a lot to do with stress and the violent headaches I'd had. I couldn't see Chuck and Wendy, but I could see Lily! WHAT THE FUCK WAS THIS? How could this be happening? Sat next to Lily....oh my goodness....what the hell was she doing sat next to Lily? They didn't even know each other! I started to have palpitations and I had to slow my breathing down. I suddenly, from nothing, began to sweat. The two black lads sat behind me could see I was suffering some kind of trauma and said, "Hey English, what's the mother fuckin problem?"

"Do you see the two woman sat together across to my right? Well the one on the left is my wife and the one she is now talking to is my ex wife Donna!"

"Holy shit, look at the pair of bitches, mother fuckers the pair of them, you can see it!"

A deputy came across and told them both to sit down or they would be in trouble with the judge who'd just left the room but was coming back shortly.

Lily hated Donna for what she had done to me and now they were sat together like old buddies.

I was wondering where Chuck and Wendy were and I was hoping they would be here, but I couldn't see either of them.

The Judge was now entering the room and we were asked to stand as he took his place. Lily and Donna were sat across to my right and Judge Rothschild was across the room straight ahead in front. As I look towards Lily, Jesus Christ, she was now crying but blowing a kiss to me and mouthing the words I love you. I was totally lost for words. The two black lads saw exactly what happened and they were shouting loudly, "Holy shit nigger, bro, big five, have you ever seen anything like that in your life? The English motherfucker is in serious trouble, you can smell the bullshit from here. The judge looked across and the officers came across again to silence them. I was feeling really ill. I heard them behind me saying quietly to one another, "I wouldn't want to be this white mother fucker now, wait till we get back and tell the bro's about this!"

A young lady then came across to me telling me she was from the Public Defender's Office. Could she have left it any later? She then told me that she could only spare me five or ten minutes at the most. She told me she could only talk about my bond as this was a bond hearing. I told her that I didn't even know I had one and that I'd been desperately trying to get one by putting in request forms asking for a hearing and wanting to see my case worker.

"How can we possibly prepare my defense now? We haven't got time!"

She then told me we were not going to discuss anything to do with your case. This is only to discuss your bond.

All this was happening so fast. I couldn't get my head round how to begin trying to get her to talk about my case. I told her in my desperation that I was innocent of any wrong doing and that no one had interviewed me yet to hear my side of the story. I needed to speak to the judge and tell him. She said I couldn't discuss my case today, just the bond and then told me not to upset Judge Rothschild, as it wouldn't do me any good.

I then asked her, "What is my wife doing here in court, with my ex wife sat next to her?"

She told me to calm down and that she had no idea who my wife or ex wife was.

"What?"

Once again she stated, "I'm just here to discuss your bond, I know nothing of your case, you will need to phone the Public Defender's Office tomorrow to ask for a public defender to prepare your case, you are legally entitled to representation."

"I have been asking for weeks for a public defender and you are the first person I have spoken to from your office."

She just looked at me with a blank expression on her face. I told her I was due in court at 10am, so I must have another hearing to go to, a continuance of a restraining order. I told her I had friends coming to court, but I didn't know if they knew of this hearing as I didn't myself. She asks me nervously,

"Are you friends now present in the room?" she asks me nervously.

"No, not as yet."

She then told me we couldn't spend much more time discussing it. She asked me, "Do you have any money?"

"No I don't, but if the judge will reduce it to 6/7 or a maximum of 8 thousand dollars, I know my friends would put up the bail and I would stay with them whilst preparing my case."

I told her this was a more realistic amount for a misdemeanor charge. She then said, "I'm sorry but unless your friends are present in the room to put up the bond personally, then the judge will not reduce the bond."

"How can I possibly do that, if I didn't even know about the hearing? That being the case, how can I tell my friends to be here? They obviously have not been told, or they would be here now."

I started to tell her that my friends were coming here to testify on my behalf and are witnesses against Lily, my wife. I told her my wife is trying to get me deported for a crime I did not commit and that Lily was trying to sue the Calder Race Track for Two Million Dollars. I hadn't even finished what I was saying when the judge had left the room. As he returned she said, "I'm sorry I can only discuss the bond." She then left me.

So, now I was alone. Nobody had come to help me and my anxiety was now beyond comprehension, in other words, sorry to swear, but it seemed I was fucked, in a real mess and I was desperately trying to keep myself together and at the same time wondering what could possibly be coming next? As Lily and Donna were sat together, what could they possibly be up to? The black lads were pushing me and saying quietly trying not to be loud, "English, what the hell is going on with the bitches?"

I just looked at them both. I didn't have a clue. I turned to face the court and heard one of the lads say, "Good luck English," while the other one said, "He's fucked bro, they're here to stitch him up."

It was announced that the court was now in process, "Judge Rothschild, now proceeding, quiet in the court please!"

I could swear I was going to be told off for my heart beating so loudly.

The Public Prosecution called Donna Vanburan to the stand and she took the oath. The two black lads were as speechless as I was.

She started to tell the judge that I was her ex husband; she then told the judge that I used to stalk her and harass her at her place of work. She told the judge that I had harassed her both at her work and at her friend's house by phone, and that I had followed her home from work in my wife Lily's car to find out where she lived. She then told the judge that she feared for her life and had to put in for a small fire arm certificate to protect herself from me and that she was looking over her shoulder all the time.

At this point I was nearly falling off the bench. I was having really bad palpitations and sweating really badly. It was a wonder I was not having a heart attack. All I could hear from behind me was, "Holy shit, holy shit bro" and the guy sat next to me said, "You're really in the shit now English!"

Donna sat down. How was it that the young lady from the Public Defender's Office told me I was not allowed to discuss my case, yet a woman I hadn't seen for some time was allowed to take the stand and tell all the people in the court room an absolute and utter pack of lies, ridiculous, serious claims against me and I was not allowed to say a single word.

At this point I was in so much shock I was totally speechless. How could Donna do such an evil thing to me?

Whilst writing this part of the story I had to stop as I was so overcome with emotion. I was re-living this whilst I was crying and I even began to laugh at the same time. A sign of loosing the plot a little I thought. I just wished that my dear friends had been in court to see this ridiculous spectacle.

I know now that Lily had George, the private detective, track down Donna. Donna was in a lot of trouble with her finances and it was obvious to me that Lily had to be paying Donna to say all of this. It was like a script. They must have sat down together and thought out what would really make me look bad and help Lily to have me deported. But they had gone far too far with this. Lily now took the stand.

Lily took the oath she started to tell the judge that I was at present her husband and that she was divorcing me. She then told the judge that I was stalking Donna and that I was harassing her to such a degree that she feared for Donna's life. Lily also told the judge that I used her car to follow Donna home from work to find out where she lived. Photos were then passed to the judge showing Lily's bruises. I was totally blown away with the things being said about me and none of my friends were in court to help me. The prosecutor told the judge that I was a menace to society. He then told the judge that Lily was to have a special x ray on her breasts as she had breast implants and that it was possible one was leaking. If that was the case he was going to raise the charge to a felony.

I just sat in silence, very, very frightened and totally shook up. The judge asked me if I had any money and I told him no. I said I would like to say something in my defense but he replied, "This is a bond hearing, do you have any money?"

How could this be happening? Donna and Lily both testified against me with terrible accusations and I was not allowed a single word in my defense and my so called public defender was not saying a word to help me. The judge told me if my friends were not present in the room he couldn't reduce my bond.

"How can they do that if my friends haven't been told about the hearing, I wasn't even told about the hearing."

He then simply said "Bond remains set at Twenty Five Thousand Dollars."

Lily then sat down. I wanted to stand up and clap my hands saying "Bravo, Bravo, can we all see the performance again please?"

"Wait till we tell the bro's back at the stockade about this, its unbelievable English, you sorry arse, they're gonna throw away the key." said the black guys next to me

As Lily sat down I raised my hand. The judge looked a little surprised but he then asked me what I wanted to say. I told him that apparently Lily had sent all my clothes to England without my permission and that I thought she still had my master tapes to my songs, 17 years of my life's work. They were priceless to me. I told him that without those tapes, I couldn't continue working. Lily also had my photographs and promotional stuff. The judge looked at Lily and ordered her to hand over these things. Lily then told the judge that she had sent all my things. Everything had been sent to England.

The judge then told me that he would see me in about 2 weeks for my arraignment.

At that point I just sat down, too weak to even try and say a word. Not one word had been said about what actually happened and why I was arrested and there were no witnesses at all to say they had seen anything on the night of my arrest. This whole thing was based on Lily's word only without a shred of evidence of any kind...incredible!

Lily's detective friend George was sat quietly at the back. I know he played a big part in writing this script.

As I was taken away, both the black lads gave me a high five and said they would see me back at the stockade.

"Maybe," I said, "I have another court to go to yet."

One of the black guys says very slowly "M..o..t..h..e..r.....f.. u..c..k..e..r."

"Yes it is isn't it bro's."

I was then put in yet another holding cell. It was so cold. I was starting to cough again. I was sweating in the courtroom and now I was freezing cold again. I was given nothing to eat or drink and I missed breakfast. I was thinking to myself, "I hope I get pneumonia and die."

I sat alone a little tearful. What a morning it had been. The way things were going, I would be doing autographs back at the stockade. I was totally alone. I wondered if I'd ever get to see my good friends again?

Chapter 9

# A Friend in Need

*When you're in jail, a good friend will be trying to bail you out. A best friend will be in the cell next to you saying, 'Damn, that was fun.'*

Groucho Marx

I felt really drained as I was handcuffed again and led away down some corridors till we entered a room. It was a small room, a little like an office with a large table in the centre and chairs all around. As I entered the room, I immediately saw that Lily was there with Donna. I then saw Chuck, Wendy and Randy. I went to give Wendy a hug but the officer stopped me and I was told no contact was allowed. I was a little emotional. I had never needed a hug so much in my life and I was a little tearful. I told them that I had been to a bond hearing already and that they had missed a wonderful performance from Lily and Donna. They said nothing. I could see Lily was finding it difficult to look me in the eye and Donna didn't even try.

Chuck asked why I hadn't told them and that they would have been in court. I told them that I wasn't even told myself and that the bond remains at Twenty Five Thousand Dollars. Very soon a judge arrived. He sat next to me at the end of a long table. Lily and Donna were away from me at the other end. It was quite a shock to see them both close up and very eery to say the least. Chuck then told me that sadly Wendy had laryngitis and that she couldn't speak a word. Wendy had prepared a lot of what she wanted to say and I could see that she was very upset at not being able to speak. I felt very sorry for her. Wendy was a wonderful lady. When Chuck told me this I looked across at Lily and saw her smile. The judge now started to speak to us. He told us this was a continuance of Lily's restraining order. Both Lily and Donna were allowed yet again to stand up and repeat what they had said at the bond hearing. I asked Chuck if he would say something but he was so shook up and angry all at the same time he didn't know where to start as Wendy had written her own notes and had prepared herself.

So here I was again with no one to represent me from the Public Defender's Office. Wendy couldn't speak and Chuck was in a real mess with himself. I just thought to myself, I hope Lily and Donna are pleased with themselves putting two really nice people like Chuck and Wendy through all of this!

I told the judge that I wished to talk about what had happened on the night of my arrest and try to clear up what Lily and Donna were both saying about me and I was told by the judge that it was ok to speak. I said Lily had told Judge Rothschild that I stalked, harassed and followed Donna home from work in Lily's car, to find out where she lived. Lily just stayed silent. I said how could I have been harassing her if I phoned her work as a gentleman to speak to her? She was out of the office at the time and I left a message for her to return my call. I also phoned Pam who was a friend of both Donna and me. Pam actually married us. I asked Pam if she would speak to Donna about some money I had loaned her.

She was renting a town house in Kendall and the air conditioning stopped working. It happened in summer and the house was very hot and the family staying there had children. Donna was in a real mess at the time and we had split up although we were still seeing each other occasionally. I gave Donna the money as a loan for the new air conditioning unit. it took just about every penny I had left. It was over a thousand dollars. I told her I would still do this even though we were not living together but she had to promise to pay the money back and she said she would. So the only time I phoned Donna was as a gentleman to ask when I could have my money back. As to following Donna home from her work to find out where she lived in Lily's car. I was still married to Donna, long before I even knew you were born Lily. Donna had moved into her new apartment and I already knew where she lived as she had invited me to stay with her at this apartment for a weekend. Donna's own mother and father slept in her bed whilst me and Donna slept on the floor on an airbed and Eric, Donna's son sleeping on a sofa to our side. We had a wonderful weekend. How could I have used Lily's car to find out where Donna was living when I hadn't even met Lily yet?

Now Donna, you had my beeper number and you said you put in for a firearms certificate because you feared me. If I was stalking you why didn't you make a call to arrange to meet me, to give me my money and have me arrested instead? Lily and Donna both sat silent. I told the judge I would like to make a statement as to what happened on the night of my arrest. He told me that if I did that anything I said could be taken down as evidence and maybe used against me later. I told him I wasn't worried about that and that I had nothing to hide, nothing to fear as I was a totally innocent man. With that he asked who would be representing me. I said again no one as nobody had contacted me from the Public Defender's Office. The judge could clearly see that I had caught both Lily and Donna out telling lies. He ruled against me not being allowed to make a statement and told me to get an attorney. I believe he was actually looking out for me and gave Lily an extension up to a year. I was still not allowed to talk or hug my friends and I was sent back to the holding cell and then later back to the stockade. Wasn't it about time I got to say something? If the police had given me the opportunity to make a statement and then had done an interview with both me and Lily in the same room, Lily would have looked a fool very quickly. Plus as I said a lot earlier, after looking at Lily's statement then looking at her injuries, Coco the Clown would have seen it wasn't possible for me to have thrown her up and down a flight of concrete stairs without her legs, arms and feet being torn to pieces.

At the bond hearing the photo she showed was only showing her from the waist up, showing her breast was bruised. She did slip on the spaghetti and then fell down some steps and her eyes were swollen but as I said before, when she cried her eyes puffed up. She told my brother over the phone that she had a broken collarbone and bruised ribs. Lily actually told our friend Randy that I had ran off and that it took three days before they found me. I found this out later! How pathetic was that?

When I finally arrived back at the stockade the other cell mates were talking about what had happened to me in court. The guys that were in court with me had arrived back at the stockade some time before me and were telling everyone that they'd never seen anything like it before. Some of the guys followed me to my bunk asking me what had happened at my other court hearing. I told them that I didn't wish to discuss it, as I was far to upset at the time. I was so tired and I hadn't had anything to eat or drink all day. I hadn't been back in the stockade long when my name was called out. I was told I had visitor and I was taken through to the visitors' room. It was like telephone cubicles with thick glass and a telephone in each booth. You could see the visitors through the glass. It was the closest you could get to any form of contact.

When I entered the room I was told which cubicle to sit in, at this moment I still had no idea who it was. I thought maybe it was Chuck, Wendy, or my friend Doug? But it was our friend Randy. Randy told me that he didn't have long and that they had told him fifteen minutes only. He said I wasn't looking at all well and he could see clearly the terrible trauma I was suffering going through all this. He said what Lily was doing to me was horrific and evil. He then told me that he had a message from Lily.

Randy told me that Lily had said she still had all of my belongings and that she wanted Three Thousand Dollars or she was going to destroy everything.

Randy then told me that he had told Chuck and Wendy this as well.

"This is extortion Randy,"

Lily had lied to the judge in the first court that I had to go to about my bond hearing. Lily was ordered by Judge Rothschild to release all my belongings and return them to me through my friends. She told the judge that she had already returned all my belonging to England. She lied to the judge, straight to his face and that in itself was a very serious crime. I was sure when Judge Rothschild found out about this he would be very upset with Lily and to then go on and try to commit extortion against me for Three Thousand Dollars. What a stupid woman. How could she possibly think she could get away with that? I then told Randy that he would have to testify on my behalf that Lily had said all this to him. Randy told me at the time that he would prefer it if he didn't have to get involved, as Lily knew where he lived and he was worried about his van and his car. He was convinced Lily could damage both in revenge and said Lily would certainly provide enough rope to hang herself. It was just a matter of time before all this caught up with her and when it did, she would be in an awful lot of trouble.

"But what if it doesn't happen that way, will you testify then?"

"Yes," he said. He would definitely testify if it became necessary.

Randy was a good man. Lily introduced me to him. He had a cleaning business and I started to do some work with him part time to help make some money. Randy was a very good person.

He had told me then that Lily had said I had been on the run for three days before the police finally caught up with me and arrested me. He said it was all very sad and that Lily wasn't right in the head. I then had to go back to the stockade.

Chuck and Wendy now had a system where I could phone them sometimes and they would accept the charge. This system was also set up for me with Doug.

When I finally got to speak to Doug for the first time, it gave me a much needed lift. Doug told me that he was in the court building but couldn't find me and everyone he asked couldn't tell him either. By the time he found where we were everyone had gone. He told me that Chuck and Wendy had told him everything that had happened. I then told Doug about what happened in the first hearing. He said he was blown away with the tenacity of the two of them, that it was pure evil and was very, very angry with Lily in particular for everything she was doing to me. I then told Doug he was right about Lily.

After I phoned Chuck and Wendy they passed all the information on to my brother John. Apparently John told them that this could not possibly happen under British Law. Chuck and Wendy then set up a three way call, so Chuck, Wendy, John and I could have a conversation. As the officials at the stockade refused me a call to my brother even when my brother said he would pay for the call. It was very emotional to finally get to speak to my brother, John, as we are very close. He told me that he was absolutely horrified at what was happening to me. He told me that he couldn't understand how the American legal system could possibly allow anyone to get away with this. Lily was making a mockery of the police and laughing in their faces. I then thanked Chuck and Wendy and they said that they would like me to talk to John again. John said he was going to put something in writing to send as evidence for when I went to court.

Doug was now going to find me an attorney to represent me. It wasn't possible to trust in the Public Defenders Office, so I was now waiting to hear from Doug. Within a few days Doug found me an attorney, Mr. Mick Rocque. Doug gave me Mr Rocque 's phone number and when I finally spoke to him, he told me to make some notes as to what had happened along with information on both Lily and Donna. Then when he came to see me in the jail, we could discuss everything and he could leave with whatever I had written down for him. I had to wait until he could tell me when he could actually get to see me, but he told me not to worry as he would make sure he had plenty of time to interview each of my witnesses and study any statements.

*The Aer Lingus receipt that clearly shows (on the right, under the date) that Lily's parcel contained nothing more than my old clothing.*

A few days later I was told by Chuck and Wendy that after my brother John had phoned them, that a package had arrived at Manchester Airport from Lily. John knew that Lily had told Judge Rothschild that she had sent my valuables back to England after she had been ordered by the judge to do so. My sister Maggie went to collect the package and had to pay £222 as Lily had sent it cash on delivery. My family didn't have a lot of money, so to find £222 out of thin air wasn't easy to say the least, but they found it for me. My sister Maggie then drove 75 miles to John's house and together they opened the package only to find old work clothes. They were not at all happy. Lily had put a sticker on the package saying, "I'm a winner."

My family was now very angry at Lily for this. When John phoned Lily to ask her what the hell she was doing Lily just hung up on him. He did later manage to speak to her again and she admitted that she still had my valuable belongings and that she wanted three thousand dollars for them. Remember my brother is a police officer!

I think now is a good time to tell you about Donna and me and then we will continue.

One night I was out with Doug at the Boca Club, Boca Raton and I was watching Sister Sledge. Donna was stood in front of me with a friend and a guy was trying to chat her up and would not give up. He was standing in my way so I tapped him on the shoulder and said to Donna, "I'm sorry I'm late dear." This shook him up and he said he was sorry and that he didn't realise she was with someone.

"That's ok, you weren't to know she was with me."

He then left. Donna was so thankful and asked me if I wanted a drink as a thank you, I said no and that I wasn't chatting her up, I just wanted to get him out the way as he was blocking my view of the show. She insisted in buying me a drink and asked me to stand with her to watch Sister Sledge. I did and we hit it off. She gave me her number and said to call her.

It was a week later before I got to drive down from Doug's at West Palm Beach to where Donna lived and when I did we got on like a house on fire.

It all happened so quickly. It was a real whirlwind romance and after a week, she actually insisted I stay with her for the rest of my time in the USA.

I was introduced to her son Eric. Eric almost immediately started stealing from me and Donna informed me that she had problems with him. He stole money from me and his mother. He had a problem with drugs and was stealing from school and would often not attend school. Donna ended up sending him to Savannah Hospital in Point St Lucie for 4 weeks to help him sort out his problems. Sadly it didn't work.

Donna and I were now very much in love. A couple of nights before I was to fly back to England she took me to a fabulous restaurant called The Cove. She asked me to go for a little walk near the restaurant and we sat by the intercostal, which is an in land river. "I'm going to shock you now Ricky. We are going to be together forever. I've found you now and I'm not going to lose you."

We then discussed the possibility of me coming back to live with her.

I returned to England and we were apart for 3 months. Donna wrote to me nearly every day. She sent me cards and gifts and when I had a cough, she even sent me honey in the post.

Donna came to England for 2 weeks and met all my family. We went to the Lake District, York and London where we attended a show, The Phantom of the Opera. Then we also went to Windsor Castle and attended a family wedding where she announced to all my family, including my mother that she was going to look after me and make me very happy. Everything seemed great. I told Donna I didn't want to rush things and she said ok but we would marry in the end.

When I left England to live with Donna and start a new life, I rented out my home in England, sold all my furniture along with my pride and joy, my car, a Granada Gia, a superb PA sound system and I left lots of work behind. I had a permanent agent who lived near my home and I lived near my family. I was giving up an awful lot to be with Donna.

When I arrived in the USA, Eric had been in hospital, but was now home, still stealing and doing drugs and was very untidy around the house. Donna asked me to have a word with him. She asked me to check that he had done his jobs that she had put on a checklist and posted on his bedroom door.

I took Eric to watch American football, it was very different but Eric became more and more of a problem. Donna still remained in touch with her ex, Eric's dad, which I didn't have a problem with, as it was good for Eric. She told me that Scott, her ex, still loved her and wanted her back, but he was now history to her and that she wanted to marry me. I had to wait 3 months until I could work, to qualify for my work authorization card, but Doug had introduced me to a friend who owned a removal company. I started to work for his company called Father and Son in West Palm Beach. It was very hot, really hard work and long hours for very little money, but I told Donna that I wanted to prove to her that I was a worker and a hard worker at that. I wanted to give her money, so until I could find work singing, I would work for the furniture removal company. Some days I would be out 12 or 14 hours and come home absolutely exhausted and totally dehydrated.

Scott, her ex, was now phoning more often, and I asked if I could speak to him. I tried to be friendly with him, but he was hard work on the phone. It was a really wonderful time in my life although I missed my family very much but I had regular contact with my Mum and son Craig. I was also badly missing being an entertainer. I was somebody back home. I had worked on TV doing stunt work in films; I was hard working and always a very busy man.

Donna was so sweet but it became a little over the top. When we were out, many times during the course of the day she would say to me in a really high, silly voice, "Have I told you how much I love you today?" It's sounded stupid, a little bit like Miss Piggy, nice but a little too often.

One day Donna had been on the phone with Scott. He was flying into Miami, staying in a hotel over night and then flying out again. She told me that she was going to the airport to meet him and have dinner in the hotel he was staying in.

"Wait a minute Donna, he's your ex husband who still loves you."

I told her we could go together, pick him up and bring him to our home. We could cook him a nice meal and we could all chat together which would be good for us and Eric.

Scott was a cruise director on the ships, a fellow entertainer, so we had a lot in common.

I told her that Once I'd met him and got to know him, maybe in the future then maybe I would feel better about it.

I also told her that if Scott and I became friends maybe he could help me with work through his work as a cruise ship director. However I began to question his intentions, as he never made any attempt to get into conversation with me. She told me I was being unreasonable and said she thought it would be a good idea if we went to see a therapist. I told her I had no problems with that what so ever.

Donna made the appointment with the therapist and we went. She seemed a very nice lady, very professional. Donna told her what had happened.

"So you left your home, your son, your family, work and country to be with Donna, correct?" she said.

"Yes."

She then continued "and you are happy to pick Donnas ex husband up, allow him to stay a night at your home, knowing this man still loves your now wife, correct?"

"Yes."

"You have a serious problem," she told me

"What? I have a serious problem?"

"Yes." She pointed at Donna. "She is your problem and I suggest you get away from her as soon as possible. She then continued to tell Donna she should never have married me and that she was the one being unreasonable. We paid the therapist, thanked her and left. Donna was not a happy camper at all.

At this time Donna was renting her town house out to a family in Kendall, south of Miami. The air conditioning unit was working but not properly and a friend told us it would cost over $1000 to buy a new one so he fixed it the best he could but did tell us it wouldn't last. The next day I was up at 4am. Donna made me a coffee and I set off for West Palm Beach, which was a 45 minute drive. Normally when I returned she was always very happy to see me with a glass of chilled white wine waiting on the table. I would take a shower and then she would give me my dinner. She was always very loving to me calling me sweetie or darling, but not today. She was very distant, no wine and very off with me. I asked Eric what was wrong with his Mum and even he wasn't pleasant with me. I was very tired and Eric was sarcastic with me when I said I was tired.

I told him that he couldn't possibly understand what it felt like to come home after a very hard days work, as he had never done that in his life. Eric was still very much in my face with a very threatening stance and Donna was saying and doing nothing.

"What the hell have I done wrong?" I asked her "I want an explanation!"

Eric was now really annoying me and I told him to go to his room as I needed to talk with his mother. It was getting a little heated and he refused to go to his room. I told Donna I was going to take a shower, have something to eat and then I was going to Doug's for the night or there was a possibility me and Eric could end up in a punch up as he was constantly coming at me. When everyone had calmed down tomorrow, we would talk about what was wrong as I had no idea what was going on here.

When I came out of the shower, she handed me my car keys.

"I don't need them yet, I haven't eaten."

"No you said you are going to Doug's and here are your keys."

I noticed my house key was missing.

"Where is my door key?"

"You told me you're going to Doug's!"

"This is all very silly," I told her. I took my jacket and left.

The next day I went back to see Donna but when I got there she opened the door and Eric came out with two large suitcases and a bunch of other items belonging to me. I was totally and utterly speechless. Then I was given a bankbook that was in both our names. She told me to cancel the account and do one in my own name. She then said she had organized a P.O box for me and gave me the details. Eric put my things in my car, refusing to discuss anything, then they got into her car and drove off. I still had no idea what was wrong. I was simply thrown out with no explanation. I knew she was in a lot of debt because the mail was always red and without even opening it I could tell what it was. Anyway I left the house and went to Doug's, but he had gone away for a few days and I couldn't contact him. I had to sleep in my car.

At this point we were married and I was devastated. Whenever I tried to phone her there was no answer so I gathered she had gone away for a few days. When Doug came back, he couldn't believe what she'd done.

Doug said he thought it was all to do with money. He thought she might be contemplating going back to her ex husband and it was possible that was what Eric wanted. He said to give it a few days and see what happened.

I was in a very emotional state. I was now living at Doug's hoping things could be worked out.

I had an appointment with a casting agent and Solomon King. Yes, THE Solomon King, She Wears My Ring, Solomon King.

We had a breakfast meeting and after this he invited me to visit their home in Jackson Memorial Avenue, Inter Coastal Towers. They lived in the penthouse suite. His wife was a really lovely old lady called Evelyn and I sang to Solomon in his living room with no mic, just my backing tapes and he fell in love with my voice. He said he wanted to be my manager and me to be his manager and we set up an agency Solomon King Inc. I became very close to Evelyn and I told them all about Donna and me and that I wanted things to work out between us.

I started to see Donna again and she invited me to stay the weekend at her new apartment with her Mum, Dad and Eric. This was the weekend that I had talked about earlier at the second hearing where I talked about Donna and Lily in front of the judge lying to him.

I was now living with my new manager and his wife however still seeing Donna. She received a phone call from the Town house in Kendall to say the air conditioning unit had completely broken now. I gave her $1000 and told her it was a loan and she had to pay it back as soon as possible. In total she owed me near to $1400. Things seemed to be going well between us. It looked good and as if soon we would be back together until one night I phoned her to see when I could see her again. She told me that she was still not happy about not being able to see her ex and that she had changed her mind about the situation again and we ended up having an argument on the phone. We then decided we would not meet again for a while.

As all this is happening Solomon's wife wanted to adopt me. She said I was more of a son to her than her own. She said I wouldn't have any problems with my immigration if she adopted me. I told her I loved her dearly, but I only had one Mum and I hoped to get back with Donna.

Very soon I met with Donna at the Immigration Office for my work authorization card. Now I could work legally and Donna wanted to go ahead with the Marital Fraud Interview even though she said it was over between us. I told her that unless we were going to be together I didn't want to go ahead with the final interview. We had words in the car park and I tore up the papers for our final interview. When I told Solomon about this he became very worried about us being married but it was over between us. We had a possible recording deal on offer but Solomon was not prepared to go ahead with it while I was still married to Donna. He said Donna could cause us problems and that if we had success, she would come at me for half my money.

I phoned Donna at her work place to arrange to see her and she told me I could meet her at her work, which I did.

I told her everything about the possible record deal and that my manager would not go ahead with anything while we were married. We both agreed it was over and our meeting was relaxed and pleasant. I told her I would still be needing my money and she told me she had non at that time but promised to pay me back. Solomon made the arrangements through an attorney for our divorce and paid for it. It was all very sad.

Chapter 10

# The Plot Thickens

*The rights of every man are diminished when the*
*rights of one man are threatened.*

John F Kennedy

Some weeks later I had a car accident. My car was wrecked! I
needed some money, so I phoned Donna, told her about my
car accident and that I was driving a car that was smashed
down one side and to get out I had to climb over the passenger
side as the driver door was so badly damaged it wouldn't open.
She said she could only send me 39 dollars. That was all she
could afford. A short time later my car blew up and I phoned
her again to ask her for my money. Doug bought me a car for
$600 and I had to pay him back so I really needed my money
back from Donna. Still she said she didn't have any to give me.

At this time Solomon and I were no longer in business
together. It just didn't work out. When my car engine blew up,
I had serious problems as I desperately needed a car. Doug,
being a dear friend in my desperation, knew I had to have a
car and therefore lent me the money, but I should never have
had to take the money from him.

I made a phone call to a friend of Donna's called Pam. Pam
was a notary who actually married us and she became a good
friend to me also. I explained to Pam the situation with Doug
and him lending me money for the car. Pam was a really nice
lady and very professional. I asked Pam if she would speak to
Donna. I told Pam, that Donna had not re paid my money after

I had helped by lending her money for the air conditioning unit that had broke down.

Pam was very disappointed with Donna and agreed with me that I shouldn't have had to borrow the money from Doug. I asked Pam if she would ask Donna to give me the money she owed me so I could give Doug the money for the car. It was Pam's husband Tony who actually supplied and fitted the new air conditioning unit that I paid for.

Whilst talking to Pam about this situation, she told me that Donna had a new boyfriend. I told her I wanted Donna to be happy. Donna made no attempt to phone me and my luck was running out. Any luck I ever had ended when I met Donna. Everything I touched seemed to turn to shit, not gold as it does for some. Now things just seemed to be getting worse and worse, I was now told by my brother John in England that the person renting my house has not paid the rent to my bank for some time and I needed to send money to England. I phoned Pam and explained I was sorry to call again. She said it was terrible and that Donna should have paid me back my money before now.

I had now started to see Lily but wasn't living with her. Lily would help me when she could by letting me use her car. I was using Lily's car sometimes, just before Doug lent me the money for my own car, but still sadly nothing from Donna. When I told Lily about Donna, she called her a fucking bitch. Considering what happened with Lily in the end that last statement coming from her was hilarious.

I made some more phone calls to the reception where Donna worked, leaving a message for her to phone me, but never got a reply. I had spotted Donna driving a different car and Lily told me to go to where Donna worked and get the registration number of her car then she would get George, her private detective friend, to run a check on the plate to find a phone number to contact Donna. Lily said not to go into the office where Donna worked, just to get the registration number of the car. I did what she said and unfortunately got part of the number wrong and George wasn't able to locate anything. Lily said to phone Donna again and I got a beep from Donna's boyfriend asking me why I was phoning her. I said "Hasn't she told you?" He said no. I told him the whole story and he said he was sorry to hear that and that he would talk with Donna and call me back. He phoned me back and told me that Donna had told him to tell me that we were divorced and she had no intention of paying me back and that I was entitled to nothing. I told him that she had still promised to pay me back after the divorce.

The conversations I had with Donna's boyfriend were always cordial, we had no problems at all, but he said she wasn't going to pay me back and that he was sorry, that was the last time I spoke to him. I told him that when I had some money, that I would be taking her to court. Now you can imagine how I felt when as the next time I saw Donna, she was sitting in court next to my then wife Lily, telling the court I'd been harassing her and that she feared for her life to such a degree that she put in for a fire arms certificate and that I was stalking her. At this point I hadn't seen Donna in person for 18 months. She accused me of following her home from work to find out where she lived in her new apartment after we'd split. As she was saying this in court, all those nice people had no idea that she was the fucking idiot as she had invited me to this apartment to stay with her for the weekend along with her Mum and Dad, and her son Eric was there and Donna and I had slept on the floor, remember me telling you earlier?

I was sat in a dock in court with a bunch of imbeciles cuffed to my seat, in orange outfits, black guys giving me big fives saying yo, fuckin bro! Why didn't someone just simply ask Donna, if I had done all that she claimed, why didn't she have me arrested? I suppose that would have been far too easy, don't you think?

How would you feel, all this going off around you and your not allowed to say a single work in your defense, even your own public defender says your only allowed to discuss the bond.

Throughout all this, I often found myself thinking back to my beautiful home. I couldn't tell you the hard work I put into my beautiful garden, my lawns were like putting greens on a golf course, borders around my lawn full of colour, bedding plants and rockeries full of colour and inside my house was also beautiful. I was very proud.

My son Craig was living near to me with his mother. I spent hours playing with my son, teaching him colours and shapes, but my ex moved away to Wales. This was to play a part in my decision to start a new life, a new love, a fresh start. I would of gladly worked to the end of time, if it meant I found true love and happiness.

I was able to visit my mother regularly as she lived only 20 minutes drive away from my home and I phoned her everyday. My two brothers and five sisters all lived within a short car journey. I gave all this up to be with Donna. I was a very well known entertainer and I missed it so much, walking out in front of an audience and singing beautiful ballads with all my heart and then to power into Springsteen's Dancing in the Dark or Roy Orbison's, I Drove All Night.

All that had gone, all gone. I was accused of marrying to get a green card. I married for love. My only crime if I had committed one was to stand by my marriage vows. It's a very cruel world we live in and money being the route of all evil. I had everything but the love of a wife.

As I was writing this I often had to wipe away my tears in disbelief, wasted tears as there would be far more important things to cry over, life would make sure of that like the loss of a loved one in death.

None of this should have happened or been allowed to happen, where were my basic human rights? To be protected by the law from this pair of heartless bastards. Innocent until you are proven guilty and to hear from a police officer, a protector in society that in fact I was guilty until I prove myself innocent and then with a sick grin on his face he said, "Welcome to America... could be a good title for a book, don't you think?"

As I had been writing this, I had become very much aware of people thinking I was a bit stupid. I had actually felt a little embarrassed at times, but I had come through a tunnel. I now thought more than ever, yes I had made some decisions that I could have made differently and sometimes made a complete prat of myself.

There's a fine line between being stupid and naive, but sometimes we need protecting from our own inability to make the right decisions. How many times have you heard people say, I wish I knew then what I know now when I was younger. I dearly hoped at some point in my life, that with all I had been put through, maybe, just maybe, I might have been able to stop it happening to somebody else. If it could be possible through this book to make changes, some kind of solid procedure could be put in place to make sure people are protected from the likes of Donna and Lily and if someone fails by not keeping to a procedure they would be prosecuted.

Back to the stockade...

I was now back in my bunk, my head is spinning with everything what had happened in the two courts and Randy's visit. Lily was trying to get 3000$ from me therefore committing extortion.

How wonderful, I was totally exhausted, both mentally and physically drained, very emotional and not well in myself at all. Looking around I saw guys playing cards, dominos, some just walking around the tables as if they are walking round the block for exercise. The weirdo had gone for his afternoon shower. The black guys are shouting at him in their kind of happy disgust with big fives going around in some kind of celebration.

I was looking at my feet. They were covered in insect bites.

I felt very weak, but I needed to make a request for some paper as my attorney Mr. Rocque was coming soon to interview me. I would make notes for Mr. Rocque like he asked, writing notes on Donna and me, Lily and me then putting a list of my witnesses together, giving him the names and telephones numbers and information as to what they are going to testify to against Lily.

It was nearly feeding time at the zoo. Dinner had arrived. Here we go again. I was eating more nowadays; I just gave what I didn't want to the other animals. I couldn't stand the arrogance of some of these black guys, they walked straight to the front of the queue and then pushed you out the way. I hate to think what some of these guys would do if I bumped into them outside of here.

The Mexican was quite a nice chap, he was no harm to anyone and he often asked how I was doing. He was not very bright, however you might say who the fuck am I to say that? He asked me how long it took me to drive from England. He really didn't know about the ocean, I didn't want to be horrible; it just made me smile which was something I didn't do much anymore. He was arrested for stealing a car....or was it a boat? Sorry, he said he'd like to go to England one day and I very nearly told him that he'd have to steal a bloody boat then.

I was still waiting to see Mr. Rocque and time passed so very slowly. We had new faces in there and one day I was actually invited to play cards again. I knew they only wanted to talk about my case. You could only keep yourself to yourself for so long so one day to their shock I said, "Can I join in but you'll have to teach me?"

They did and some of the stories I was hearing, you just knew most of it was bullshit. I was told not to trust any of these motherfuckers bro's and that came from a black lad.

"They'd steal the steam off your shit," he told me.

The two black lads that were in the doc with me now seemed to be okay with me. Sometimes as I took a walk around the room and passed where they were stood they would give me a big five and say "Yo, English mother fucker."

I started to notice that some of their brothers didn't take kindly to them showing me any kind of friendship at all. They'd say "Hey man are you motherfucking black or white? You'll be the white English piece of shits bitch next nigger"!

Sometimes they'd say. "English its okay man, you've got enough shit to deal with those two white bitches in court! Man, you can see the evil in them, it makes me shudder".

One day we had one of the black guy's playing cards, he'd never played at the table. They called him Joe; he was huge like Mighty Joe Young from the film. Sometimes I thought I was really starting to loose the plot, my mind slipping a bit.

One day, I don't know to this day why but whilst we were playing cards, I decided to say, "Have you all put your names on the list?" At first I didn't think anyone heard, so I said it again but louder. One or two asked, what list?

"Haven't you heard? I thought you all knew what the list was? You know Pavarotti is in Florida, singing live in concert on South Beach?"

They said "Yes, so what!"

"You haven't seen the notice?"

"What notice?"

They were all still playing cards and I told them that Pavarotti was singing again tonight and apparently all the mess and rubbish on the beach had turned out to be a bigger job that they thought, so they are asking for volunteers to go after the show and clear the mess up.

"Fuck off"

"Please yourself. They want all us pieces of shit inmates to clear up all the shit left and they don't have to pay inmates, anyway my names on the list, I just thought I'd tell you."

"Fuck off English." They were laughing. Suddenly Mighty Joe said, "South Beach tonight, do you think we are stupid enough to believe that English.

"Well, you can't say I didn't try to tell you about it, look there's the sergeant, he's just about to leave, you can ask him about it if you want to go. Suddenly Mighty Joe stood up in a panic and this giant of a man ran across the room. You could almost feel the ground shake as he took each stride. He took hold of the bars with each hand and shouted in horror to the sergeant like he might be missing out on something.

"Sergeant, sergeant!!" The sergeant walked across to Joe.

"What's your problem?" Joe replied. "I want to put my name down on the list sir!"

"What list?" the sergeant replied.

"The one to go to South Beach tonight, to clear up the mess after the concert."

The sergeant looked across to our table.

"Have you been talking to English? He's not right in the head either, you dumb shit!"

Well, no one could stop laughing but me as Joe turned and looked straight at me. He then came bounding towards me and all I could hear were others saying English is fucked now when Joe gets his hands on him! I started to run around the table as he chased me but Joe was too slow. Even the black lads were laughing. I was saying as I was running that it was only a joke, it was only a joke.

I was thinking I was dead for sure. Joe suddenly stopped, took a deep breath and started laughing himself.

"You English motherfucker, you got me a good un!"

When all calmed down, we sat back down at the table to play cards again. Up to a week later the others were still asking Joe if he was going to the beach. It could have been very nasty, but it seemed to go the other way. Part of the depression was lifted a little and it was needed as the O J Simpson trial was starting to stir up the black lads and tension was definitely building up towards any white guy. It became a topic of conversation and even some of the officers said that they were worried what would happen in the prisons if O J was found guilty.

I was sitting on my bunk when an officer came over to me.

"Your attorney is coming to see you tomorrow night," he said.

I'd managed to finish my notes for Mr. Rocque and just had to wait now to see if he would turn up and whether he would take on my case. It was now ten or eleven days until I was due back in court. There was a definite buzz around the place and other inmates were saying they hoped my attorney would take your case and give it to my ex's. They should both go away for a long time!

I couldn't sleep that night. Going through in my head, over and over and over again what I was going to tell Mr. Rocque , but then I also thought what would happen if he didn't take my case? I felt constantly queasy in anticipation as to what was to come.

Chuck and Wendy were coming to see me at the stockade. They were declined a contact visit and I didn't understand why they had to be so cruel. Chuck and Wendy were such loving, wonderful people. I remembered being invited to their home, to large family get togethers. The food was always wonderful and they sure knew how to put on a spread. All the brothers, sisters and grandchildren would come and there was a small pool at the back and a constant supply of cold beers for the guys. The kids would paint faces on eggs and it was always such a happy occasion. Lily never wanted to get involved in any of this, which was sad. How could anyone want to miss out on such wonderful occasions? It actually made me feel sorry for Lily. I knew it hurt deep inside, but she couldn't handle the closeness of family. Mind you it wasn't the kind of setting where she could show off her boobs, that would have gone down like the Titanic, a one legged man at an arse kicking competition, a lead brick, yes best Lily and her tit's stayed at home.

Later in the day, the kids always played together and the grown-ups caught up on what was happening in and around their lives and normally the kids would sleep over. Wendy just loved every minute.

The way I met Chuck and Wendy was through my work as a singing telegram. I did all sorts of singing telegrams. I was once a singing frog. I went out as a rabbit and as a gorilla with a pink tutu. I was a hairy fairy and even wore a ballerina's outfit with large pit boots and sang to an office full of females. It was hilarious! Once I did a telegram that was the same as when I met Wendy, but what was different was that I was actually asked by the boyfriend to propose to his girlfriend for him and I was to give her the ring. This was to take place at a beautiful mansion. All the family were there and I sang Lady in Red then Three Times A Lady before I did the proposal. When I proposed, she fell into a deadly silence and was clearly not happy with the situation. I was so embarrassed and it seemed to take forever before she suddenly answered my question and to the relief of everyone she said yes. It was as if the whole world stood still at the time. I was asked by her fiancé if I would sing at their wedding and that money was no object so I said yes. His mother said she would phone me with the final details. They even said if I was out of the country that they would pay flights first class for me and my wife to return, pay for the hotel, then fly us back to where we had come from.

I hadn't heard from his mother in a while, so I gave her a call, she told me that the wedding was off and that her son's wife to be had committed suicide. She had a cocaine problem and when her parents found out she couldn't face them so she killed herself. All because of drugs. The entire family was devastated. How sad because of cocaine, I wonder how many other people are dead because of this. How many people's lives would never to be the same ever again?

One of the most fascinating singing telegrams was when I had a call from the telegram agency, all the office were shouting and whistling in celebration. I was told that the sister of tennis star Chris Evert had booked me to sing to her at a Boca Club Restaurant. It was her 40th birthday bash and Hello magazine were to be there. I had sung to Chris's sister at her anniversary and then she told me she would be booking me to sing at her sisters 40th birthday, but she wouldn't tell me who the sister was. My brother John and son Craig were in America at the time to be best men at my wedding to Lily, therefore John, Craig and Lily were also there when I sang to Chris Evert Lloyd. I was always a big fan of hers myself.

They were such magical fun filled times. Alas they now seem a million light years away.

Chapter 11

# A False Optimism

*For myself I am an optimist – it does not seem to be much use to be anything else.*

Winston Churchill

When Chuck and Wendy came to visit me for the first time, I did my best to make myself look as well as I could but it was always going to be difficult as the strain of it all was obvious for anyone to see. I sat in my cubical and took the phone. Chuck and Wendy were standing on the other side of the glass. We started to talk and I could see that Wendy was having problems holding back her grief. What she was looking at was not the Ricky that she had always known. I was trying to smile and make light of the situation the best I could but Chuck was also visibly not happy at what he could see. Wendy had to walk outside and leave Chuck to talk to me. It was difficult, but I was so happy to see my beautiful friends. I felt so sorry for what these wonderful family folks were being subjected to.

They were not allowed to stay long. Wendy came back in but she had clearly been very upset. Not the kind of day out they were used to. When I was able to get to the phone, they would always pay and put a little money in a kitty for me so if I needed anything, for example, chocolate was a total luxury in here. When they left I was devastated at what they had been subjected to because of my situation and I felt a deep sense of shame.

All this was happening and yet Lily and Donna were still free to lie and commit crimes that they both would have gone to jail for. Perjury in a court of law was an extremely serious crime.

It was now the day when Mr. Rocque would be coming to see me. Everything was very much the same that day and I went outside in the exercise yard where I did some light bench presses.

I'd lost a lot of my strength. I was super fit and super strong for many years. I did triathlons, swimming, cycling, running, 65-70 mile cycles, then 13 mile runs. I was very good, but not good enough to get near to a win. I also ran marathons. I ran the London Marathon, which I completed in 2 hours 48 min 30 seconds. I did cross country and 10k road races. What I had become now was a shadow of my former self. I was once a model working for a big company in London, Ugly's Enterprises Male Models. I had a casting company in Leeds and I did TV and Films including Aufweidersain Pet, Butterflies, Emmerdale, many TV ads and I gave it all up to end up here.

Ugly's Enterprises?? Yes I can hear you....honestly they were a top company to work for. I was going to tell you that I modeled for gargoyles on churches... ahhh I bet some of you don't know what one is? See I'm, not as daft as I look, well I hope not anyway. If you don't know, I'm not going to tell you, you'll have to look it up.

Waiting for the time to pass till Rocque got here was ridiculous. I just didn't think he was going to turn up. I had one or two of the guys wish me good luck for that night.

By the way we had a new guy there. Well I say "guy", he looked and walked around more like a model on a catwalk. He's obviously gay, outrageously camp and I was told a romance was in the air already.

Another new mate was another huge black guy, not a nice man at all, evil. Even mighty Joe didn't want to mess with this one. He had put a really bad feeling into the room, not that it needed a lot of help. The word was that this man would hurt you if you pissed him off.

Eventually my name was called out and I was led to an office. I sat alone for a while and then an officer brought Mr. Rocque into the room and he introduced himself to me. He told me Doug had hired him and that Doug had told him I'd had a rough time and then asked if I had made some notes for him. I told him yes I had and he then told me to tell him what had happened. We sat for quite a long time. When I told him he was horrified and said Lily was a real bitch and that he'd not come across anything like this. He told me not to worry and that she wasn't going to get away with this. He was clearly shocked by many of the lies Lily had told, all because of her lawsuit and he told me Lily would be in serious trouble when it all came out about lying to the judge, trying to extort money from me then bringing to court a false witness who also lied to the judge. Lily and Donna committed perjury in court to the judge himself. Mr. Rocque then told me, that we would have no problems winning this case. I gave him 22 pages headed Lily and me, 6 pages headed notes for Mick and 8 pages headed Donna and me.

I also had notes with the names of my witnesses, Chuck, Wendy, Doug and Randy with their phone numbers and how each person could testify against Lily in my support. I also had the name and phone number of my immigration attorney, Mr. David Kilpatrick. I told him that letters were being sent from England, mainly my brother who is a police officer. Mr. Rocque told me that we were going to ask for another bond hearing so he could get me out and prepare my case but he told me if that wasn't possible, not to worry. He had 7 maybe 10 days to meet with all my witnesses and read testimonies and also to contact my immigration attorney Mr. Kilpatrick. He said he had plenty of time and we would nail the bitch and I would be fine. This would be the only time I met with Mr.

Rocque . The next time was in the court room. Now, at last, I had an attorney and he was firmly out to kick Lily's arse on many serious charges plus the attempted fraud of Two Million Dollars. As Mr. Rocque left I shook his hand and he said he couldn't wait to get to court with this one with a big smile on his face. What a feeling! I was then taken back to the stockade. When I got back I had already missed a bit of aggravation with the new inmate and it seemed he was marking his ground. He was really evil with staring eyes that pierced right through you when he looked at you and he didn't seem to like the attention I was receiving.

I then had the guys asking me about my meeting with Mr. Rocque. I could feel the new inmate's eyes looking at me, trying to intimidate me. The only other good news was that the weirdo in the next bunk had been moved to a mental hospital. That was the end of the entertainment for the black bro's when the weirdo had his daily shower.

It was all about hanging in there now. I have kept copies of all the papers I gave to Mr. Rocque that he had to work with to prepare my case. You must read through them as there are many things written in the Lily and Me and Donna and Me notes for Mick. Many things that you will find very interesting to say the least. Obviously you will also read things that have already been said, but may come across in a different way. You have to remember the mess I was in. In this book you will find that I have gone into more detail although I am finding it very traumatic and at times extremely emotional. I am still in a far better state than I was when I wrote the notes for Mike Rocque.

By the time Mike met up with all my witnesses he had been given testimonies from witnesses in England, more ammunition against Lily. I did make one mistake in part of my statement to Mike Rocque but I was going to correct it with him. As I said when I went to the Immigration Offices with Donna, for my work authorization card after 3 months. I said in the notes for Mike that Donna said she was not prepared to go to the next meeting, that's not correct, she was, but I wasn't unless we were going to stay together and be happy. I had said earlier that she was going to go to the next meeting, so I thought I had better tell you. Now before you read Donna and Me, it's here you will see that I said she wasn't going to go to the next meeting......confused? Sorry it was my error at the time, I could have said nothing but I've left it as I wrote it.

I'm going to tell you something now that I haven't mentioned, I still don't need to so, and I have personally decided to write it.

In the notes Lily and Me, you will read, whilst away for a few days Lily and I had words. We were in a hotel and Lily had just been on the phone late at night to Doug. We were having words, Lily was in one bed and I was in the other. I was giving Lily a bollocking over her rules for her and her different rules for me. She jumped on me whilst I was in bed hitting me very hard, angry at what I was saying. I slapped her across the face. All this is written in the notes for Mike. What I'm going to tell you now, however, I didn't put in the notes.

The next day when Lily woke up she was laughing as she woke me, she had a slight black eye from when I slapped her in my own defense. She thought it was very funny because she said it would make me feel really bad when people asked how she got it. She said they would never believe me when I said it was in self-defense. It was like some kind of trophy to her.

"I will never let you live this down." she said to me as she smiled, gave me a kiss and a hug and said lets go out now.

We left the hotel and continued on our few days away. It was very strange as she kept smiling at me all day, it was the happiest I had seen her for a while. The next day she made me take pictures of her until she got the one that looked the worst. When we got back she stuck the photo on my mirror. I had to keep it there, so when I had a shave I would have to look at it. I told her no, that it was sick and was her own fault it had happened but she just laughed and said it had to stay there for a day or two.

When you read the notes Lily and Me you read about my beeper and car keys, where they "lived" and what she did to me, thumping my arm, tapping me hard on my head. I won't spoil it for you but make sure you read the notes. It's all there. I'd actually forgotten about that until I read my own notes headed Lily and Me for Mike and there was more in there that I had forgotten. So much was coming back to me that must have been locked away with the trauma of it all or maybe I felt such a dickhead and was embarrassed to have put up with so much shit from Lily. Not only did Mike take my notes, he also took a lot of notes himself throughout my interview. He went away with an awful lot of information to prepare my case with more to come from England and my witnesses when he met with them.

What do you think to the show so far?....Rubbish!! So I had every reason in the world not to be ok. Seriously depressed, obviously not looking shit hot as we say. A feeling you could say of being let down a little by the legal system. Horrified at being living proof that it was most certainly possible for people like Lily mainly but also Donna to simply pick up a phone, make outrageous accusations about someone without a single witness to any crime then be allowed to rule a court room, bring to the court a false witness, then together with their legal team, make a total mockery of the American Legal Judicial System and continue to attempt to defraud the race track of two million dollars and send a personal friend to the jail who later ends up in court in my defense. To commit extortion against me through a message through Lily, and terrorize my family. I have a saying, "eleven o' clock will arrive, my day in court will come."

When you see some of the photos I have with some of my well-known acquaintances do I look like a man who needed to marry for a green card to stay in America? I don't think so, do you? I had lots of opportunities with my work and I could have married a very wealthy lady if I'd wished but I married two devious idiot's with no money. It was them that married me for all the wrong reasons, come on, even the village idiot could see that I didn't need to associate myself with women who had nothing.

Chuck and Wendy were also at the time running a kind of fan club hot line. I had two fans fly from Washington DC to Earie, Pennsylvania to see a charity show I was doing. One of the ladies was a very large lady and she'd bought a red dress so I could sing Lady In Red to her on stage at Serones Restaurant and Sports Bar. I lost contact with them, with all this lot. Wendy and Chuck used to hand out flyers for me at my show. Lily thought the ladies from DC were lovely people. The show that I did in Earie was for a family to raise money to send all the family to Disney, Orlando. Three young boys were caught up in a fire, 2 managed to escape, however one of them didn't and suffered brain damage. I did the long drive from Fort Lauderdale especially to do this show. I set up the sound system in the day and News TV companies came to my sound check. It was on the news, 3 different news channels on every half hour covering the build up to the show. There were lots of TV interviews and I was very tired. All three news companies were at the show and it was very emotional. I sang Through The Eyes Of A Child, written by Rob Freeman, who was to be my partner in a new production company based in Miami, it was a very beautiful song.

Aaron, if I remember correctly, took his first steps with the aid of his Mum to me on stage and then I sang the song. The mother was a personal friend of Lily's and they did go to Disney.

I now can't even enter the USA, try and get your head around that, I'll tell you more about this later.

All the videos I had showing my interviews are still to this day with Lily, priceless memories that are denied me.

I met Lily's mother in Earia. She was an alcoholic. When Lily was not in the room, she even asked what a nice man like me was doing with her daughter and to make sure I looked after myself. She said she knew Lily could be a very difficult woman.

# Chapter 12

# Joking in the Face of Adversity

*Sometimes you climb out of your bunk in the morning and you wonder if you're going to make it, but then you laugh inside as you remember the good times that made you feel that way.*

Ricky Dale

Every minute of every hour was passing so slowly. It was as if someone wanted to torture me. To drag all this stupidity out and make me suffer. I knew I was a good man and I had my place in heaven, if there is one. If He was waiting at the Pearly Gates, I was going to knock him out and say, "You know what that's for."

Only Joking, but it all just made me feel so angry. Look at the earthquake in Haiti and all the wars throughout the world. It made me question everything. Obama on the news today said he was stopping the space project. Bush was pushing ahead for man to walk on the moon again, I think Obama was right, the money was needed for far more important things.

One new guy on the block was definitely not liked by anyone. He was feared. He pushed to the front when it was meal time and no one said anything. It was funny really, but in here they made bets using food as money. It could be a baseball game or football game or anything else you might want to bet on. It could be your breakfast, lunch or tea or a simple bar of chocolate or some cigarettes. One day a big American football game was on TV, I think it was Pittsburg against Miami Dolphins. The new guy was taking bets against the Dolphins, he was a real arrogant bastard with a chip on his shoulder. I was not in a good frame of mind at all, really down in myself and not well. We all stood watching the game and The Dolphins were way down at half time. They all said the game was well and truly over and this guy was being a real prick saying," I can't wait until I collect my winnings."

I don't know what came over me but I walked up to him and I said, "I'll have a bet with you. I'll bet my breakfast tomorrow that the Dolphins win this game."

He burst out laughing and said, "If you want to bet on the Dolphins, I'll take your breakfast you dumb mother fucker English, that is you isn't it? What the fuck are you trying to prove ten minutes into the second half?"

"I'll make that my dinner as well on Miami

"Ok."

Another ten minutes passed and I told him to make it my evening snack as well. Everyone else thought I'd lost the plot. I went to my bunk and lay on it. I couldn't see the TV but I heard the volume of the guys building up, shouting and cheering. Well would you believe it, The Miami Dolphins came back to win the game! As he walked back to his bunk, I shouted, "I'll see you in the morning bro, remember, for your breakfast you owe me, the Dolphins won!"

The look this man gave me was enough to send cold shivers through an Eskimo. I was told by the guys not to push my luck and that I should be out soon. They said he would hurt me if I really pissed him off.

The next morning I shaved as usual. I think my face had grown thicker skin as the razor didn't seem to cut me up as much now. Not a word was said about the bets and everyone knew he was never going to pay up. So here it was, breakfast time, yes the big twat walked past everyone to the front and pushed the guy at the front of the queue out of the way. He picked up his tray and walked straight past me towards one of the tables. Everyone carried on. I just couldn't tell you what came over me but I shouted.

"Oi. Oi!!!!"

He stopped and the whole room fell silent as he turned around. The guys looked on horrified at what happened next. I told him I had decided to let him have his breakfast. I wasn't that hungry anyway. He just stood in total disbelief. Then he breaks the silence.

"You're definitely not right in the head English."

He then turned away and walked back to his table. I don't know why I did that. I spent most of the day in my bunk. I felt disturbed by all of it. Dinnertime came and once again he walked to the front, took his tray and walked passed everyone. Again I couldn't tell you what possessed me but again I shouted.

"Oi, excuse me!"

He turned around.

"I've decided out of the goodness of my heart that you can also have your dinner."

He shook his head and this time looked around the room at all the other guys, as if to say what's wrong with this guy? I just couldn't let him get away with it.

I had to see the nurse to get my medication. I was quite tired so I slept a lot on this particular day. I didn't even bother to play cards. A snack arrived and my new found friend was asleep on his bunk. He hadn't realized it was here so I took my snack and walked over to his bunk. I heard some of the other guys speaking.

"What the fuck are you doing English? Don't even think about disturbing that evil bastard!"

Well it was too late. He was on the top bunk and I gently tapped him on his forehead. He opened his eyes and for a second he must have thought he was dreaming. Before he said a word, I said to him, "Here's your evening snack. I've decided to let you have that as well."

I then simply turned away and headed back to the queue to collect my snack. He was now shouting at me.

"You crazy mother fucker English, you crazy mother fucker. He's one crazy mother fucker guys isn't he?"

He started to laugh and so did everyone else. I think they all thought the shit was about to hit the fan, but I had one over on him.

The next day, everyone was outside in the exercise yard. Not far away was a boot camp and sometimes the boot camp guys would jog passed with the sergeants screaming at them, singing in time as they jogged. I was stood by my new found friend watching him bench some seriously heavy weights. I was flexing my chest in a comic fashion when he suddenly pulled off his heavy sweaty T-shirt. The man was built like a brick shit house, solid as a rock. He was stood right by me and looked straight through me. I looked at him.

"Now I bet you're fucking glad I didn't make you pay your bets yesterday, aren't you?"

He looked at me in disbelief and then started howling with laughter. He put his hand on my shoulder.

"I must say English, I like you,
and you're okay, not like this other bunch of mother fuckers."

When I went inside I felt a little sick and could feel this incredible pressure building up inside me. I really believed at this point that I must be close to having a major nervous breakdown. I just didn't know what to do with myself.

When I get back to my bunk, the Mexican had gone. He was an ok guy and I actually felt sad that he had gone. This was a situation that I just couldn't get used to. Every hour of every day was very difficult. I was up and down, my emotions running all over the place. I often found myself going back in time to my son, my family and how I adored my shows. It runs through my blood, I thought to myself. How can my life ever be the same again? Even though I was totally innocent, I couldn't win.

At some point I would tell my mother about this, but where would I start? It would upset her incredibly if she knew. My Mum was also my best friend.

Over the past few days, I had managed to speak to Chuck and Wendy and they had told me that Mr. Rocque hadn't contacted them or any of the people on his list. I told them not to worry, Mr. Rocque was really upset with what Lily had done to me when he left me and he was all fired up for the case. He still had time to do what he needed to do.

Also my caseworker had finally come to see me. What an arrogant man. He showed no real interest in me or my case and basically did nothing. I asked him where he'd been all these weeks, all the request slips I'd put in without an answer but he said nothing, just that he had to leave. What a total wanker this man turned out to be. The guys were right about him weeks ago.

Again we had another new comer. He was an older gentleman, clearly intelligent and he was my new bunk neighbour sleeping where the Mexican had slept. He was also very well mannered. He told me that I seemed very popular in here and apparently some of these guys seemed to respect me.

"They call you English, why's that?"

"It's just the way things have turned out," I said.

He replied saying he didn't want to call me English as it sounded a bit primitive so I told him he could call me Ricky if he wished. The situation with this man just didn't fit. He said he was being bailed out almost immediately but he seemed to need to talk. He was very stressed.

"I can't believe what's happened to me, it's not legal," he said suddenly.

"Tell me about it!"

He told me he had lost his wife a year before and that he lived near to an area that was slowly turned into a bit of a red light district, not too bad but slowly getting worse. He went on to tell me he had been very lonely and had no family.

"I just parked my car on my own drive when a very nice lady came up to me."

"Do you live in this house?" she said

"Yes."

He told me he was on a real downer and she said that I seemed a nice guy and I thanked her. He then told me that he went on to ask her if she was lost and if she needed directions.

"No silly. Would you like some company for a little while? It wouldn't cost me a lot of money."

"She seemed so nice and I realized she was a prostitute. I had never in my life been with a prostitute but I was feeling very lonely, so I said yes, I would like some company. Then as I walk to my front door to let her in, she told me she was a police officer and arrested me for picking up a prostitute on the street. I'm being bailed out and my attorney is coming to get me," he said.

Well, what can you say to that? The policewoman came onto his drive and cohorts him and then arrested the man. He was so upset in case people found out. He said his wife must have been turning in her grave.

In a very short time he had gone. He wished me well and said he felt very sorry for me. He said it must be horrendous being in here with these disgusting animals. He had heard some of the guys talking about my case and said he could not understand how this could be possible, to be keep you in here for so long. He thought it was disgraceful.

Throughout my stay, whenever the church came, which wasn't every week, I would attend. I found it very difficult to sing the hymns and I became overwhelmed by it all. The Chaplain said they always had a word with someone in the office about my situation as I had told them all about it. They also said that it was against the law and against my human rights.

That was another day gone and another day closer to my final day in court. Let the battle commence. Lily was going to shit herself as all my witnesses lined up against her. Randy was definitely going to testify against her and finally I would have the chance to tell the judge everything that had happened. I just wondered what they would do to Lily in the end but that was not my problem. Both Lily and Donna married me for all the wrong reasons.

One of my witnesses was called Sari. She was a children's entertainer and we were very close friends. She saw straight through Lily right from the start.

One night when we were out Lily had had a bit to drink. Sari and Doug were in the bar and Lily pointed at me.

"See Ricky there, I'm going to get him to fall in love with me, marry me and then when he's a star, I will want for nothing."

"In your dreams Lily."

Sari was coming to court to testify to that. I had found out that apparently for an American to marry someone for financial gain was against the law and they could face a 10000$ fine and even a possible jail sentence. It was obvious to anyone that was the reason they both married me and between them had destroyed my life.

As the days passed, I was just watching everyone from a distance. I played the odd game of cards but I still had really bad headaches. I had another unpleasant thing happen to me. I suddenly started to get lots of spots above my dick and I had to see the nurse about it. All very embarrassing I can tell you.

It appeared that our she-man has been giving out sexual favors to some of our black bro's. Mighty Joe seemed quiet smitten by him/her. It was near comedy to just sit back and digest what went on in here. All the officers were really unpleasant even though they had all heard about my very serious situation. No one, including the sergeant, had lifted a finger to even try to see what could be done to help me. My cough seemed to be getting worse. If I went out to sit in the sun a while I felt a little better. It was still a little cold inside.

I hadn't spoke to Chuck and Wendy but I would see them the next day as today was my last day of being locked up. I spoke to Mr. Rocque later that night. I felt like my brain was itching and I wanted to scratch inside my head. I felt agitated beyond words. I can hardly bear this annoying feeling in my head. I couldn't sleep even though I feel desperately tired. I also had a headache.

When I got out of my bunk, I went for a walk around the room. I was unsteady on my feet and the anticipation was so overwhelming. I would have those two bastards tomorrow in court....yes, I would have them tomorrow. Justice would be done and I would have a party with my friends to celebrate.

I then had to go to the phone to speak with Mike Rocque. When Mike answered, he told me he was late for his next meeting and that he would talk to me tomorrow in court. He quickly told me the prosecutor was after my blood.

I laughed and said he was going to get his arse kicked tomorrow. That bitch would be going down for a long time. He then said he had to go and he would see me in court. Tomorrow was going to be a really big day in my life. As you can imagine I had no chance of going to sleep that night.

# Chapter 13

# I'm an Alien, a Legal Alien.

*It takes a man to suffer ignorance and smile, be yourself no matter what they say*
Sting – An Englishman in New York

It was early in the morning when they came to get me. As I walked to the cage, some of the guys were shouting.

"Good luck English."

One of the black lads who was in court with me before shouted "Get the mother fuckin pair of bitches English!"

A couple of them give me a big five.

"I hope not to see your sorry white face again bro," said Mighty Joe with a big smile, I even got a little wave from the he/she.

It was all a little emotional. I was taken to the police van and when we arrived at the courts I was put in a holding cell. It was so cold in there it was a wonder some people didn't get pneumonia. You were always cuffed to someone and I tell you now it was so degrading. They left me in this cell with no drink or food for a long time. I felt like a gladiator waiting to go into the arena and I was ready to battle. I just couldn't wait until I was asked, "What is your interpretation of what happened on the night of your alleged crimes Mr. Dunphy?"

I had gone through it over and over again. To see my dear friends one by one stand and take the oath then deliver to the court their own personal experiences with Lily and some of what Lily had said and done. I wanted desperately to see Lily's face when Randy told the judge that she had sent him to visit me in jail to tell me she still had my things. Despite the fact that Lily only hours before had lied, perjured herself to the very judge she would stand before today. Also I couldn't wait until Randy told the judge that she had demanded $3000 or she would destroy my things bearing in mind she was demanded earlier by this judge to release my things and to which she said she had already sent my things to England.

I also couldn't wait to hear Mr. Rocque tell the judge that he had a letter from my brother, my brother a police officer saying that Lily had sent a package of items but it only had in it old work clothes, papers and some photos and she even had the audacity to put a smiley face on the package with the words, "I am a winner" and she also sent it cash on delivery costing my family hundreds of pounds and a 75 mile drive to Manchester Airport to collect the package. In this letter Lily told my brother that I had no friends anymore as they were all disgusted in me and wanted nothing to do with me, yet lined up in court would be Chuck and Wendy, Doug, Sari and Randy. The judge would be told that Lily also told my brother John that she had a broken collarbone and bruised ribs. I really needed to see the look on the judge's face and then turn to see the dread on the face of Lily.

What would she think when Chuck and Wendy took the oath and told the judge about when Lily went to visit them and told them both over a cup of tea that she was so happy I had them as friends because I would be needing them very soon. What would Lily say in reply to that when the judge asked her what she meant by this? Lily also said that she'd spoken to my ex wife in England and that my ex had told her I'd beaten her on several occasions. A letter is now with Mr. Rocque from my ex-wife in my defense. Lily also said I had beaten my ex father in law. Also in his possession Mr. Rocque would have a letter in my defense from my ex father in law. Both of these letters stated I had never touched either of them. Of course she wanted to say as much as she could to make me look like some kind of monster. Obviously it would all have a serious effect on my case because of the huge case going on with OJ. Remember Chuck and Wendy were out with us the night of the alleged incident.

Doug would also take the Oath, my good friend. He was going to tell the judge that Lily actually asked him to lie in court and say that at some point I actually confessed to him that I did do all these things that Lily had said!....What would the judge think to that? Also my dear friend, children's entertainer Sari was going to be in court and would tell the judge what Lily told her in the bar that she was going to make me fall in love with her and that when I became a star she would want for nothing for the rest of her life. In reality Lily had broken the law yet again by marrying me for financial gain. Then of course bringing in my ex wife Donna. Lily and her detective friend must of thought this would be a massive strike and that I would obviously be totally blown away with it. No way could I have anticipated what they probably thought was a masterful piece of genius between their very evil, twisted minds.

When finally given the opportunity to speak, I would make mincemeat of Donna's part in all this. Being able to tell the judge what I'd suffered with Lily, trying my best to be a good husband and standing by my wife when I felt she most needed me. Her cocaine and drink problems, being unfaithful to me for cocaine, how I took her back and nursed her, telling me in graphic detail what happened and why she was unfaithful. I wanted the same graphic detail told in court. I wanted to turn to the public gallery and tell them I had held my dear wife in my arms, already beside myself with grief at knowing she'd obviously been with another man. I wanted to tell them as I was comforting her, looking into her eyes with her nose gently bleeding from the cocaine, almost a pathetic innocent child like look, exhausted and dehydrated with a pale white face how she then told me how she'd been to a hotel with another man only for cocaine. That she'd never seen so much cocaine in her life and how he was a nasty perverted man, making her do various sex acts and that he'd fucked her in the arse with a double headed dildo. This is now fucking killing me to write this, I'm going to have to stop, I'm trying to catch my breath as I write this, I'm so upset, sobbing, trying to keep control as I write, no I'm loosing it now, I will have to come back to this later....

Why hadn't some simple procedure been put in place, where someone very easily would have spotted that something was seriously not right with Lily's version of events. Then if they had investigated further, all this could have been prevented.

There were so many things I needed to tell the judge Mr. Rothschild. But to be honest after Mike had interviewed all my friends and put all this together with the letters he had from England I thought there would be overwhelming evidence against Lily and the judge would simply throw Lily's case out of court. Case dismissed, me released and then Lily arrested on many charges. I thought that Calder Race Track, for the attempted fraud of two million dollars would bring charges against Lily. You would think the court would have to tell the racetrack what has happened? After all Lily did all this to get me out of the country to protect her lawsuit against the racetrack. How ironic, if after I was released I was actually called to court as a witness on behalf of the racetrack.

The doors to the cell opened. Yes! I was taken out and led to the courtroom. The courtroom door opened and I could see across the room. I noticed it was the same room I was in before when previously in front of Mr. Rothschild. To my utter delight, I could see Chuck, Wendy, Doug, Randy, Sari and Mike who was is in conversation with the public prosecutor. Lily was in the room and I could also see her detective friend George.

All my friends were at the far side of the room and it was impossible for me to speak to them from where I was. I was now cuffed to my seat and all my friends gave me a wave and smile.

Rothschild entered the room, I have no words for my feelings at this point, I felt like a sprinter waiting for the starter to fire the gun and then I could sprint to take the gold.

Rocque came across to me.

"Hello Mike and how are you today?"

He started to tell me that the court was not going to hear my case.

"What? They are not going to hear my case against Lily today? Then what are we doing then? Why are all my friends here in court?"

He then told me that while I had been in court, Lily had divorced me and this now meant I had no legal status in the country. What the hell did that have to do with this case? I wanted my day here today in this courtroom and for my friends to testify against Lily with me being able to speak directly to the judge in my own defense letting them all know what I had suffered. It was only right they let me do that! I had rights.

Mr. Rocque very sternly told me "I'm sorry Mr. Dunphy that's simply not going to happen today."

"But you're my attorney, talk to the judge and make it happen."

I could see across the room that my friends were looking and could obviously see the look on my face as I was speaking to Rocque. They could clearly see I wasn't happy about something. I could see Lily with a smile on her face.

"What do my witnesses think to this?"

"I haven't told them yet."

Rocque told me that the public prosecutor said he and the judge wanted to deal with this today. They wanted the case out of the way.

"Well can you please forgive me for being a little confused, but how the hell can we do that if my case against Lily is not heard? It doesn't look like she has confessed to it all, so we can all go home."

"No Mr. Dunphy, she has not confessed to anything."

"Then what the fuck are we going to do now Mr. Rocque? I whispered in his ear. "I suggest you go and demand we certainly do hear my case today."

"That's not going to happen Mr. Dunphy, a deal is being put to you."

A deal. A deal!! This wasn't a game of cards; this was my fucking life we were playing with.

"Here's the deal Mr. Dunphy. Because you are now divorced you have no legal rights. You are in fact now an alien.

"What? An alien? I've been called some things in my time but never an alien. You must be on another planet if you think for one minute I'm going to take any deals."

"Let me continue Mr. Dunphy. If you take a plea of no contest...."

"No contest? I've done nothing wrong! Lily is the criminal. She has to go to jail today! I've done nothing wrong Mr. Rocque, I'm not guilty of anything!"

"No one is saying you're guilty."

"No contest means no one wins, we all just go home. No chance. Mr. Rocque, I demand my legal rights to my day in court, a jury trial even."

"Let me continue," said Mr. Rocque, "if you take the plea of no contest you will be deported immediately."

He then told me I could return to the USA after 12 months but if I was to return before, I would have to serve a 12 month sentence because they were going to give me a 12 month suspended sentence on probation with no costs. This would be served in the UK. I would have to fill out a form once a month and post it from anywhere but the USA

"Are you totally mad Mr. Rocque? How can you possibly tell me to accept no contest, me thinking no one wins but I have a 12 month suspended sentence from the UK? I am an innocent man, I have already been in jail now for 6 weeks for a crime I didn't commit. I have 5 friends in this court room that are witnesses to testify against Lily, five American citizens that started out as personal friends of Lily and they are here now to testify against her. All of my witnesses are willing to take a polygraph test."

"That's not going to happen Mr. Dunphy."

"I want a jury trial then. Why can't we do that today?"

"Mr. Dunphy, if you have a jury trial, I've been told that you can..."

"Then that's what we'll do. Today my friends will bail me out and then we'll prepare my case while we wait for the jury trial."

"Mr. Dunphy because you are now no longer married sir you have no legal status in the USA, no sponsor, nothing. The judge has told the prosecution that if you demand your jury trial you can have it, but you will have to go back to the stockade for 6 months pending your trial, then if you win or loose, because of your divorce, because you have no legal status you will have to be deported the very next day Mr. Dunphy, win or loose."

"My witnesses will sponsor me, take responsibility for me, whilst I'm living at Chuck and Wendy's pending a jury trial. Put it to the judge.

Mr. Rocque then became really pissy at me, saying, in his opinion; I would never win a jury trial.

I demanded to speak to my immigration attorney Mr. David Kilpatrick; I had rights I told him. Although not happy, Rocque agreed to phone Mr. Kilpatrick from the courtroom but I would not be able to speak to him personally as the phone would not reach to where I was sitting.

Mr. Rocque returned from making the call and told me that Mr. Kilpatrick advised me to go home.

I then told Rocque to go ahead and tell my friends about all this bullshit and that I still wanted to fight my case. He just looked at me in total disbelief. Mr. Rocque then went over to them and as he was telling them I can see the shock and anger on their faces, trying to gesture to the judge so they could be heard. Mr. Rocque then went to talk to the public prosecutor and they both left the room.

I sat in absolute devastation. How could this possibly be happening to me? How could Rocque do this after meeting my friends and taking their testimony and reading the letters of support from England? How could my own attorney do this? He had been paid $1000 up front after meeting me at the jail. He was so outraged at Lily, telling me he couldn't wait to get her in court and that she was going to be in very serious trouble. Then he turns up in court to supposedly to fight my case and was now saying go home. Nobody could possibly begin to understand what I was feeling at that time. It was simply impossible. I would defy the best actor in the world to try and act out how I felt.

Rocque came back and told me he had been on the phone to the immigration people and had told them about my situation and had asked them if they would accept me staying with Mr. and Mrs. Norman pending trial. They said if the court agreed they would permit this, but then Mr. Trip (I think that's what his name was) then asked the immigration people if they would be prepared to allow me to be freed to possibly murder my wife whilst I was out? The immigration people said no so Mr. Rocque again said it was either you took the no contest or went back to jail for 6 months pending a jury trial.

At this point I was in a terrible mess. Not in any physical or mental state to be sat in the dock. I told him to speak to my friends and tell them what had happened.

For 6 weeks I had been to hell and back so many times. I wanted to fight on but what I couldn't begin to imagine is what state I would be in in 6 months. I could hardly sit in my seat with my grief and all my friends could clearly see the state I was in now. Even Lily couldn't even look at me. What a horrible mess! Rocque told my friends and came back over to me trying to be nice telling me win or loose my case in 6 months time, I would be deported, so whichever way it went, I was still to be sent home and because of my mental state and my heath they wanted me to go home to England now and be with my family so they could care for me. Then if I still wanted to I could return to my friends here in the States.

I was now so weak I was bent over supporting my head with my arms, so desperate for someone, something to stop this horrible nightmare, I couldn't even see the paper I had put my name on saying I would go home. No contest.

"Guilty until you prove yourself innocent," as the officer said at the beginning of all of this and then "welcome to America."

Even when I was in court with all my witnesses, I was denied my legal right. Everyone was in the courtroom. The judge could so easily have heard all the testimony without the need for a jury trial. What were these people doing? All my friends were clearly devastated. So many people deeply hurt by all of this. A trauma they would never forget for the rest of their lives.

How could I blame the immigration people? They knew nothing about my case. How could they know what I could or couldn't do? The prosecutor finally stuck the knife in and twisted it, finally killing my chance to be with my wonderful friends that night. I was not even allowed to spend 5 minutes with them. I wanted so desperately to comfort Wendy because I knew how devastated she was across the courtroom.

Back to a holding cell, freezing cold in my desperate condition, I seemed to feel the cold worse than ever and again

I hadn't had a drink or food all day. Not that I could eat at that moment but I really did need a drink. My mouth was so dry.

I arrived back at the stockade. Even the officers were shocked to see me. Everyone thought I would be free that day. Everyone could see I was in a total mess and were sympathetic towards me. No way could I even begin to discuss what had unfolded that day. I was given a drink but I couldn't eat and I just simply went to my bunk.

It was now Friday morning. To my surprise my name was called for a visit, but it was not visiting day. I thought maybe it was Rocque, not that I would want to see him after he obviously sold me out to the prosecution. When I first entered the visiting room I was told to go to the cubical at the end so at this point I still had no idea who it was that had come to visit me. As I turned into the cubical, to my absolute shock and horror, it was Lily. She could see the look of shock on my face. What the fuck was this... the finale? Lily told me not to be angry with her and that she'd come to talk of nice things. I just sat totally dumb struck, unable to get any kind of grip of the situation. She then told me that she had been down to the courts and that she had to really fight to get a special permit to see me. Could you imagine the look on the faces of the people in court when they realised she wanted to visit the person who allegedly had beaten the shit out of her? She then went on to tell me that she thought I was a wonderful person and a gentleman and that nobody had ever loved her the way I did.

"You have had me branded a menace to society and a dangerous man and now finally you're having me deported for a crime I did not commit! Why are you here? Why are you telling me this?"

Lily was now crying. She told me that a day never went by without her missing me and that she often cried wanting me home. She told me that she really loved me and I was now starting to cry with my hands shaking uncontrollably. She then asked me if she could send me a gift to England.

"And what would that be?" She told me she wanted to send a guardian angel to look after me.

"A fucking what? A guardian angel to look over me????"

I could hardly believe what I was hearing. Then she told me that she was worried about me. I was now laughing and crying at the same time. She asked me to calm down before I gave myself a heart attack and started calling me sweety. She then went on to tell me that Poo Poo the dog had been doing well as he had not been well, telling me that I was Poo Poo's daddy and always would be.

"Fuck Poo Poo the dog!" I said. "You have no idea what I have been through. I've been in a hell hole for 6 weeks!"

My friends had been through hell because of her bloody law suite against the racetrack. When back in England I'd lost my home, I had no money, no car and no sound system. Without these things I could not work at all. I told her I had ill health, that my immune system was low, that if I caught a cold or flu it could be really harmful to me.

"You're having me sent to England, to a damp and cold English winter"

As I was saying this I actually fell off my stool then climbed back on it again totally bewildered. I told her when I had done kissing and hugging my family, I would have nothing and that I would be a burden to them. Lily then said she might be able to get me a job in a circus somewhere warm. She knew lots of people in the circus. I told her to leave me alone and asked her if she had sent the rest of my things to my brother. She told me she had. I then asked about the master tapes and she told me that she had written a letter to me, telling me about my tapes. The deputy then walked in and told Lily she had to leave. Her time was up. As she was walking away I asked again about my master tapes but she didn't answer. I could only assume that she still had them.

When I got back to the cell I told the others. They all said she had to be simply mad. A little later I spoke to Chuck and

Wendy. They told me that Rocque had not contacted them, had not answered any messages that they had left and had made no attempt to meet with them to prepare my case. A meeting wasn't set up until the very last minute. They had to meet him at 1pm which was only about 1 hour before the hearing. So Chuck Wendy, Doug, Randy and Sari all went to his office for 1pm. Mr. Rocque had had all week to meet and call my witnesses and read all the written testimonies from England. He had left it all until the very last minute giving him not a chance in hell to prepare for my case. Wendy then told me that Rocque didn't get to his office till 1.40pm, giving himself no time to talk to anyone or read the testimonies. They all thought he was a disgrace to the legal profession. We all knew he had sold me out and done a deal with the prosecution. He made no attempt to fight my case. The notes I had given to Rocque at the jail/stockade would, on their own, have been enough to win this case. As long as my witnesses were in court to testify, as they were, then Lily had no chance. I wondered what deal he had done with the prosecution. It must have been something big. To let go of such an easy case to win as mine was and to let Lily walk free from the courtroom!!!

It was Friday night and I was not getting much sleep. At approximately 5.30am I was woken up by one of the officers and told that I was going back to court. What! Back to court? I had already been to court. They must have the wrong person. I was to be deported immediately so unless they were taking me to be deported they must have the wrong man.

"No," he said, "it's you, James Dunphy, to go to court."

I had to get dressed quickly, didn't even have time for a shower and I put into a van and off we went. All I could think was what the hell was happening to me now? What court would this be? Was it possible they wanted to behead me like they did in medieval times? When you think about it, these bastards could do just about anything they liked.

So, I was back in a holding cell. The holding cell was full and I had nowhere to sit and no one was saying a word. It was all totally wrong! I was in there for a total of 4 and a half hours. I happened to hear someone in the cell say that everyone in there was on a felon charge or was being up graded to a felon charge. When I heard this I said it was impossible as I was on a misdemeanor charge and did a no contest plea. I was being deported back to England.

Then a really mean looking black chap perked up.

"Well mother fucker, if you're in here they have probably found some other charge to put on you and it must be a felon charge, they do that sometimes, sort one offence out and then find something else to do you on.

I was struck into sheer silence. I felt so ill. Even in this cold holding cell I could feel the sweat running down my back and I had a very bad headache within seconds. I was now having palpitations. I must have a bloody good heart to stand all this. Finally I was taken into a court again. It was a big TV screen with a judge and I was in there some time. By the time I got to the front, the judge, a woman, simply said, "Immigration hold, no bond"

"Jesus," said the guy behind me, "what have you done to have your bond cancelled? You must be a really bad lad!"

I was then quickly taken out of the room and into a holding cell on the fourth floor. With all this stress my mouth was like a camels arse in a sand storm, so dry I could hardly move my tongue about and I had to practically beg for a drink. Why did these people have to be so mean and hard, I really didn't understand? When I did ask for anything I tried to be as polite as I could. Even in this very cold and empty environment, God had forsaken this place even the women were really mean.

When I got back to the stockade, one of the deputies asked what it was in the end? When I told him, his words were, "It's a wonder you haven't had a heart attack." He actually seemed sympathetic towards me.

I was now so depressed I just stayed in my bunk. I should have been deported by Saturday and it was now Tuesday night. Well how about that! When they finally came to get me even the deputies seemed happy that at last I was to be deported. It was a surreal moment as I left, high fives, smiles, even the giant evil bastard that lost his bet on the Miami Dolphins gave me a wave and mimed the words to me, "Good luck English!"

## Chapter 14

# In the Depths of Despair

*Even in the grave all is not lost*

Edgar Allan Poe

I was on my way to Broward again. It was now dark and I was put in a holding cell yet again. They then called me. I was taken to a kind of warehouse to strip off and was given a really horrible orange/red outfit to wear, worse than the last and placed in my arms was a bundle of bedding and this really huge giant of a man was cuffed to me.

So I was cuffed, my arms full of bedding and a pillow, this guy towered over me and we were led down some long hallways with cells both sides and then out into the open and led along a path with Stalag 13 type fencing on both sides with the top of the fence pointing in. If you were to climb the fence you would never get over the top. This guy was a white man. A really mean looking bastard. As we were walking, following him down this pathway, there was a building totally by itself. I looked up at this guy. It was like looking to the top of a block of flats, looking at his mean, hard chiseled face.

"Officer," I said, "where am I going sir? Last week I was told in court that I was going to be deported back to England. I know you don't want to hear this but I have committed no crime. Why are they doing this to me?"

With that he stopped abruptly.

"Look here you piece of shit, if there's any truth in what you're saying, which I doubt very much, then I would not breath a word of it in the place I'm about to put you in now. You are entering a high security felon cell with some really evil mother fuckers who will eat you up and spit you back out again! Speak to no one and keep yourself to yourself."

I had to lean on the fence and my legs buckled under me. I was feeling so dizzy, couldn't even try to say how I was feeling psychologically at this point.

When we got to the door, it slid open from right to left. Another officer had to then put in some kind of code. It opened slowly with a droning buzz noise and as it opened you knew it was not going to be good. You then took a short step to a metal jail type door and the door behind you closed before they opened this second door. At first all I can see were some long metal tables running down the middle of this room with metal benches running parallel to the tables. Everything was bolted down to the floor. Four rooms were also attached to this room and I was taken to the far right where they opened a door. It was dark and as the lights entered the room and I heard one or two groans like they were pissed off with the light cascading into the room disturbing their sleep.

I was showed a toilet and 3 bunks although I didn't have one. I had a rolled up mattress about an inch and a half thick and told to sleep on the floor right by the door with my feet touching the toilet. The officer left me to unroll my mattress, put my pillow in place and put my blanket out. As I was doing this I heard a voice. Not the best start you could possibly have waking people up at this time! This was a very, very frightening place. A blind man on a galloping horse could see this was not a good place at all. I curled up on my matt wondering what I was going to wake up to. Why, why, why did they have to put me in here? Why not just keep me at the stockade where I'd now lived for the past 6 or so weeks? What were they trying to prove by putting me in here? It seemed to me that they simply wanted to punish me even further. I was now remembering my beautiful house that I no longer had. I had no intentions of ever selling my home. I could see my lawns, flowers and rockeries. I really had had some happy times with my son in the garden on the back lawn, chasing him through his little tunnel and pushing him on his little swing. He had a little sand pit and other little kids would come and play with him. I'd do pop and crisps for them and take some of them home in my car and sometimes my son would go round to their houses. Now I had lost my home! What would people think of me? How quickly your life could change. My brother would have been OK. He was a good, strong man but I simply could not think of my brother maybe having a heart attack over the stress of the situation with the house. At the time of my niece's phone call, I was totally incapable of doing anything else but telling my brother to sell my house. I made very little after paying Mr. Rocque and Doug for the car. There was very little left for when I got back.

I just couldn't sleep. It was almost getting light and I soon learnt I was amongst a very uncaring bunch in this room. Three bunks with 8 of us in here. One guy was on the other side of the room in a plastic coffin type bed on the floor. No one would talk to me! There was a toilet but it was in full view of the room, so when you used it anyone else in this room could see you. Taking a piss, not much of a problem, but to sit and have to take a dump in front of a load of guys, I don't think anyone would enjoy the prospect. I felt very frightened, very alone. It had always been difficult before, but I already knew being in here would be an extraordinary experience to say the least.

All these guys were getting up and stepping all over me, some of them deliberately kicking me. One guy even stood on my chest. He was a real prick.

The razors were bought in. It was the same type of routine. Razors then breakfast but there was no room to move about. It was all very up close in each other's faces. It was all very intimidating. I found out very fast that the other 3 rooms were black guys only and it was a very strict thing. A white guy just did not walk into the other rooms.

The food arrived and it was much worse than at the stockade. No one says excuse me, you were just pushed to one side. At the bottom of the room is a very small TV in the top right hand corner. This was totally dictated by the black bro's and all they wanted to do was watch shows like Oprah Winfrey.

I just couldn't eat. I left it on the table and walked away and said nothing to anyone. They would sort it out I was sure.

At last some one spoke to me. Frank was his name. What an awful man, bald and white with very large round eyes, sunken cheeks and a big gap in his front teeth. He looked like he was from an asylum. Looked a complete nutter! Frank was a trustee if you needed something. If you had money put aside for you or something to trade, Frank was your man. He just didn't like me.

"Who the fuck are you looking at," he would say.

"Look at me like that again and I'll smash your face. This is the white house, if you don't keep yourself to yourself, you'll get fucked up in here."

So I just said okay and sat on the floor in the bunkroom or I should say the White House. As you entered the room to your left a guy was drawing a full sketch of the White House in pencil. I must say it was very impressive. He must have been an artist. He was on the top bunk and the sketch was along the top of his bunk, the full length of his bed.

I was now very tired but I couldn't lie down. If I did I was in the doorway. I would just get the shit kicked out of me if I tried to lie down.

When someone used the toilet and you flushed it, it was like a jet plane taking off. The noise was so loud it was very annoying. If someone took a dump, I was told as the turd came out of your arse, before it hit the bottom of the toilet, you flushed it. Doing this sucked the smell out straight away. If you get it wrong you were screamed at by the others. Can you imagine, someone teaching you how to use the toilet? It was very crude! The guy in the cradle type bed didn't move. He just stayed asleep and he didn't look at all well. When I went into the main room was unbelievably intimidating. I thought I was disliked by the black lads before but I had no doubt that nobody wanted to talk to me in there. I went to look at the TV talk show and a young black lad 21 or 22 pushed past me so hard that I fell over onto the table. I just knew I was going to have a problem with this guy!

"Get the fuck out of my way, you piece of shit!" he shouted.

I just moved out of the way and said nothing. Two minutes later he came past me again and caught me with his elbow. He stopped and looked at me, a cold empty stare.

It was important they got me out of here soon. They must be coming to deport me soon? There was a speaker near the ceiling and when they called a name that person went to the door. If you had medication the nurse came to the cell type door and handed it through to whoever was in the line.

I was so tired and I had to lie by the door. I felt so ill and I just put up with being kicked and stood on from time to time. To be honest I was past caring. I then some how closed my eyes and tried to catnap. Someone tripped over me on to the floor. He actually said sorry which really surprised me. He then went into the room and sat at the table. I began to nod off to sleep again but I was woken up by loud banging, shouting, laughing and whistling. I wondered what the hell all the noise was. It was a bunch of black lads playing cards. As they played a card from a hand, they raised the card above their head and slammed it down onto the top of the metal table and shouted at each other. Hey nigger, big five, yo bro, mother fucker. They didn't just speak. It was as if everybody was deaf. They also acted the same when playing Dominos. Can you imagine the noise of a domino being slammed onto the metal table? If there was a game going with the white lads, it was just normal, therefore one table could be having a quiet game while on the next table it was all out war.

You always knew when someone was about to be called on the speaker as it made a noise just before the announcement and there was a pause from the unbearable noise in the room. After the name was announced, it was back to the mayhem.

"Hey you, what's your name?" said Frank

"Rick or Ricky."

"Are you English?"

"Yes," I said

"OK English, get the fuck out of my way, learn to move faster English."

I then sat next to the guy from our room, the white house. I looked at him and he looked at me. I thought well here we go.

"How are you?"

He looked at me with a troubled look.

"Not very good."

"Neither am I."

He then told me that this was a terrible place. There were a lot of really bad men in here and the noise was so loud. He says it was better if you wished to talk that we sit on the floor in our own room, so we did. He seemed to need to talk.

"You can't speak to anyone in here, no one is interested. The black lads talk or should I say shout a lot. I've been here 3 days now, it's like this all the time, but a little later in the day, the noisy bastards go to their bunks or watch TV. Then you can hear yourself think."

"Oi English, I thought I told you to keep yourself to yourself." I heard.

"We're having a chat, he's ok."

Frank then put his nose next to my nose and looked me right in the eyes. "You're trouble, I'll give you trouble. Then he climbed onto his bed.

"Fuck you English."

This guy then spoke to me.

137

"English, is that what Frank calls you? What's your name?"

I said he could call me Rick and I asked him his name and he told me it was Ken. He then asked me what the reason was for me being here and I told him of my deal with the courts and I was waiting to be deported back to England. I continued to tell him that I didn't know why they had put me in here. I was innocent of any crime, I was on a misdemeanor charge. Frank was also listening.

"They don't put you in here if you're on a misdemeanor charge you lying bastard" Frank said.

Ken said to just ignore him.

I didn't even have to ask Ken why he was in here, he just started to tell me.

"A few years ago, I lived in New York. I had a pistol under my drivers seat. I did not have a license but I kept the gun for my own safety. Some parts of New York can be very dangerous. I hoped never to use it, but I was pulled over by the police and they did a search of my car. They did me for possession of an unlicensed gun. I did time but was let out on parole. I came to Florida, just for a couple of days, without the permission of my parole officer and met the lady I'm now living with. We fell in love and I moved in with her and her two kids. I never went back so I had jumped my parole. I'd been living with her and she worked for a firm of attorneys. One day I just had to tell her. She had a word with her boss and he told her to tell me to go and see him and that he would sort something out. He said they might give me a fine and parole me here so we notified the police but they arrested me. Now I'm here waiting to return to New York. I may get 2 or 3 years I'm told. We were so happy and I think I'm going to loose my girlfriend. I was so happy with her."

I then told him about Lily. Frank was still listening. 'Bullshit English."

A little later I went and sat at a table. It was a lot quieter now and I heard two of the guys speaking.

"What do you think to the English guy?"

"He's not one of us. We think he might be an undercover cop, put in here to spy on us. He's not a criminal, no way is he one of us."

I just felt a cold shudder down my spine. I was well and truly in the shit if they believed that! I just had to get out of here very soon. Frank also heard this.

"I told you to keep yourself to yourself English, no one in here is on a misdemeanor charge."

"That's right Rick it does look a little suspicious, especially to the black lads, all kinds of stuff is discussed in here, some of these guys are running all types of illegal shit. They don't stop because they're banged up in here."

"If they believe that they might as well kill me now! You can tell them and Frank to get on with it. They'd be doing me a favour!"

In this room there was a phone mounted on the wall. If you had credit or someone to take the cost you could use the phone at certain times but there was always a queue. I did get chance to ask the sergeant if I could call Chuck and Wendy and was told I could but had to wait.

I had been here a couple of days and I was on eight pills a day. I was really struggling with it all and I was still sleeping on the floor. Ken was also getting more and more depressed. He talked to his girlfriend but he felt it was not good. When I got to talk to Chuck and Wendy and told them what had happened, they had no idea where I was. They thought I was still at the stockade and were even more horrified. They told me that they were meeting Doug and that they had to deport me as that was the arrangement and part of the deal. It's just outrageous! What were they doing, putting me in a felon cell? They told me not to worry and I told them that I was in cell 9.0. They said they would tell my brother and said I had to phone and tell Rocque and he should demand that I be moved back to the stockade pending my deportation.

After a couple of days I was sat at the table in conversation with the other guys in the white house. I was losing a lot of weight and looked really bad. Frank was always leaping off his bunk and threatening me so one day I leapt up, stood on the bottom bunk and looked Frank in the eye.

"You can beat the living shit out of me now, you fucking arsehole, or leave me the fuck alone!"

Frank looked at me. "Well you surprise me English; you're not a chicken shit are you? Get out of my face English."

So I did.

Somehow it really made a difference with Frank. Later, he was playing cards with some other guy from the white house and as I watched Frank, he suddenly spoke with a grin on his face.

"Do you play cards English?"

"Yes, but not very well," I said.

"You can join us then."

Later that day I was the only person in the main room from the white house. I was sat at the table and some black lads also sat at the table to play cards. One sat opposite me and began to shuffle the cards, so I asked if I could play.

"Fuck off," they said.

"I was only trying to be friendly."

The big black guy stood up and to my horror, punched me in the face. With the force I was thrown backwards but my feet were hooked under the table on a cross bar so I was catapulted back up right. This shocked him. It could have been straight out of a comedy sketch. I then simply stood up.

"So you don't want me to play I take it."

I walked back into the white house. The side of my face was quiet a mess.

"Look Frank," Ken said "look what they've done to Rick."

Frank went to get some cold water on a towel to put on the side of my face.

"What were you trying to do, you stupid Englishman?"

I was in a lot of pain. It really set my headache off even worse. I just couldn't for the life of me understand why they had so much hatred. I was just a simple guy, trying to get by in life, just the same as them.

I put in another inmate request form for medical assistance, telling them about my left black eye, my left cheekbone and that I was starting to cough at night again. No wonder as it was so cold in the cell. They must be preparing us for arctic warfare. I looked a right mess. That bastard really had hit me hard, but he now knew this lad from Doncaster, this Yorkshire lad born and bred, this son of a miner, wouldn't break that easily. He would have to do an awful lot better than this if he wanted to crush my resolve. I admit though my face bloody hurt something chronic.

I would love to see that wimp Rocque take a punch off my black friend. I think I would piss myself laughing. To be honest I was in here and it really should have been him.

In the days I'd been there, we had not been allowed outside. By law apparently they had to let us out at some point everyday but if you talked to the officers you were wasting you're time.

I needed someone to press a stop button. I simply couldn't cope much longer with the rate and speed of events. Any one of these situations alone would be very traumatic for anyone to cope with, but the old saying "Just when you thought it was safe to back into the water, another shark turns up." Sadly for me, this was my situation. Within a very short time of these latest events, I was still trying to go forward. When I was lying on my bunk, I heard my name being called out. I thought that when I went to the officer they would say get my stuff and I would be out of there. I must surely be going to be deported but when I got to the officer he said "Post." I was given two envelopes, one of them a pinky red colour, the other yellow. I couldn't begin to think what they might be, so I began to open the red one. I saw immediately it was some kind of greetings card. It said on the front, "I just thought of something nice." It

141

had some kind of cartoon character dancing with some little clouds above its head, with a little pink heart in a cloud. When I opened it I saw a big "YOU" inside and arrows pointing to a circle with the letter L in the middle. I can't say a word of how I felt. I opened the yellow one and there was another card with two photos. One was of me standing singing with Lily in my arms at the Chapel as we were being married and the other was a photo of me and Lily standing together smiling as we'd just been married. At this moment I was starting to struggle with my breath a little. Written as a part of the card on the front was, "I wanted to send you this note, to let you know I'm thinking about you and wishing we could talk and just be together a while." When I opened the card, Lily had written a letter to me.

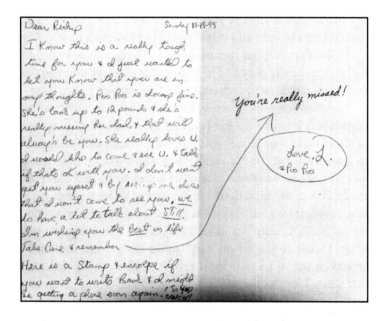

142

What a mess I was in now. I fell to my knees shaking and crying at the same time and I had dropped everything on the floor. Frank and Ken helped me to my bed...yeah, was this when I had a heart attack? They put me in my bunk and told me to calm down. I felt so tired and I just wanted to die. When the guys picked up my cards and photos they read what Lily had written and all I could hear was "What a fuckin bitch... what the....what.....look at this." while some guys I heard asking "What's happening."

The guys then went on to say, "It's English, his mail, he was telling the truth about his crazy ex wife that put him in here when he'd done nothing wrong."

I then heard someone say "Imagine being in here with us mother fuckers and you're innocent, poor bastard. What a nutter she must be, evil."

There were another two photos, one with the dog Poo Poo, and another with my son Craig, mind-blowing stuff, don't you think? She missed me and wanted to come and visit.

It was a good day or so before I could really find the strength to get up and walk about. Some of the guys showed the officers my mail. You'd think they'd come and take me out and have Lily arrested, but no, "poor bastard" was all they said. Just as I was picking my self up, I went to see what was on the TV. Some shit talk show. Suddenly the young black lad that had pushed me over when I first arrived sat at the side of me. He was sat at the end of the table right next to me. I thought I really didn't need any problems with this guy now but after a minute or two, really nasty, he told me to move up, so I did. He then moved and sat right next to me again.

"I thought I told you to move up motherfucker," he said.

Again I did and once more he moves right next to me again.

"Hey English, white piece of shit, I remember asking you to move the fuck up.

As I was at the end of the table I stood up to walk back to my bunk thinking I was not playing his game. Then he hit me without warning. I was now on my knees and he hit me again twice then walked past me saying "Mother fucker." another black lad gave him a high five.

"Yo bro, whitey needs a lesson on good manners at the table."

You don't need to be a rocket scientist to know what state I was in, however he did not hit me as hard as his bro did. I wanted to say so as well, but I thought what was the point. If I did retaliate and the officers came we would both be in lock down and in trouble.

It surely now had to be soon that they would come to deport me. The guys in the white house looked at me and said,

"Jesus, not again."

"Not to worry chaps, just another day in the office," I said in stupid, posh, well spoken English and I got into my bunk.

"What was that? Why did he speak in that stupid voice?" I heard one of them say.

I felt really ill and I knew myself that I was slipping a bit. I had lost quiet a bit of weight. I couldn't eat anything and didn't look good at all. Now was my darkest moment. I was getting to the point where I simply didn't give a shit. They could kill me if they wished and part of me really did hope they would or a heart attack... either would do, at least I would be out of it.

It's a strange moment when it comes to you that death may just be the best option. I went to sleep that night and wasn't really worried if I woke up, I was at the stage where the sleeping nightmares were preferable to the ones I was waking up to.

*Horses always featured prominently in my life. Above, a BBC Production, 'By The Sword Divided' 1985.*

*And above, in 1972 riding for the British racehorse Trainer Bill Elsey.*

*Lily and I on our wedding day.*

*Above, yours truly.*

Photo by Keri Owen

Actor, Philip Michael Thomas, star of television and movies; entertainer, Ricky Dale; Director of the NAEA, Laurie Hannan-Anton; and manager, Solomon King attend National Arts & Entertainment Association meeting.

*A press cutting with Soloman King, Philip Michael Thomas (Miami Vice) and Director of the NAFA Laurie Hannan-Anton*

Chapter 15

# A Song in the Darkness

*Those who dance are considered insane by those who cannot hear the music*

George Carlin

**Academy Award Show 1994**

I was invited to appear on this show by the owner of a management company model and talent agency, Boca Raton, it was to be the first ever East Coast Academy Award Show with a satellite link to the West Palm Beach Academy Awards Show, red carpet and all the trimmings. This was being done because the film industry in Miami had grown so much, many stars could not get across to the West Coast because they were working on productions in Miami and many now lived in the Miami area. I was asked to sing four songs and had to sing one song from the film The Lion King (Can you feel the love tonight) Elton John/Tim Rice wrote the song. The Lion King that night took nearly all the Academy Awards. I sat at dinner during the awards show next to the black guy out of Police Academy; he made all those silly noises. What a phenomenal night for a Doncaster lad. J

I appeared in films such as The Drop Zone (Wesley Snipes) and The Specialist (Sylvester Stallone/Sharon Stone/James Wood) and also many other smaller productions. As I mentioned I was putting together a new production company in Miami with Rob Freeman, No 1 Billboard producer with eight platinum albums to his name. The company was to be called Title Wave Productions. Rob and myself were to be 25% shareholders in the company, my salary $38.000, paid to do my own backing vocals, I was initially the only artist on the label. Rob then wanted me to go out and discover a female artist to record four songs, and to find a band to do four songs. We would have had 3 artists on our label and I would have been co producing my own songs with Rob. Rob produced Kiss and discovered Blondie and worked on many film sound tracks too. The Bee Gees Attorney was also to be our company attorney. Teddy Mulay, Gloria Estefan's then MD wanted to be my MD when our company was ready and a merchant banker of Brikel Ave agreed to finance it. Teddy and I got on great, I met him after I'd done a show with Miami Sound Machine and he said when I sang seven original songs, I blew him away. What a night that was.

Rob always told me that our production company would sponsor me, so again I could have simply divorced Lily and moved on but I wanted things to work out. Rob wrote a letter to the Florida Bar complaining against Mr Rocque that my prolonged incarceration and subsequent deportation ruined all of our plans and finished the company after we had all worked so hard to get it up and running.

I brought all these people together to form our own company and it would have been huge and I was proud of my achievements. How silly was Lily, she would have wanted for nothing for the rest of her life!

I forced memories of my home, family and son into my mind. It seemed like I was looking down through a mist and climbing higher and higher. My past felt like an old dream that was fading away. Would they come to rescue me tonight I wondered? They did come for people in the night.

Ken asked me how I was.

"Never mind me Ken, you have a woman, a home and some kids to hold out for."

"I've lost her now," Ken replied, "she'll never wait for me. She's very angry. Why didn't I tell her sooner? It's all my fault," he muttered. "I'm on the phone most days and she says she's not coming to visit for a while. She needs to think things out. I'm finished. I've lost everything now!"

"All is not lost my friend, not until the fat lady sings."

The last time I had spoken to Chuck and Wendy, I had told them nothing about my encounters but I did get David Kilpatrick's phone number as well as Rocque's phone number. The next day I would hopefully phone them both. We still hadn't been allowed outside yet. It had been over a week or so. How could they get away with doing this?

The next day I phone Rocque and Kilpatrick but they were both out of the office until the day after.

I had to eat something. Some of this lot ate like pigs. I was a little worried for Ken. He really looked out of it now.

Whenever you were on the phone, the noise was deafening. People could hardly hear a word, but later in the day when it was quiet you knew who was on the phone and you simply couldn't make a lot of noise if the bro's were using it or trying to watch TV for that matter.

I played cards more. I don't like dominos and I spent most of my time in my bunk but I had started to do some exercises to try and boost my self esteem although I became tired very quickly. At least I was doing a little more.

I hadn't mentioned this before now, but I did overhear the odd comment that "English would make a good bitch." There were two shower cubicles in there. The water was always bloody freezing by the time I got to shower. We were supposed to have a rota system but it never worked out the way it should.

All day and all night all I heard was talk about crime, murders, drugs, rapes, fights they'd been involved in. It was all very low life as most of these guys had spent most of their lives in here

Frank had calmed down now he was not so aggressive. I now just told him to shut up and to stop being so nasty and he did. Frank did seem to have a good side. His problem was drugs and he ran drugs and classy prostitution. He had spent 15 years behind bars so far and he must have been coming up to his late 40's.

That night in the white house we were all in our own bunks or sat on them before lights out.

"I'm sick of listening to you lot going on and on about crime, don't any of you like music? Talk about something else." I said.

"Ok English, what have you got to talk about?"

One of them asked what I did for a living when I lived in England and I said I was an entertainer.

"Fuck off, what kind of entertainer?"

"He's a cocksucker ." They all burst out laughing.

"What kind of entertainer?"

I tell them a singer.

"My arse." one of them said.

"Yeah Kermit the Frog."

"You can say what you like, I'm telling the truth."

It was now lights out but some were still talking.

"Hey English, If you're not bullshitting about being a singer, sing us a song now."

"Yeah come on you lying mother fucker."

It was that dark in there you could hardly see your hand in front of your face.

"OK, but if I can sing, then you're a bunch of arseholes, Agreed?"

They laughed.

"Most of us are anyway English," they said.

"Shut up and give me a chance, I'll sing a song I wrote myself called Beautiful Eyes."

They were cat calling and jeering as I started but within just a few seconds you could hear a pin drop and when I had finished they even gave me a polite round of applause.

"Yo yo man, way to go you mother fuckin dark horse." Someone said and others muttered in disbelief from the dark.

It was time to calm down now or the officers would be pissed off.

"Will you sing again for us Rick?" said a voice from the dark. It was Ken's voice.

"Maybe, but who's the arsehole now?"

"You, you married that Lily," someone said.

They all then laughed and it went quiet again.

The next morning, razors, shave, then Frank approached me.

"That way really nice last night Rick, I've never heard that song before."

"I wrote it myself Frank."

"It must be very difficult for you, what can I say Rick?" You will overcome all this one day and we'll see you on TV."

I could use the phone again so I phoned Rocque. Bingo! His secretary put me through.

"Well hello Mr. Dunphy, what's the weather like in England?"

"You idiot."

"What do you mean?" he said.

"You don't even know do you?"

How could it be possible that my attorney didn't know that I was still in the USA? "

Not only that you arsehole," I said, "I've been put in a high security felon cell and I've been beaten up twice already. You had better get your arse on the phone and get me the hell out of here! Why did you let that lying bastard get away? Why didn't you do what you said you were going to? You didn't tell me the night before going to court that you hadn't met with my friends and my witnesses to prepare my case! Get on the phone now and get me out of here!"

What an incompetent ........Again I simply had no words.

My name was now called out. Could it be now at last? No, I was given some more mail but what I was about to read was way beyond words. Way, way beyond words.

I had 5 American witnesses in court to testify against Lily, backed up with testimony from England. I wish I could have got my hands on Rocque now!!!

Lily should have to face charges of:

- From me making false accusations about me.

- Perverting the course of justice by bringing into court Donna Van Buran. Between them conjuring up charges to make me look bad.

- Lying to the judge Mr. Rothschild by telling him she had sent all my belongings to England. Therefore committing perjury in a court of law.

- Trying to get Doug to lie in court, again this was attempting to pervert the course of justice. Asking someone to commit perjury in a court of law by asking him to say that I confessed everything to him.

- Committing extortion against me by sending Randy to visit me asking for 3000$ for my belongings after she has told the judge, Mr. Rothschild, that she'd already sent everything to England.

Lily would have to then face charges of attempting to defraud the racetrack of two million dollars.

Mr. Rocque told me that the prosecution had told him I was now divorced, so obviously without checking the facts, he told me that I have **no legal status.** Despite how much I demanded that my case be heard along with my witnesses, I was given a no win situation. It was beyond doubt that Mr. Rocque could clearly see the distress and duress I was in. It turned out that Mr. Rocque had made absolutely no attempt what so ever to meet with my witnesses and to prepare my defense despite having met with me for up to 2 hours and taking my case after excepting $1000. He had told me Lily didn't have a chance and that she was going to be in a lot of trouble and that I'd be free. The night before going to court he told me the prosecutor was after my blood then failed to tell me that he had not met with any of my witnesses therefore had nothing to defend me with.

The document shows that on 21 September in court I was still married and that today which was 11 days after the hearing I was in fact still married to Lily and remained so for another 4 days. How about that? My own defense lawyer had lied to me in a court of law before the judge himself and the public, therefore committing perjury in a court of law. To then coearse me under duress to change my plea to no contest and be deported immediately, then failing to carry out the deal they had put to me by not making sure I was deported. By lying to me they had perverted the course of justice. It was obvious now more than ever that Rocque had sold me out to the prosecutor. He must have done a deal with another case totally at my expense, disregarding the fact that I was an innocent man.

Mr. Rocque had far more evidence than he needed to bring Lily to justice and was clearly not in the slightest bit interested in justice. He should never have taken my case. When he did, he was very happy to do so.

I now made a phone call to the clerk of the court. I told them a bit about my situation and asked if they would do something to get me out of there. They showed no interest what so ever.

"Aren't you going to do something to get me out of here?" I asked them again and again.

They simply said that they were coming to get me and put the phone down.....No words eh?

What a total uncaring bunch of bastards!

I was now looking out of a window. Well I say window. It was just a thin long window, about 6 inches wide. I was watching a rabbit popping its head out of a hole. Part of me wished I was the rabbit, but knowing my luck if I was turned into that rabbit, two minutes later, I'd be shot by some twat and eaten for dinner.

Ken said he was off to the phone and I do hoped he would be ok? He seemed a nice fellow. I heard Frank say he thought his relationship was fucked.

The noise in the main room was overwhelming. Again I could see Ken with his finger over one ear and by the look on his face, things were really bad. I stood closer and he shook his head to indicate things were bad. I didn't know what suddenly came over me but I just stepped forward and took the phone from him.

"Hello I'm Ricky," I said "Ken loves you desperately and thinks he's losing all that is wonderful in his life. He's a good man and he shouldn't be in here. Please don't give up on him, this is from him to you."

I started to sing Richard Marks song, Now and Forever. By the time I was half way through the song the room had gone very quiet. Ken was in tears, she was in tears and I gave the phone back to him. I was given some high fives by some of the guys and one or two of the black bro's made comments. "Who does he think he is, singing in here, doesn't he know he's in jail? The dumb shit!"

I went back to the window but my new friend was not playing out at the moment. I thought to myself, would I ever get over this?

"Nice one English." Frank said.

"What? What? It's the least I can do for you old chap. He's a spiffing fellow, don't you think?" I replied in my posh English voice again.

Then I climbed into my bunk. Ken came in numb with emotion.

"Thanks Rick," he said still a little choked as he got into his cradle on the floor.

The cards and photos Lily had sent had a serious effect on my mental state. I couldn't make my mind up if I simply hated her and that she had only sent the cards to soften me up so I wouldn't go the race track but did really sincerely love me but couldn't deal with her feelings because of her inability to believe in the love I had for her.

I was so horribly confused now about what to think. I had lost the ability to work out anything anymore.

Tomorrow I was going to phone Kilpatrick to see what he thought about all this mess. Could you imagine I had been here over a week and we hadn't been outside yet?

Every time I heard the speaker buzzer, I thought it was my time to go, apparently no one stayed here too long. It was just a holding jail where you stayed before going to the courts and penitentiary. Some of these guys said they couldn't wait to go to the penitentiary. What does that tell you about this place?

My feet were now in a right mess. On the bottoms the skin has gone really hard. I had tried to peel some strips of skin off so the skin was not too think and as I had done this it had gone too deep and stung like a bitch and as I now had some really painful sores it was really painful to walk on.

The next day it was the usual start. What was the problem with these people, now they all knew about my situation, why the hell was I not priority to be moved out of here. Today I was able to speak to David Kilpatrick. When I told him I was still in the jail he was horrified and told me that he had had a phone call from Rocque from the courts and that Rocque told him about the deal they were putting to me. Mr. Kilpatrick told me that he had told Rocque not to take any deals. That even if Lily divorced me I still had rights as I'd successfully got through the marital fraud interview. I told Mr. Kilpatrick I was horrified because Mr. Rocque had told me that he had told Mr. Rocque to tell me it was best if I went home. David then said that Mr. Rocque was lying. That he would come to court to testify that Mr. Rocque had lied to me in court as to what he said. So Mr. Rocque yet again had committed perjury in a court of law to get me to take the no contest deal. Mr. Kilpatrick then said I should sue Mr. Rocque when I got out. I told David that I was now in a high security felon cell and that I'd been beaten up twice. He just said it was terrible.

I then told him that I was still married until 5 October. He was simply astonished and told me he should be able to keep me in the country for a while and that if I could get a sponsor in that time they could not deport me. I told him the chances of me getting a sponsor whilst I was in there were impossible. I would need to be out. As a result of all this I asked Doug to go to the hearing for me and contest the divorce on the grounds that Lily was not well and that she would need me after what ever was to happen to her. Maybe it would buy me some time to get out. It was all a bit ridiculous don't you think?

Apart from the main conversation being crime in this jail and the other being sex, I can honestly say I hadn't managed to raise a single hard on in all the time I'd been here. That was not normal was it?

Ken had been on the phone again and his girlfriend had said she was coming to visit him and that she would stand by him when he was sent back to New York. His demeanor really had picked up.

I had seen my rabbit friend today. I felt I could escape a little just watching my little pal play. He jumped out of his hole, hopped about and jumped back in. I hadn't seen any others as yet.

Chris the artist guy asked what I was looking for.

"It's my buddy," I said in my English mans accent. "I used to do a spot of shooting you know old chap. He just looked at me, smiled and went to his bunk.

When I was able to speak to Doug I told him everything that had just come about. I told him I was still married and he was so angry.

"I'm gonna find you another attorney Rick to get you out and sue that incompetent lying bastard. I'll say it again if only someone when you were arrested had interviewed me and simply investigated as a police officer should."

You can imagine. Your wife/girlfriend simply picked up the phone, said you'd beat her and you'd been through all this lot! Then you pay an attorney good money, provide him with enough ammunition to sink a battle ship but you're still in this situation. How outraged would you be? So much was happening so fast. It was not long now before the divorce hearing later today. Frank said there was someone who wanted to talk to me in the White House. Everyone was asked to move out whilst one of the black lads had a word with me. This guy I didn't know, but he was one of the more friendly bro's.

"I've heard all about your problem and I can help you," he told me.

"How can you help me?"

"Apparently you're still married yes?"

"Yes, so?"

"If your wife doesn't go to this divorce hearing, then you can't be divorced and they can't deport you."

"What are you trying to say?"

"Well if she disappears, never to be found, all your problems will be solved English and I can help you, give me her address with that photo she sent you. I've been told all about it, just leave the rest to me."

"I can't do that bro."

"Why?" he says

"That would make me as bad as you, no offence...but I could never live with myself but Thank You bro."

I gave him a big high five.

"If you change your mind, just let me know."

I was just speechless.

# Chapter 16

# A Chance to get Even

*It's necessary to have wished for death in order to know how good it is to live*
Alexandre Dumas – The Count of Monte Cristo

Chris the artist was a diabetic, he got quiet ill. He told me that sometimes he got so ill that he had collapsed in the past but it had not happened while he had been in custody. If he had enough insulin it didn't happen.

We had more newcomers. I just continued to keep myself to myself. On Sunday it was church. Yes in here some black guy, an ex murderer who was now a reformed character came in. Well some of this bunch of idiots sat around one of the tables and of course things were very quiet then. The lads from the White House would re treat to their bunks. By the way, Frank was the president of the White House. One day I decided to go to church. I was told by Frank and Ken that it was not wise.

"We'll soon see."

They said I was crazy. I approached the table and asked if I could join the table. The guy taking the service said yes and asked my name.

"English, he's one crazy mother fucker," a couple said at the same time.

I was then asked to sit down.

"Before I do can I say something?"

"Yes you may," I was told by our kind of vicar.

"In England, I have many black friends, even neighbours who come into my house. If they knew how I'd been treated by our black bro's in here.... I've been beaten twice for doing nothing but being white, but I'd like to say I forgive the bro's that beat me."

I then sat down and our vicar gave me a smile.

It was really beyond words. No one was yet making any attempt to come and get me. I was going to phone Rocque to see what he was doing to get me out of here.

I had been told that my brother John had phoned the British Embassy in London but they couldn't find out anything about me. He was given the phone number of the British Consulate in Orlando, but they couldn't find out anything from Broward County. Then when he was told where I was when he phoned, they wouldn't even acknowledge that they had me in custody. In England, if someone like a brother/family member phones to a police station or a prison, they have to tell you if they have the person enquired about in custody. It's against British law to not do this. They don't have to give any other details but they do have to say yes or no.

When Chuck and Wendy found out I was still married they told me not to worry as surely they now had to release me?

I managed to get hold of Rocque again, and I told him not only was I still married but also told him that I'd spoken to Mr. Kilpatrick and that I now knew he had lied to me when he'd said that even my immigration attorney David Kilpatrick says you should go home when Rocque spoke to him from the court room.

"When am I getting out of here Mike? Why did you help that lying bitch to get away with what she did?

"Why would Lily lie, Mr. Dunphy? he asked.

"Two million dollars you idiot...if you don't get me out of here, I'm going to hire another attorney to handle my case and I will see you one day in court but you will be in the dock this time for perjury in a court of law and serious mal practice by

163

not meeting with my witnesses as paid to do so and preparing my case."

The next day nothing happened, I just waited, pacing up and down. Every time I heard the speaker start I thought it had to be me and I now knew in myself that I was going to crack up soon. This morning when I first woke up I stretched my arms and loudly said in the posh English man's voice,

"Goooooood morning chaps! What's the weather like today? Anyone fancy a spot of golf? What...what?"

Then I went to see if my rabbit friend was about. I couldn't begin to tell you how slow the time passed in this mental institution.

The young black lad that attacked me was going before the judge the next day to be sentenced. I would be glad to see the back of him.

Ken had been told by his girlfriend to expect to be taken out and returned to New York very soon.

The speaker called out my name. When I went to the gate they didn't tell me to get my stuff, they told me I was going to see the doctor, but when I was taken out they took me to an office on the other side of the prison. I was sat at a desk and two officers came and sat with me. I was asked if I wanted a cup of tea of coffee. Was I dreaming? They were actually being nice to me, I said I would like a cup of tea. This couldn't be happening. What were they up to?

"We know you've had a hard time in 9-0 and that you've been attacked twice. We know the young black lad that was responsible for one incident; he's going to court tomorrow, he's a real piece of shit. He's up on violence charges; maybe he'll get 2 or 3 years. We want you to put in a complaint against him as he's been violent again. Though he's in jail, he could get another year or up to 18 months added on top of his sentence."

"So you haven't come to get me out yet, despite the fact you all must know by now that I'm innocent and that my wife has mental problems?"

"We'll move you to a different jail if you put the complaint in so no one will know what you did, they will just think you've been deported."

"Let me tell you something, if that young lad is to get 2 or 3 years already then I'm not going to add to that. It's a real hellhole; I hope he's learned his lesson. I don't condone what the man did and I dislike him for what he has done, but unless you're going to deport me then put me back with the imbeciles."

They weren't happy with me at all and took me back to 9-0.

After all I had been put through by these bastards they had the audacity to ask me to help them but not release me. Yes, Ok, another jail would have to be better than this but I wanted to be around for Ken till they took him away and they now had to let me go soon anyway.

When I got back, I told Frank what had happened. A little later I was playing cards with the real shit pack when one of the black bro's stood right by me with a real mean look on his face. What was going to happen to me now? This guy was huge. One hand alone was twice the size of my penis. He put his fist over my hand nodding his head.

"What do you want?" I asked him.

"Open your hand English."

When I did he dropped a brand new pack of cards into it, still in the plastic cover and unopened. This was like gold dust.

"Thank you for looking after the young bro. We know what you did for him. You didn't have to do that; no one would have blamed you if you'd have made a complaint. He's not that bad really; he's just had a bad upbringing."

He then when back to his bunk. The young bro said nothing. He just stayed out of my way.

Doug went to the divorce hearing but the divorce went ahead. It had been more than 2 weeks since I should have been back in England.

Oh my goodness the officers were here and apparently we were being let outside.

"Bloody hell chaps, spiffing stuff, we're going out. Tally ho old chaps, Tally ho!"

Even the officers just ignored me as if I was some nutcase (which I suppose I was) not to be taken any notice of.

"Why do you keep doing that? Frank asked.

"Because I bloody well want to old chap."

"You're fucking mad English, definitely!" he replied.

We were then put out into a fenced compound that was also a basketball court. I just walked round and round not stopping. It was very hot and I was wet through with sweat. A container full of water was provided but it had lots of black bits in it and flies floating around in it. We were outside nearly 2 hours.

One of the guards today was a real nasty, horrible man. When we returned to 9-0 we had a new man in the White House. There was something about this guy and even Frank picked up on it. He was just too distant. He didn't look like a hard case but a really snidey looking man. He never let go of his papers. Everyone had papers with their charges on.

The last time I got to talk to Wendy, she told me that when they last met Doug and told him I was in cell 9-0 that Doug became a little tearful which was not like Doug at all. He said he knew all about 9-0 and that I couldn't survive in there they had to get me out

Doug had then found another attorney from West Palm Beach called Burt Winkler. Doug felt really bad because it was him who had found Mike Rocque. When Doug set Burt Winkler on to work on my case, I had to pay another $1000 My brother sent the money to Doug out of what I had left with the sale of my house. My house was worth approximately £68000. I sold it to someone for a quick sale and it was sold for only £37000. After paying off the mortgage and legal fees I had next to nothing left. 17 years of my life gone and all my hard work. I gave up all I had to be with Donna for her to simply drop me very soon after we were married. How callous, with not even a word of explanation.

This new guy in the White House let it be known that he was arrested after being involved in the theft of a truck but no one believed him. We had a guy who was involved in stealing luxury cars from Miami. Cars would be stolen from New York, then half way the cars stolen from Miami area and these from New York would be switched around on a transporter, so Miami cars went to New York and New York cars went to Miami. All new documents and plates were made and they had contacts in the road traffic section to re register the cars. That was what I was told.

The black guy who offered to make Lily disappear came to have a chat.

"English, I've had an idea how you can get your own back on your wife."

"How's that," I asked?

"You give me the address of your wife or your now ex wife, a contact I have who is a road traffic cop, a bro. He follows your ex, stops her and has her spread against the hood of the car. He then goes into where the spare tyre is and plants some cocaine with an unmarked pistol. She then gets done for possession of drugs and possession of a firearm without a license. Both serious felonies!"

"You can actually do this?"

"Yes, definitely English. You helped a bro."

"Thank you so much but I'm sorry, I know you'll think I'm mad but I can't possibly do that. Thank you all the same. I know what Lily's done, but I just can't allow that to happen. It would be wrong!"

Days were passing. The same old shit and Burt Winkler wasn't getting anywhere. I was just rotting until they came to get me. What else could I do? I was totally powerless to do a damn thing. I was just going downhill. I had lost so much weight I looked a totally different person I spent hours and hours in my bunk.

It was now time for Ken to go. I was so happy for him. He told me that at some point hopefully his girlfriend would get to visit me. She wanted to thank me for singing "Now and Forever" down the phone. Ken told me if I got out and they didn't deport me I always had somewhere to stay and that he would never forget me and he hoped to see me on TV one day.

I had been in 9-0 eleven weeks at that point. It was impossible to understand how this was happening to me and why. The OJ Simpson case was still going on and it wouldn't be long now before we found out if he was guilty or not. It was too scary to think he would be found guilty.

Even though I had been told I was being deported immediately I was languishing day on day, week on week in a lunatic asylum even though every man and his dog knew I was innocent. What kind of country went about pulling stunts like this? AMERICA!

If they could do this to me, they could do it to you!

Chuck and Wendy were out of their minds over this. I'd had to see the doctor a few times now and they wanted me to see the prison psychologist. That would be entertaining. My family, what must they have been going through? I desperately needed to hold my little boy in my arms. He must have thought his Dad had abandoned him. How would he possibly ever be able to understand? I had always phoned him every few days I became very emotional when I thought of him asking for his Dad. My Mum would also know by now something was very wrong.

I had asked for help from officers, sent sergeants request slips and asked doctors. What these morons were doing to my family and friends was completely out of order and totally against the law not to mention violating my human rights. They had got what they wanted and they hadn't had the decency to honour their part of the deal that never should have been put to me!

## Chapter 17

# An Inner Hatred Bubbles to the Surface

*Perhaps, after all, America never has been discovered.*
*I myself would say that it had merely been detected*
Oscar Wilde

Another morning waking up to the reality of the hell I was in. I couldn't believe what I did myself. I woke and stood up.

"Good morning old chaps," I said, "which suit should I wear today? The grey one or the black one? Are we off to the beach? We'll have to call somewhere for a spot of tea, don't you think?"

There was one guy, a black bro, again a really big man. He was one of the top dogs among the black lads and no one liked him at all. He started making comments again when I went to the shower, saying again that I would make a really good bitch.

I was told by some of the other bro's to stay away from him. He doesn't like the way that some of the others were starting to like and respect me. I was also told he was a very violent man but I was not afraid of him or anyone anymore.

Simply being here was utter agony and every minute I was constantly listening for my name to be called out.

"James Dunphy, get your stuff, you're out of here."

Oh how I would feel when I left this place. It was beginning to feel like a hopeless dream and I feared that if I stayed in here much longer I would slowly become like some of these and it already felt like I had been in here forever. I suppose that if I had been given a sentence at least I would know when I was coming out, but this, every second of the day thinking the very next time someone was called it was going to be me was pure torture.

Something else that happened now was that when someone farted in the White House I said really loud in my posh English gentleman's voice "More tea vicar."

It was actually starting something as the other guys also now said it in their attempt to copy me. It was dumb but they said, "Moooooore tea vicar." I suppose I would be remembered for something eh?

This guy I've told you about the new guy who said he' was in here for stealing a truck was going to court the next day to be sentenced. He gave me the creeps. I just couldn't be bothered to try and make conversation with him. Another was going to court, the black bro who gave me a pack of cards. He was sat at the table silent with his head in his hands. It was being said that he' was going to get a stiff sentence. I sat next to him and after a while I noticed a little tear. When he saw that I had seen it he quickly wiped it away, embarrassed.

"It's ok bro, your only human," I said quietly then went back to my bunk and left him for a little of privacy.

The speakers came on. Was it for me? No it was for the new guy who said he had stolen a truck. I didn't care what anyone said, when you heard the speaker coming on, it was the fastest way to get quiet in here. It didn't matter how hard or tough you were everyone's heart missed a beat hoping it was their turn to be moved out of this disgusting festering place. Even flies didn't want to hang around here!

Then he was gone. What a strange man. Distant... but in a different way. As if he had something to hide.

There was a bit of a commotion in the White House and I over heard Frank and Chris saying what a disgusting, evil man! He'd left so quickly that he had left his court papers on his bunk. I felt a real sense of tragedy when Frank showed me his documents. I had been sleeping within feet of a man who sexually abused a baby. In graphic detail it said the baby's rectum had been torn. I was stunned in a silent sickness, a feeling of hatred. Never in my life did I ever think I would experience this. If this man came back here, he was fucking dead! I had a desperate need to tear his dick off from the roots and stick it up his arse. Pull out his tongue and then push it down the back of his throat. I couldn't believe the horrendous hatred I had within me towards this man. I was shocked at my own thoughts. It was horrible. How could I possibly be affected to this degree? I was a little chocked at what that poor helpless child must have been subjected to, unable to stop his deranged abuser from committing his vile act of perversion. This had gone way past disturbing me, maybe I had been in this den of iniquity for too long. Was it possible that my feelings were over the top? The irony was that he probably got a fair hearing. The officers were coming back and they walked straight to his bunk. Frank had put the papers back so they didn't know we had looked. If they had known we'd seen them, there was no way they would bring him back in here. He must have told them that he'd forgotten his court papers. When the officer picked them up he looked around as if to say, "Have you lot seen these documents?" Then they walked away with them.

I have cold shudders down my spine. You can imagine what the topic of conversation was for some time after that.

Someone was quickly brought in to replace him. Everyone that read those words had definitely suffered a kind of deep sadness and I could see it written on their faces.

The new guy was an Italian American from New York. This one was so full of himself and introduced himself to everyone as if it was an old pals reunion. He would clearly rob his own granny, sell you a chocolate watch and give you a lifetime guarantee. He was over friendly and told me that he knew all about my case and that if we were in New York he would have had her sorted out in no time.

"I might be a criminal but I do have a code of conduct, there are some things that you just don't do," he said.

"I'm sorry old chap but I haven't a clue what you're talking about with codes of conduct."

"That's why I'm in here as my partner broke his code of conduct."

"How?" I asked.

He then went on to tell me. Remember this guy knew nothing about me.

"I was arrested at Miami airport carrying some cocaine. We were working as a team. If one or the other was arrested, then the other had to try and bond you out. Of course you then jumped the bond, but my partner just left me and now I'm stuck here. They will soon find out that my passport is a fake and I'll have another charge against me. But when the one who left me gets back to New York, he's as good as dead. It's only a matter of time before our boss has him."

"Are you sure you're not on drugs now?" He just laughed.

This guy was very annoying kept coming to talk to me all the time. At the moment of writing this it was 9th Feb 2010. Simon Cowell had the song out to raise money for the Haiti Earth Quake and Michael Jackson's doctor had been given bail of only 75000$. His defense said it should be only 25000$. This doctor was up for involuntary murder of a world superstar, a legend. I had a bond in 1995 of 25000$ for a misdemeanor charge. How outrageous was that?

I was born April 1st 1956. Yes it figures, doesn't it? Mum, Dad, 5 sisters and two brothers. My father was Irish. He worked in the mines on the coal face and he was a very staunch union man standing up and speaking on behalf of the other miners. He was a good looking man and very well respected however that was where it ended. As a husband to my mother he was a real bastard. Knocking her about and beating her. He was a male chauvinistic arsehole most of the time. When he wasn't at work he would be in the pub or the bookies betting on the horses. He would come home drunk, have his dinner and then sometimes go out and get drunk again. He was also a womanizer. We were a very poor family and my mother was a very hard working mum. We didn't have a TV for many years and when everyone else had one, we just had a wireless. Mum never had a vacuum cleaner and outside our house was a brick coalhouse with a washhouse attached to it. In the washhouse was a cast iron hopper. You filled the hopper with water and there was a fireplace with a cast iron door beneath it and the fire would heat the water. Clothes would be boiled and washed then put into a dolly tube. You then scrubbed the clothes with a rubbing board, rinsed them out and then they would go through a mangle to squeeze out the water. The clothes were be put on the washing line to dry and then Mum would iron them with an old cast iron. The iron was heated up on the fire in the living room.

Our Mum cooked everything herself. We had a very large back garden and we grew everything from potatoes, cabbages, carrots, peas, lettuce, green beans, beetroot and even parsnips. We also had a green house with cucumbers and tomatoes. We had chicken so we had eggs and we had a cockerel, pigeons and rabbits. As a child I had to work for hours in our garden and our so called father was very strict. If you didn't do it right you'd get a slap or even a belt across you.

At the age of 12 I could drive a tractor as I worked at a farm mucking out cows and helping to milk them. At 14 I could plough a field and if it snowed Dad would say, "Get your wellingtons, gloves and balaclavas on and grab a shovel."

He'd tell me to go and knock on some doors and offer to clear the paths and driveways. My fingers got so cold that I'd get chilblains. When I returned home he'd ask how much money I'd made? Sometimes he took most of the money and then went to the pub and if I hadn't made much he'd send me back out again. Usually he'd take half my money and said if I told my mother I knew what I would get!

Then after I'd been warmed up by the coal fire Mum would ask how much money I'd made. She'd then say she was sorry but Dad had told her I had to give her half so I did but never told her about the money Dad had taken.

Dad was always shouting and as children we all saw some really nasty arguments. Mum would often have bruises and from a really young age I had a really bad stutter. It was hideous. I could hardly say a word. I used to have horrendous nightmares as a kid and bad nose bleeds. Because of all this I was practically backward as a child. I was beaten and slapped a lot by Dad and bullied a lot in school and out of school.

Often I would be up at 6 in the morning, go down to the farm, feed everything, come home to go to school, run home from school for dinner as most of the time we couldn't afford school meals, then run back to school. It was a good 2 miles and then after school run home again for tea. Then I'd have to go back to another farm that was also a wood yard and saw mill. Railway sleepers were cut into smaller pieces, then with an axe chopped into logs and put into stacks. Twice a week we would load a truck up with sacks of wood, then go round the street delivering the logs to houses to burn with coal. Also we had a machine to chop the logs into sticks that we put into clear plastic bags with a twisted top and delivered to shops for sale.

At school I worked very hard. My marks out of 10 for effort would always be 10, but for actual achievement were always between 1 and 5. I was very good at sport, running, football, rugby and I was very good at fencing with a foil, a type of sword. I was bullied at school and laughed at because of my stutter. I never had a girlfriend. I had a horrible haircut, the crew cut, or a basin cut. My dad would often cut my hair with metal hand clippers. I was only very small with a freckled face. When it was near to Christmas, all the girls would stand one side of the school hall and the boys the other side. The teachers would tell the girls to pick their partners. I was always left without a partner or the really ugly girl that was left who would even pull a face when told she had to be my partner. Then other girls would laugh at her having to have me. No one ever wanted to go to the Christmas party at school with me. It was a really bad time in my life but I never told my mother about being bullied at school. When things got real bad, I would skive off school and I would go over the fields to some ponies where I would watch them for hours and I would befriend them. Slowly I started to ride the pony's bare back. I was very good at it.

When we did eventually get a 16-inch TV Dad loved watching a good western. He also used to watch racing on TV and I used to dream of riding in a race. Sometimes I ran home from school pretending I was in a horse race, pretending to walk around at the start, going into the starting stall and then I'd be off and I'd go running home doing my own commentary as I galloped along. At every lamppost I'd pretend there was a hurdle and jump. I would slowly come through the field of runners, then in the final furlong of the race would take the lead and it was always a fight to the finish line. I was the winner with everyone cheering and patting me on the back. I was a good jockey!

About the bullying, I'd never tell Dad. He'd probably give me a slap for being a recline.

Coal was delivered to our home as we had twenty bags of coal as part of Dad's wages working at the mine. My job was to count the bags to make sure we had all twenty bags that we were entitled to. Sometimes the men delivering the coal would try to steal one of our bags of coal, so I had to tell them, "Oi you missed one!" Then I had to shovel what coal had piled up outside the door into the coalhouse and close the door. I'd be as black as the ace of spades when I was finished.

We had an outside toilet at home with a nail knocked into the wall by the toilet then newspaper torn up into squares stuck on the nail that you used to wipe your backside. If we ran out of newspaper we used old glossy magazines if we had one that was a little more difficult to wipe your bum with.

Dad and I had ladies bikes and we peddled for miles across fields to a railway line then we walked up the lines picking up coal that had fallen off the trains coming from the pits. We filled sacks, tied them up and put them on top of each other then walked home pushing the bikes. We then had extra coal for our fire.

When our garden was empty of potatoes and other vegetables I had to go across the fields at night and crawl into the potato fields with a little spade and steal the potatoes. Sometimes if a farmer saw me in the field, he'd come in his tractor to chase me off and sometimes if I came home with nothing, dad would be very angry and slap me. When Dad and Mum had a bad argument, the shouting would upset me so much I would climb into the coalhouse and hide until all was quiet.

Because we were poor, I often had to wear other peoples hand me downs. I was the only kid at senior school still with short pants. My older brother John was my hero. He was a fireman, shoveling coal on the steam trains. When John became a soldier in the light infantry I was so proud of him. Dad hated John for being in the army because Dad was Irish. He'd talk about the Black and Tans. Back in the war the Black and Tans were often jailbirds from prisons. Some really bad guys put into the army and sent to Northern Ireland. The Black and Tans did a lot of really bad things in Ireland so Dad hated John for it. I'll never forget, John had left home and he came to visit us. Dad had a really bad argument with him when he stood at the front door in his army uniform. I thought he looked amazing.

One day Dad was at a pub and I was with him. He was being really nasty, calling my brother terrible names and I chirped up.

"I'm very proud of my brother."

This was in front of Dad's mates. When we got home he beat the shit out of me and after that he was often really nasty to me. Sometimes he slapped me really hard.

"That's just in case you're thinking about joining the army like your bastard brother."

Our mother was the best Mum anyone could have and brought us all up to be good people. All our family left home as soon as possible to get away from Dad. Mum went through an awful lot for us kids.

When I left school, I went to Malton near Pickering to work as an apprentice jockey for Bill Elsey. I was even bullied there but I was very good. I left Bill Elsey's stables and worked for Bob Ward near Doncaster, not too far from my mother. I actually rode in a race at Great Yarmouth but I came last. There was only approximately a 1000/1 chance that any apprentice jockey stable lad would ever race in a public race at a racecourse, so what an achievement eh?

So that was a little bit about my childhood up to my first job after leaving school. As you see with my love of ponies and my racing home from school, my childhood dream came true. I was at the Liverpool Aintree Race Track for the Grand National. In the morning we did an early morning gallop. My trainer was a good friend to Ginger McCain and the lad on the horse next to me worked for him. At the end of our gallop the lad on the horse next to me spoke,

"My horse is going to win the Grand National today."

"Of course he is," I said

I had just galloped alongside a horse called Red Rum who that day won the Grand National for the first time. He went on to be the greatest racehorse ever to have graced Aintree, winning three Grand Nationals and achieving two second places too. How about that then?

This was another reason why all this with Lily was all the more ridiculous. It was because of all that I had seen as a child that I swore never to do anything similar. I hated violence and

I had always been very anti men who hit women. The only time I ever hit anyone in my life was in my own self-defense. Whether it be a male or a female it was impossible for me to be anything like my father. I have never drank or smoked and never taken drugs other than from a doctor if I'd not been well. So all of this had been all the more upsetting to me to be accused of such a vile crime.

Back to 9-0, time continued to pass incredibly slowly, I was still there, waiting for the immigration to come and get me. Mr. Winkler hadn't been able to get me out. No one had come to my rescue so I was stuck with the worst bunch of criminals you could imagine. My new friend the Italian New Yorker had really attached himself to me but you couldn't trust this man at all. I had no doubt he would slit your throat while you were asleep and not even blink an eye. He had now told me that he had a really beautiful sister who lived in a Penthouse over looking a river. He told me she had always been unlucky with men. As he got to know me better he announced one day that he'd spoken to his sister about me and that he had set it up for me to go to New York and stay with her. He said he would be really happy if we hit it off and said he would be honored to have me as a brother in law.

"My sister is very, very rich, she told me to tell you, if you're as good a person as I've told her you are she isn't bothered if you have no money, as long as you make her happy."

I thought to myself that if he thought I wanted to get involved with his sister and have him as a brother in law, he needed his head looked at more than I needed mine looked at.

Talking about this subject, I was waiting to go and see the psychiatric person. Maybe he could help me to get out of here. I was slowly going more and more down hill. I would probably make Frankenstein look good right now. How could my life ever be normal again after this?

The evil black bro was making more comments about me making some bro a good bitch. This was becoming a real worry to me. I really did fear it was possible he might try to rape me at some point. I needed to make some kind of statement somehow but I had no idea what that could be at this point. I had often heard talking about how sometimes when there was really bad blood between some of the inmates, it had been known for someone to stick a pencil into someone's neck and then snap the pencil, leaving the rest stuck inside the neck. I wouldn't put it past some of these guys.

People came and went in here. Frank and some of the guys in the White House were joking that if ever Frank left our cell I would have been in the White House the longest. They said it would be funny if English became the leader of the White House when he was in here after not committing any crime. Totally innocent. I was horrified at the thought. It was true though. I had never been arrested for anything in my life.

I must say I was talking like the posh Englishman a lot now but I couldn't explain why I did it. I didn't plan to do it, it just came out from time to time. I think it must have been some nervous reaction, some kind of release of tension that was building up inside of me. This thing when people farted and me saying, "More tea vicar" was very obscure. I remember how I came about the more tea vicar. I was sure it was a Monty Python sketch, a tea party at the village hall where the vicar let one go and some guy in a posh voice said, "More tea vicar" and then pours the vicar a cup of tea.

Lights out then late into the night suddenly all hell broke loose. Several officers came charging in shouting.

"Everybody out!"

We were all taken outside and stood under lights with mosquitos flying around us. All our bedding, pillows and matrices were thrown all over. They were searching (so I was told) for contraband. Things smuggled in somehow that we were not supposed to have. When we were allowed back in it' was all very nasty, near to violent. Everyone was searched and

I mean searched. Apparently this happened every now and then. About an hour later I could smell something.

"How the fuck has someone got their hands on some weed in here," the guy in the bunk opposite said in the dark.

"All that searching has been set up for someone to bring something in."

"Well if that's the case it has to be an officer that bought it in for someone." I said.

"That's usually the case English. I'm the trustee but it's impossible for me to get anything like that. Someone must have some serious connections to pull that off in a high security set up."

Everyone then went to sleep.

The next day all the usual stuff and a new comer had arrived to join our bro's. What a disgusting, dirty looking man. They all said he was a hobo, a tramp that talked to no one, a little bit like the weirdo from the stockade. If you left anything at dinner he ate it, going into the bin rummaging through the waste and eating it. No one liked him. He didn't wash himself and he smelled. The black guys kept complaining about him, saying he should be moved out now because he was so disgusting. To see this man literally turned your stomach. No one would sit anywhere near him when he was eating. He even took bones from pieces of chicken out of the bin and sucked and chewed on them. Everyone found this particularly bad. What I'm about to tell you, if it doesn't turn your stomach, then nothing ever will. Some of the black lads decided to pull a really disgusting and nasty, vile stunt on this animal. Some of them took some leftover food; some chicken bones and they masturbated and came over the food then mixed it into the left over food. They left it on the table, knowing he would take the left overs and he did. He sucked and chewed everything on the plate not knowing anything about his special treat. What followed was incredible. They shouted and screamed.

"Jesus, fucking hell, the dirty bastard."

They gave each other high fives while laughing and shouting and he had no idea what the commotion was about and just carried on seemingly enjoying every mouthful. I had to go to my bunk. It made me feel really sick.

Chapter 18

# Ricky Dale- President of the White House.

*The pendulum of the mind oscillates between sense and nonsense, not between right and wrong*

CG Jung

My little friend had come out to play again. I had decided to call him Bugsy and sadly he reminded me of another terrible thing my Dad did to me. I was allowed to have a pet rabbit. It was a big white rabbit and it was beautiful. One day Dad said, "We're having the rabbit for dinner, he's nice and fat now."

"But that's my rabbit."

"Yes it is," Mum said.

Dad told Mum to shut up. I was horrified. He killed the rabbit in front of me saying that was how you did it, so the next time I would know how to do it myself. He then hung the rabbit up in front of me and made me watch him slit down its stomach, pull out it's intestines and skin it. The smell of the warm rabbit's blood made me feel sick. I was devastated by this and cried at the death of my beautiful white rabbit. Dad said that I would have to kill, gut and skin the next rabbit and sometime later, that's exactly what he made me do. I had to learn to be a man he said.

I forgot to tell you about something when I was at school, you may even find this a little funny. I entered a speaking competition and I set out to learn a poem by William Shakespeare "Blow to blow Thou Winter Wind."

I recited the poem perfectly and took first prize. When I was given my certificate for winning, the head teacher said "Well done, what do you think of winning?" I then stuttered like an idiot in my reply. It was, I suppose to some, hilarious!

I once played a donkey in a school play, E OR E OR, it always seemed like the perfect part for me and I played it well. Don't laugh, you nasty people, it was funny though. Even I could see the funny side.

Back to 9-0. The comments about me being a bitch were getting more often and he started to really stare at me with a really sick perverted smile and sometimes would stand and walk towards me as I set off to the shower. I just went back to my bunk.

One day the artist, Chris, who did the drawing of the White House, was ill. He was saying he needed some food or he would be really ill. Dinner was late and he kept going to the gate asking an officer for food as he was feeling really faint.

"If I don't get some food soon I could collapse."

They just took no notice of him then he actually collapsed on the floor. Some of the guys just stepped over him, one even kicked him.

"Get up you arsehole and stop play acting."

I went across to him.

"Are you okay Chris?"

He just muttered, I say, "You evil bunch of mother fuckers, you thick set of bastards. He's not well!"

They just looked at me, I was talking to them all and I could see it really took them by surprise, but I'd totally lost the plot and just didn't care anymore. Thinking about it, I must of hit breaking point and they knew it. I could see it on their faces. I shouted at the gate. I'd definitely lost it now. I shouted at the officer.

"You fucking arsehole get the nurse now or take him to a doctor or you'll personally be held responsible for him, he's really not well!"

They took him to the nurse. Everyone was really shocked by my outburst. When they brought Chris back he said, "I was told what happened, I can't remember but thank you. Everyone is saying you had some real bottle to say what you did."

I was now giving up hope that they were coming to get me anytime soon. I was now thinking it was just a matter of time before I was going to become someone's Bitch. My entire mind was totally dysfunctional, all normal rational thinking was going. I was thinking over and over about my black bro's possible plans. What I did next had to be one of the biggest, most dangerous and insane things anyone could ever do in this place.

My black friend was sleeping in his bunk. I walked into the room, knelt by his bed and woke him up with a firm tap on his forehead. When his eyes opened, he must of thought he was dreaming. His eyes widened with shock, his disbelief was obvious to me.

"I know what you're thinking about, but if you lay one finger on me, I'll come back when you're sleeping and, just as I have now, I will pencil you, and we don't want that do we bro?"

I then stood up and went back to my bunk. He never said a word, no one did, they just thought, English had finally lost the plot and I think they were right. I was now definitely mentally unstable. He never said another word after that or made a similar gesture ever again. My gamble paid off. Even the officers never said anything but I was told the next day I was going to see the prison psychologist and later I was taken to a holding cell across from where the doctor's office was.

Always cuffed, I sat quietly. When the other guys in the waiting room were talking about 9-0, my cell, they were saying they were a bunch of violent, evil mother fuckers in there. Some of them were psychopaths it was said.

I wanted to say "Hello chaps, I'm from 9-0" but I said nothing.

When I got to see the Psychologist, he was a very nice man. After half an hour he told me he wanted to speak to me more and I would have to wait in the holding cell and he would call me back soon. I spent the best part of two hours talking to him. I told him everything.

"I don't know how you keep smiling," he said. "I have been doing this for many years and this will catch up with you, big time," he said.

He then asked me what was my approach when meeting people?

"When I meet someone, I quickly decide if I like them. If I do, I then give them my trust and wait till they either break it or develop a friendship."

"You must get hurt an awful lot in life being like that."

"Well, it's a fast way to find out about someone, because it's better to find out sooner rather than years into a friendship, so if I'm to be hurt and let down, I'd rather it be now rather than later. It would hurt even more years later."

"Fascinating." he said.

"Are you going to get me out of here?"

"I will write a report stating you should be taken out of here as soon as possible and deported back to your loving family. I must say if what you have told me is the truth and I do believe what you've told me then you have suffered badly. I hope you find happiness Mr. Dunphy, but it will be a long time before you get over this, if you ever do. Good luck."

Maybe now they would come to get me soon when I got back to the cell?

Frank is going to be a trustee in another part of the prison. They said he would possibly come by with stuff for our cell from time to time.

We now had new young guys. My Italian friend told me that these were known as jitterbugs. Very aggressive, with big mouths, always running their mouth and full of shit. If you got one of these alone they were nothing. They were arrogant, lippy, noisy, taking the piss and threatening all the time. Laughing like everything was a joke but they were shitting themselves really.

My big black friend who wanted to be my sweetheart came in and told them to my disbelief.

"Look you mother fuckers, this is English. He's the president of the White House. Do as he says or you'll have me to deal with."

My goodness, he was looking out for me. They must have known I couldn't take any more. It seemed unbelievable but it wouldn't be long before I had been in here for 10 weeks. Staggering stuff eh?

My Italian friend told me that his partner had now been shot. I told him that I really didn't want to know. That night I was fast asleep when I was woken up in the pitch black. I was being pissed on all over my head. I had piss in my mouth and I covered my head with my blanket. It stopped. They were all having a laugh.

"One by one while you're in here I will piss on you in turn, the same way you have done to me in the middle of the night. Sweet dreams arseholes. If any one of you wishes at any time to discuss this with me, I'd be more than happy. Oh and by the way, I've asked the trustee to get you some KY jelly. It's best you know now that our black friend who introduced you to me, well at least once while you are in here, will make you his bitch and he has a really big dick and he'll fuck you hard up the arse but that shouldn't bother you because you are big arseholes anyway. Don't say I didn't warn you guys, remember the KY."

Some of the others were now laughing.

"Yes English is right but maybe you will enjoy it lads."

They had stopped laughing now. Then everything in the dark calmed down.

"I'm busting for a piss!" I said.

"Which one will it be first," laughed Frank. But our new friends were not laughing now or even making a sound. I say nothing more.

The next day I asked the officers for a new blanket.

I joke with them. "We have some kids with a bed wetting problem."

Over the past few days' things had been given a paint job outside and the food had been better. We were allowed outside everyday and were told we were having a prison visit by the powers that be. They would come into our cells and look around asking if there were any complaints or if things could be better. The prison warden would be with them. One guy joked.

"We can ask if we can have some drugs and booze and some girls sent in."

They all started laughing.

No one would say a word to the warden or make a complaint it simply wouldn't be wise at all being at the total mercy of these people in here. So the visit was tomorrow then things would get back to normal. When the warden came in I asked politely if I could have a word sir. He wondered what I was going to say as I saw a slight look of surprise on his face.

In front of these people over seeing his prison I said,

"Approximately 12 weeks ago sir I was to be deported. It was a deal put to me by the courts if I took a no contest plea. I should have been deported from the stockade. I was on a misdemeanor charge and four days later they put me in here. I've asked many times to be moved out but I'm still here, will you please make arrangements for me to be deported?"

"That's terrible," he says, "but there's nothing I can do, fill out a request slip and give it to the officer."

"I've done that," I said

He told me to do it again and now he looked a little uncomfortable in front of these people so I filled out another form. I don't think he was too pleased with me.

"You don't want to upset him, he runs this place," one of the guys said.

I was told this prison was run by a private company and they got more than $150 a day for each person here. If that's true, maybe I'd been kept here simply to make money for this company, I don't know if there was any truth in it but that could have been a possibility. Imagine that!

Frank did call by. He was a little worried for Chris being diabetic. One day Frank when he came around for laundry, I said,

"Frank can I have a quick word? If they come for me, this could be the last time I ever see you, so listen to what I have to say. I believe deep down you're a good guy but you have no qualifications. Go to school here, get the diploma you never got when you were young, take up the drugs rehabilitation program and clean up your life my good friend. Don't be a dick head all your life!"

He looked at me and I gave him an address in England. He told me he had spoken to a very beautiful friend.

"She goes out to rich clients English," he said, "very rich. I told her if you contact her, she will take you out for a really wonderful meal, you can stay with her a while, shag the arse off her as a thank you from me."

"Look Frank, no thanks, I'll get my own if I need a woman but think about what I've said then do it.

Frank then said he had to go.

This so called new attorney had done nothing for me as yet so that was another $1000 it looked like I'd wasted!

I did keep in touch with Chuck and Wendy. They had been to see me but it must have been really awful for such nice people to come and experience such a horrible place. I much preferred it if they didn't come as long as I could phone them sometimes.

I still went to church.

"One day English I think you might come back," said the vicar, "but when you do it won't be as an inmate. It will be like me, to help inmates become better people."

"I may have lost the plot big time my friend, but I don't believe that will happen."

It had been a very long day today. Chris left, so I was now the person who had been there the longest, the president of the White House.

I was able to see my little friend Bugsy today and I watched him for quite a while.

I began to hear the speaker sound and thought to myself that some lucky guy could be leaving us....but wait it was my name. I wondered what they wanted to do with me this time? So I went to the gate.

"Mr. Dunphy?"

"Yes," I said.

"Get your stuff, you're leaving."

"Leaving? What do you mean?"

The officer answered.

"Deportation James Dunphy."

I was speechless and I just stood and looked at him.

"Don't just stand there, don't you want to leave?"

Some of the other guys had gone running to the White House shouting.

"English is finally going. English is finally going!"

Even the black lads had come out of their rooms. It was ridiculous. Some were standing on tables cheering.

"Mother fucker, they're finally letting him go!"

I went to my bunk as I had to clear all of my things. As I came out most of the guys were now in the main room. Big fives were going around and some were clapping. One of our black bro's stood in front of me and shook my hand really firmly with a big smile on his face. As he spoke I could hear emotion in his voice.

"English Rick, you are a man," he said, "a real man, a gentleman. His eyes are glazed with water and I could see he was holding back the tears.

It's just incredible. As I left the room I heard one officer say good luck. At last I was to be free. I couldn't believe it. It seemed like I had been here forever. I was led to a holding cell and not long after led to a van. I was then told I had to stay one night in another jail.

"They will come for you tomorrow morning," I'm told.

"Who will come for me?"

"Immigration officers."

When I got to the other jail, it was back to the normal routine. Everyone was an utter bastard. They put me in a large room with smaller rooms around the outside but they made me sleep in the centre of the room under the lights as if I was some kind of outrageous criminal. I asked why I couldn't sleep in one of the rooms and I was told they wanted to keep an eye on me. What did they think I was going to do? Run off? I was then told to not be an arsehole and to shut the fuck up so I slept on a matt. Well I say slept. Most of the night I couldn't switch my mind off in between hearing these doors and that horrible loud wack wack wack wack, beeeeeeez, that noise was so intimidating!

The next morning, after a shave, I ate a little something then my name was called out. I was taken out, told to take off my inmates clothing and given some clothes that Chuck and Wendy had brought me. Some jeans, pants, socks, trainers and a shirt. I had a thin gold chain with a little gold cross which was taken off me when I was arrested. I now had them back. I was now dressed. I looked at my new clothes, clutched my cross with my hand and thought, yes! I'm, finally off! I was then taken out to a minibus. The driver and the passengers had a protective mesh between them. There were just five of us. I couldn't tell you the emotions that were running through my body. We had now entered the 1-95 heading south towards

Miami airport. I found myself wondering what my future would hold. I dearly wished I still had my home, my beautiful house. Where would I live? I had next to no money or clothes, no sound system, no car. If only I still had my home!

*One of the letters I received from Frank.*

My emotions were now getting the better of me and I turned to look outside so no one could see my tears. I noticed the turn off for Miami airport ahead. Nothing had been said, not a single word between anyone.

"I hope there's no delay!" I said out loud to the officers.

"What delay?" the driver said.

"My flight to England."

"What flight, we're not going to the airport."

"I don't know where you're taking these guys but you're taking me to Miami airport to be deported."

They laughed.

"Yes you're being deported but not today. We're going to the Crone Detention Immigration Centre in the Everglades. You will leave from there at some point for Miami Airport."

I am just struck into silence. Eventually as we passed all Miami airport turn offs for the airport on the 1-95 and I was just looking back to the airport with my face pushed against the window of the minibus. I was mentally exhausted unable to even begin to be able to try and comprehend what was to happen to me next. Did Chuck, Wendy or Doug know I was being sent there or did they think I was now at the airport waiting for my flight?

My headache had returned. It had to be the stress! Well, here we were being taken out of the van and were now all sat in a big waiting room and one by one we were called to a counter and asked our name. We were then given another outfit to put on. My new clothes were taken and my chain put in a plastic bag. I then had to sit back down and I was eventually taken out of the building to a big marquee, or a very large tent with bunks so close to each other that when you lay down on your bunk and put your arm out you could reach across and touch the next one. It turned out there was 120 bunks and I was told I was the only person here that spoke English. I was given some forms to fill out and just sat on my bunk. I was on the top so I could look across at the sea of bunk beds. I was also the only white guy here and I was trying to work out what nationality they all were. Some were speaking French, some Spanish. Lots of the guards were speaking Spanish. We were later called outside and put into a queue.

When we entered the building it was like lining up to go on a ride at an amusement park. Up one aisle then down another, a bit like a snake. As we entered the building, it was like a rather large canteen, really different. When you got to the front, I couldn't believe my eyes. Lots of different food and you helped yourself as if it were your dinner in a bloody hotel. Orange juice, Coca Cola, water, then a sweet section and fruit, someone pinch me! This just couldn't be real! I thought it was a trick and that when I actually got to the food someone would stop me and say "April fool," but no! All these guys were looking very depressed.

"Hey, cheer up you should see where I've been for the last 14 weeks in total."

Obviously to normal folk this would still be a really horrendous place, but after all I had been through it was now like I was stood in shit to my knees whereas before I was stood on my head in shit. I knew which I'd rather have had. In a really ironic way, these guys didn't realize how lucky they were but how could I call this being lucky?

After our banquette we could go out to a large field with a big high fence all the way round but it was grass not concrete. I took my trainers off and felt the grass between my toes. It was almost like sex, although I wouldn't know anything about that but if I was not careful I might have experienced my first hard on for a long time. Imagine getting turned on by grass. I had a trainer in each hand and I walked all the way round the perimeter. I was away from everyone and I suddenly become a little afraid and had a problem with my breathing. I just felt desperately alone and became tearful. I couldn't control myself. I was having some kind of panic attack but why? I felt I had to go back. What was I now experiencing?

When I got closer to the others I calmed down. I didn't understand, as I had been able to walk away from a confined space for the first time in weeks. Like my friend Bugsy I was able to play in the grass, run and even jump if I wished. Now a whistle was blown and we went back to our bunks. All of a sudden I thought, "I have it!"

All or most of these in the marquee were Asian and Cuban. People who had come over on rafts who had swam ashore on South Beach after the dangerous crossing from Cuba. Escaping the military regime, risking death while some even ended up dead. Those who survived were separated from their wives and children who were put in another part of the detention centre.

I tried to speak to some of the deputies but they didn't speak English.

Later everyone could go to the canteen again. In some parts of the canteen there were large TV's. I ate some food, but couldn't eat too much as my stomach had shrunk with my loss of weight. My hair was very long now and my fingernails were a little long.

The news was on, Fox News and I was watching some more people being arrested on a beach, climbing off rafts and large boats that were over flowing with depressed people, traumatised by their terrible experience at sea. The horror etched on their faces. This was at the moment a big problem for the coast guards and immigration authorities.

I then heard some immigration officers talking in English, so I asked politely, waiting for some nasty response.

"What can I do for you?"

At last, a human being! I explained my situation and asked when I could actually get to talk to someone.

"Someone will call you but they're up to their neck with all these people coming across from Cuba."

I was right!

"You will have to be a little patient, that's why they have the marquee for the overflow of people. It could take a couple of days before they get to you.

"A couple of days?"

"Yes," I was told, but at least they were nice about it.

At times you could come and go from the marquee at will to and from the field. There was a large area of picnic tables where some sat and talked. The majority of these people seemed quite nice folk, hoping at some point to be allowed to join their families and to go to live in Miami with relatives if they then qualified by law to live in America and start new lives.

Later as I stood outside the canteen a bus pulled up. It was quiet extraordinary. On TV earlier that day on Fox News, I had seen a bunch of people coming ashore and it was them getting off this bus. How surreal!

I was very tired and still felt very ill. I think the excitement of all this activity was simply too much for me after living the way I had for the past weeks.

I had been here a couple of days now and I was told I could make a phone call. They had some phone stations but the queues were endless. Everybody had the same conversation. They were talking to families here in Miami, talking to immigration attorneys organized by their families, hoping they would qualify to stay and them that didn't would be deported back to their home land.

I was finally able to speak to Chuck and Wendy. When I told them where I was they were horrified.

"They should of taken you to the airport Ricky, you should now be with your family in England!"

When I got back to my bunk I was filling out my papers and some of the people were coming up to me and showing me their papers. They didn't seem to understand so I started to try and help them, which was very difficult.

I had a little sleep. It was very, very warm and I had some big mosquito bites, swamp mosquito bites that itched really bad. You could hear the little shits but their bites came up really big.

I was suddenly woken by this black Asian guy. He spoke just a little English and he was asking me if I would help him and help his people with their papers and filling out their forms. It was a standard form I explained. He spoke French and Spanish and a tiny bit of English. Imagine me, my handwriting wasn't brilliant, my spelling was even worse and I had always been terrible with filling out forms and now I was helping these people with theirs! What had I done?

I now had a queue of people waiting for me and this guy to help them with their paper work. It looked like I had my own secretary. What had I committed myself to? But these people were all so nice!

When I lay on my bunk I could hear them all singing together, most of them were religious folk, singing hymns even though their God hadn't listened to them. What a contrast from the felon cell to here! This was an education of life that was beyond words!

Some of these men were very quiet and timid, very shy and when I helped them and I could feel their sadness instead of hatred and violence and the need to be feared as part of their survival as in the felon cell. In here there was no intimidation but gentleness, every one of them so grateful for my help. I felt so humbled in the presence of these people and I was moved to being a little emotional when I saw them close up as I watched them trying to hold their emotions back. The guy that had asked me to help them was called Paul.

The anguish was clear to see with some of these people after having to leave members of their family behind, mothers and fathers too weak to attempt the hazardous life threatening trip, not knowing when they would see them again or if they ever would. The memories of some of these people's faces have made me cry as I've written this. I could hardly see my writing.

Chapter 19

# Krone Detention Centre

*Just when you think it can't get any worse, it can. And just when you think it can't get any better, it can.*

Nicholas Sparks

Ok I'm back writing. I had just been watching TV, Sky News. I watched the Haiti Earth Quake and it suddenly hit me that many of the people I was helping back then must now live in Miami. I suddenly realized that they must have mothers, fathers, grandparents, maybe cousins and young children buried under those buildings. I became over whelmed with grief for them just weeping and unable to control myself. I felt a terrible sense of sadness at what those people must have suffered but somehow I also felt a sense of pride that I was able to be of some comfort to them at one time.

I remembered all to well my own sense of helplessness when I was with the imbeciles. When nobody would talk to me or help me in anyway. No one showed me any kindness at all. I was so happy I was able to be of some help to those people in their desperate hour of need. Everyone is capable of helping someone and it doesn't matter how little that help is believe me. What might seem a little help to you or not even worth bothering about to someone else could be priceless.

In many ways this big white marquee had turned out to be the White House. I kept thinking to myself after all this where would my life take me? How would my life unfold? It was dark, late into the night and I was reflecting on the day that had past now more than ever. I yearned for the moment I could hold my son in my arms and kiss him with all the love I could find. Yearned to be with my mother again, I hoped she was keeping well. I would run with my brother and he could beat me every time, I really didn't care. I could remember the foggy, frosty, freezing cold days when we ran for miles together, sometimes setting out to run 6 miles but running 10 instead finishing with a sprint finish up the hill near to my brothers house, steam coming off us both from the cold, frosty air. He always out sprinted me. Next a wonderful hot bath and Pat would always do us a lovely tea, oh what beautiful, wonderful memories I have of this. Also some of the shows I had performed at, I was bloody good at what I did and I was not done yet!

I remembered my good friend Taff, when he first came to live at my house as a lodger, he'd split up from his wife and he was a milkman. It was so funny as he actually managed to write off 2 milk floats and they don't go any faster than 20 miles per hour, if that...he drove the fastest milk cart in the West Taff did. What a lovely guy and his Missus Janet. They ended up back together again which was good.

Whilst I had been in there I had been in touch with Mr. David Kilpatrick and he was shocked yet again to find out I was still in America but said he was going to try and find a way of stopping the deportation. He told me Lily had spoken to him and that she told him she still loved me. He said I should stay in touch with her and even suggested that it would be possible for us to re marry. I told him he had lost his mind.

The next time I spoke to him he said that Lily had told him she was desperate to talk to me and would I please phone her so I said I would. When I first started to speak to David, I was talking in broken English...ARE YOU ...OK, very slow and very loud like a Mohican Indian.

"Why are you talking like that Mr. Dunphy? he asked.
"WHAT DO YOOOOU MEAN?"

It was because I'd been communicating with these Haitians and Cuban's for so long in broken English that I did the same when speaking to anyone else.

I now had 75 mosquito bites on my body, 28 on my feet and I had to see 2 therapists. Both said the same thing more or less, that it was possible that all of this could have sent me a little mad.

I had now found out that Doug had spoken to my attorney Bert Winkler and he now said that he was trying to stop my deportation. You will never believe what I'm about to tell you. Lily had been back to court to request to Mr. Rothschild that the restraining order be lifted so she could visit me. I would have loved to have seen the look on his face. Apparently Lily told Mr. Kilpatrick that Mr. Rothschild actually said that I seemed to be a nice guy, calm and quiet in the courtroom. When would someone realize that Lily was a very distraught woman who was trying to protect her law suite?

My life was now very different. I got up, shaved and showered with water that was always hot. I stood in a very long line to have breakfast then went for a walk. I continued to run bear foot around the field but still have problems with some kind of phobia. When it was really bad I just stopped running and went near to where there were people even if I didn't have a conversation with them.

I passed by officers asking quietly, "Do you know when I can talk to someone about my situation?" Always apologizing, saying, "I know you are very busy."

When I went back to my bunk at some point Paul would come along and often I would try to help if I could. My broken English was clearer in my attempt to communicate with some of these folks. Often my attempt would end up with both parties laughing and trying to communicate. When I did speak to someone on the phone I literally had to remember not to speak in the broken English.

It was obviously a far better place here but it was all still very daunting to say the least. No way could you get used to having your freedom and your liberty taken away from you. It was still very intimidating as you were constantly fearful as to what was going to happen next and I had learnt very quickly that you had no control and that these people could simply do what they wanted and wished with you. But you were treated more humanly here.

At last someone came and told me that the next day at 11.30am I had a meeting with the immigration people.

The days were passing by. It's nearly a week and my mosquito bites were really bad. My feet were looking really bad but the hard skin on the bottom of my feet was much better and the sores had nearly healed but the itching from the bites was awful.

I was still here so my new attorney Birt had turned out to be a waste of time. What little money I had left was money desperately needed for my return to England.

I knew I looked a mess and my mental state was really bad. I was eating better but I am desperately depressed. I sleep better but I was very tired most of the time and I had lost a lot of weight. To think I used to be a model.

A lot of my thoughts were constantly of my son, my mother and my family and friends.

What would happen when I did get back to England? Where would I live? I knew I wasn't well and how was all this going to affect me?

It was the next day and here I was with the immigration officials. I knew they had a lot to deal with here but why did they have to be so cold?

The lady I was talking to was telling me that I was going to be deported and that I had been in court and sentenced after a crime I had committed which was a battery offence.

"I'm sorry but I did not commit any offence and I was lied to in court by the public prosecutor and even my own attorney representing me. I was coerced into a no contest plea, just because I was then apparently divorced and I later found out that I was in fact still married. I was told immediate deportation, one year suspended sentence and that I could return to the USA a year later. I am totally innocent of any charges what so ever! My wife did all this to me to get me out of the country, so I would not be able to testify against her in her attempt to defraud the Calder Race Track of Two Million Dollars."

When I finished saying all of this, I could see the totally bewildered look on her face as if to say, "What the hell drugs are you on?" It was a total waste of my time. Set the scene in your head, I must now be branded slightly mad.

She then told me, "I don't know why anyone would tell you that you could return after 12 months. All I know Mr. Dunphy is that according to my papers that I have before me, you cannot return for 5 years."

"5 years?" I said in horror. "This deal was put to me in a court of law and my 5 American witnesses were told the exact same thing.

"Sorry sir but I assure you that you cannot return to America for 5 years. Once you are in England you can write a letter to appeal this if you wish."

I was wasting my time trying to convince her. She told me that my flight would be paid for by the state but I told her I would pay for my own flight. I was then told if I wished to not put my name on the deportation paper then I could stay here for up to 10 months but I would then be deported. I was then told I had a visit the next day by a Lily Barron. The look on my face made her say to me, "Are you ok Mr. Dunphy? You look a little shocked by this."

How do I go about telling this woman why I looked so shocked? I was totally devastated at being told that I couldn't return for 5 years and the double shock was that the perpetrator of all this was coming to visit me. What do you think to that my friends? In all the time I had been here at the detention centre, I had not told anyone about Lily or what I'd suffered at the hands of the legal judicial system. I had hardly said a word to anyone other than helping them with their paper work, talking to them in broken English. I told this lady I would think about putting my name to the deportation papers. She told me it would speed things up and then said she was sorry she couldn't do anymore to help me. I went to speak to Mr. Kilpatrick.

"If you cannot find a sponsor and if you and Lily won't re marry, then you will have to leave. I can only keep you here a little while longer."

I am now trying my best to tell you how I felt at this very moment. It was the next day and I was sat in this picnic/garden area waiting for Lily to arrive. There were lots of families sat together who were very emotional and at any minute Lily, my now ex wife, was going to be here after all that had happened to me and her causing it all. I felt very tearful, what was I supposed to say to her? What was she going to say to me? Part of me just wanted to stand up, walk off and stop this visit, but it was a case of curiosity killed the cat. Come on folks, right now, how do you feel? I really wish you could tell me. I have no way of telling how I felt at this moment in time.

I could now see Lily. A deputy had opened the gate and she was walking towards me. Don't forget I was supposed to have beaten the shit out of her, thrown her up and down concrete steps and told her I was going to kill her and she had 2 restraining orders out on me the second of which she had been to court to cancel herself so she could visit me.

In court the prosecutor told the immigration that if they let me out pending the jury trial I wanted, I might go and kill my wife. I was not hand cuffed to anyone and the same people have just let Lily into this family picnic area to be with a "menace to society" who was apparently going to kill her.

Now freely of her own will she felt it was safe to be with me with no protection, it was all totally serial as she stood in front of me and opened her arms with a big smile.

"Aren't you going to hold me then sweetie?"

Fucking sweetie!!! I put my arms around her which I was finding difficult to do.

"I've missed you sweetie," she whispered, "and you've missed me too, I know you have and Poo Poo misses her dad."

I'm just struck with silence. I had tears in my eyes.

"Don't get upset Ricky."

"Why did you have to do all this to me? You have no idea what I've been through and I have nothing left."

"But you sold your house."

"I've got very little left after paying for my legal fees and the money to Doug for my car. I sold the house for a lot less than what it was worth."

"Ricky, I want us to stay in touch and I will visit you in England when I have my money. We can go to the British Virgin Isles, I know of someone with a villa, pool and recording studio underneath the villa and you can bring people in to work with you when I have the money. We will get to know each other again."

"If you could do all this to me when I had done nothing wrong, what would you do if I was to really piss you off? I haven't got a big enough crucifix to stick in front of you Lily."

"Oh don't be like that, you know you don't really mean it sweetie."

I then asked her what the hell she was doing bringing Donna, my ex wife into court?

"Oh what a bitch she is. That woman will do or say anything for money. It was George's idea about the gun. She didn't hesitate Ricky. You are a lot better off not having anything to do with her. It was a good job you found me!"

Lily then told me that she still had my master tapes and that she still wanted $3000 for them.

"I've got no money and I've had to get a roomy, (that's a lodger) but everything will be OK when I win my law suit Ricky."

"All my money has gone and I will need my master tapes for work when I eventually get back to England."

She then told me that she had to leave but that she still loved and missed me and that one day we would be together again. She gave me a hug and walked to the gate.

I was now sat alone, totally confused and very emotional. I knew I really had to go home. I had a total no win situation and I felt deeply hurt. I really did love Lily when I married her and even though I was hurt I couldn't hate her and I did have some kind of feelings for her but I was not in love with her anymore the same as I was not in love with my ex Donna.

I went back to my bunk, looked around at these sad people and thought at least they are with their loved ones. I felt so empty now and desperately alone.

I was now in my bunk and Paul came to see me. He had someone with him.

"Can you come back a little later, I don't feel too good at the moment," I said in broken English.

When Paul first met me he asked me my name, what do you think I told him?

I said he might as well call me English as I had got used to it.

The next day I asked to speak to the lady from the day before. I went into the office.

"Have you come to sign the paper?"

"No not yet, but I may do sometime tomorrow."

"I looked through your file. After your divorce Mr. Dunphy you were sent a letter to your P.O. Box telling you to report to the immigration offices in West Palm Beach and that because of your divorce to Donna Van Buran you had no legal status and that without a work sponsor you had to voluntarily leave the USA. Not doing so would have meant you would have been arrested as an illegal alien and deported. I told her it was many months later that I would have passed my P.O.Box in Boca Raton. I didn't use it anymore so it would have run out of date. I called in to see the manager, just to say hi and he said he was glad I had called by as he had an envelope for me. Someone else had my box but he had kept the envelope for me just in case I did passed by. I was then living in West Palm Beach. I didn't go to Boca Raton as it was some distance.

When I opened the envelope, I was very worried because the date had way passed of when I had to leave. I was so worried that I phoned an immigration attorney that I found in the newspaper in the West Palm Beach area and he told me not to worry when you had a job and they would sponsor me then I needed get an immigration attorney to represent me and I would be ok. If I had gone to the immigration people they would have told me to leave the country if I didn't have a sponsor. He told me that the people in the immigration offices had far more to worry about with all the Haitian's and Cuban's and the problems with the Mexicans. They were not worried about an English man, as long as when I went to see them I had a sponsor. So I did what he told me. I told her again I was innocent and that the visitor I had had the day before was my ex wife Lily Barron who had accused me of all these crimes.

"Really?" she said.

"Yes, what do you make of that?"

I also told Chuck, Wendy and Doug about the visit, they were speechless. Birt Winkler had done nothing, David Kilpatrick had done nothing so I said sadly it was time for me to sign the papers and go so I did.

Now I continued to wait. I have to tell you when Lily introduced me to David Kilpatrick so that he could sort out all my immigration, while filling out the forms they asked had I ever been requested to leave. I asked David what I should put and he said we should really tell them but all it would do would be to hold things up a little and that everything would go through in the end. David then told me as we'd filled out all of the papers that we had told the immigration people about my marriage to Donna Van Buran and that I was now divorced. They had had plenty of time to dispute anything, but they hadn't after 3 months of filing for work authorization. In that 3 months they knew all about my divorce and my then application for a work visa. They gave me my work authorization card and then went ahead with the paper work for me and Lily, bank account in both names which was required legally. After 6 months of marriage you then had to have the martial fraud interview, but still nothing had been said by the immigration people. We both passed the interview so everything was fine until Lily called the police. All because of Lily's law suit. It was outrageous! Even Mr. David Kilpatrick said the same.

I had been there at the Krone Detention Centre for some 2 weeks or so now. Once again I was in my bunk. It was something like 3am. They came to my bunk and I was told I was going to be deported. I went to the main building and they gave me my clothes. I was eventually taken by minibus to Miami Airport. When at the airport I was put into a tiny cell, approximately 7ft by 5ft. It was 7am. No one came to talk to me, only to give me some food, which was sandwiches and water with a carton of orange juice. I was left there all day.

I was finding that open spaces and confined spaces were now a problem to me. Why, I couldn't possibly tell you. It had to be some kind of psychological problem and it was horrendous. I was left in this cell until 7pm before they came to get me. I was handcuffed to an officer then taken to a van and driven to the underside of an aeroplane. Still hand cuffed I was taken up some steps to board the plane then taken to my seat. Then the cuffs were taken off and I was told to sit and not move only to go to the toilet. The two officers were very abrupt and cold towards me. All of this was done in full view of the airhostesses. I could only begin to wonder what they thought about me being on the plane. I was told only the pilot and the airhostesses knew about me. The passengers were then allowed to board the plane and the two officers remained at the exit door until stewardesses closed it. I just sat silent throughout my flight home. I was totally numb by all that had happened to me but at least now I had no doubt at all that I was being deported.

Chapter 20

# Home

*When everything goes to hell, there are people who stand by you without flinching -- they are your family*
Jim Butcher

When I got to London, Heathrow Airport, my brother had booked me a ticket with a bus company to Rotherham, South Yorkshire where he would meet me with his wife Pat. It was very cold and I didn't have a jacket. I sat upstairs on the bus, at the very front, so I could look at the beautiful English countryside. I couldn't help it but at times through the trip I was constantly in tears, totally broken hearted. I could see in the reflection of the window that I really did look a mess. What was everyone going to think? I just couldn't wait to see my son and my Mum. She would know as soon as she saw me that something terrible had happened to me. I would tell her at some point when I felt up to it. To hold my son, words could not express my need for this. To see my sisters and brothers again would be wonderful and I knew I would have to see my doctor as soon as possible as I knew I had problems.

So Here I was. I climbed down the stairs of the bus and my wonderful brother and sister in law Pat were waiting for me. I could see the shock on their faces at my appearance, especially on Pats face.

After our embraces they asked how my trip was. It was all very awkward. I mean what could I say after being through all the extraordinary and awful events. How did you enjoy your stay in America would have been a strange question. Just think after being locked up in those horrendous cells!

Now I was in my brother's beautiful home with my own bed, a big double bed. My room was very nice with my own toilet and shower. I sat on the bed.

"I'll put the kettle on," I hear coming up the stairs from the kitchen as I was sitting on the bed dressed in all that I own. The room was warm with the heating is on. It was November. After a cup of tea, I took a shower and then we talked about many of the phone calls Lily had made often in the middle of the night. They were shocked by it all.

"Come on, we'll go down the pub." John said.

I didn't know if I wanted to go. John gave me a warm jacket to put on. I had a pint of Guinness and the pub was full. I suddenly started to feel alarmingly uncomfortable and everything seemed to slow down. I was looking around and it was as if the sound stopped. I told John I needed to go outside for some fresh air. I felt really ill and I couldn't stand to be amongst the crowd. My brother and his wife were really wonderful but I knew I couldn't stay too long. I just kept thinking of the stress and worry I would cause them and what would my niece Heather think if it caused my brother stress.

I still had some money left from the sale of my house, not a lot, but I managed to buy an old Ford Sierra car for £350. John and Pat took me to my mother's house and then to visit my son Craig. You can imagine my emotions. I had to go across at some point to see my doctor. He was horrified at my mental state. The pills I had been given for being in contact with TB had been barred from use in the UK. They were cheap and dangerous.

I went to visit my good friends Taff and Janet. They lived not far from my doctors and not far from where my son was living with his Mum and her new partner Steve. All within walking distance. My friends were really taken back by my appearance. I told them I would soon be looking to move near to where my son was staying and Taff and Janet said I could stay with them. I had no money and the social services wouldn't let me have any but they said not to worry. I told John and Pat my plans as I wanted to be close to my son. At first they were concerned and told me I was welcome to stay with them for as long as I wished. I didn't really want to leave them, but I thought it was best if I lived at Taff and Janet's.

My health was getting worse and I was having some kind of break down. Whilst I was at John's Lily phoned. She told me she still loved me and she got the dog to bark down the phone. She still wanted 3000$ before she would give me back my master tapes. The only music I had was on old cassettes and I told her I needed the master tapes more than ever as I was back in England now. Lily said she would give me my master tapes back when her Law Suit was over and I was only talking to her in the hope she would give them back. Recording all my tracks again would cost a fortune and I simply didn't have that kind of money.

I had to go back to see my doctor as I was having really terrible problems. I had definitely developed a fear of open and confined spaces. I didn't like being surrounded by people I didn't know. I cried a lot when I was alone and I couldn't sleep. I had constant flash backs from the jails. Bad dreams, awful nightmares and I had lost all my confidence. I needed to see a therapist every week to help me. I had never believed in therapists before but I must say I did now. My doctor put me on sickness benefit and I was paid a mere £93 every 3 weeks. I had lost everything and I now believed I am totally useless and a complete waste of space. I had lost all self-respect and was nothing but a burden to everyone. I was now suicidal and becoming a zombie with the medication I was on but the doctor said it was very important I stay on the medication for the time being. I kept remembering the prosecutor pointing at me saying I was a menace to society and a dangerous man. I constantly saw Donna and Lily sat together with Lily mouthing the words to me across the courtroom, "I love you."

I phoned Dean Murton from the racetrack and he told me that Lily's case was not going to court until the spring of 1997.

I had to talk to Lily. I needed my master tapes. If she would not send them then I would have to beg, steal or borrow to find the money to replace them. Then she would no longer have a hold over me. Deep down I now knew I was not going to get my master tapes back.

I had now moved in with Taff and Janet. I was a real mess and it was a very cold winter. I would not put on the central heating as I couldn't afford to pay towards the electric and gas bill. I sat freezing cold in the house and I could see the condensation from my breath. I was trying to get back on my feet, doing a lot of driving to see old friends with studios. They were trying to help me with finding backing tracks of songs for my shows. It was all very traumatic, especially when I was ill. My doctor told me not to do anything, just to rest. I'm sorry but anyone who knows me will tell you you're talking to the wrong man if you tell him he can't do something, he will try even harder to prove you wrong.

I would overcome all this. I swore to myself. Lily was continuing to phone me telling me how much she loved me and she then told me that she might visit me in England. She said she sat on our blanket in the garden pretending that we were cuddling and that she played my music and that the dog sat by the speaker. She also told me that she played with herself imaging I was inside her. After talking to Lily it upset me for days after. She also said that I might see her sooner than I thought and that she might just turn up at my door to surprise me

It was now 8th of March 1996. Lily had just told me that she was sending me my master tapes after I'd spent 4 months replacing them. I was still on sickness benefit and I hadn't done any shows to earn money, just a couple of charity shows where I sang just 3 songs. I had problems even doing this.

I remember after one charity show I put so much into it that I was in bed for 3 days after. All the running around had finally caught up with me.

I have decided when I was well I was going to work towards clearing my name by suing Rocque and the courts and one day I would return to America to be with my good friends. I still had faith in the American Legal System I just thought I fad fallen foul on some bad eggs. I would win in the end. I would recover from this in an attempt to fight a case against Lily, Rocque and the prosecutor.

I had contacted a firm of solicitors from London. After some time on the phone I was told that if half of what had happened was true then I had a major lawsuit against the courts, Lily and Rocque but these solicitors couldn't handle the case. They said it must be a firm based in America and it would be better if I found someone out of Broward County area.

I have copies of the letters I sent to my probation officer, Mrs. Louise Rorie. I have a document telling me I was supposed to pay a fee each month. I told Mrs. Rorie that the agreement was none payment. In the first letter I sent I gave details to her of my sad situation and asked her to pass on the letter to Mr. Rothschild, the judge that was presiding over my case. In this letter she was told all about the lies Mr. Rocque and the prosecutor had told me, committing perjury in a court of law, cohering me to take the plea of no contest then failing to carry out my so called immediate deportation. I never, ever received a reply from Mrs. Louise Rorie. All the documents I sent to Mrs. Rorie and to the head of the probation office were sent recorded post however I never received a reply. I put to them pleas for help telling them to notify Mr. Judge Rothschild. Can you imagine once they read my letters and realized the enormity of what had happened in court that they decided to completely ignore me, therefore totally failing to investigate the crimes perpetrated against me, the very serious crime committed in a court of law by my own attorney Mr. Rocque and the prosecutor. I sent two letters to Mrs. Rorie and one to the head of probation dated 11th March 96, 18th April 96, 1st November 96. I explained everything I had been through and detailed the horrors the American system had heaped upon me. Yet to this day I have had no replies.

It was obvious that the courts had not contacted the probation office telling them that Lily had been back to the courts before Mr Rothschild to have an order made cancelling the restraining order so she could visit me at the jail. I sent a copy of the order of dismissal of the restraining order plus a copy of the final divorce decree proving I was still married in court so the probation people could check it all out. I was actually writing the letter to the probation people when Lily phoned me telling me she was thinking about me. I told her not to phone me again as all she talked about is how she loved and missed me. I told her she was just being nice to me till her lawsuit was out of the way. I said it was two weeks since she sent my master tapes and I still hadn't received them yet. I told her she was ordered by Judge Rothschild to give me my things back, that she had purged herself in court telling the judge she'd sent all my things back to England. Lily had sent all my things to a friend so she could not be caught with them. I ended the call by telling her that it had now ended between us and that she had made me look a fool, that everyone was right about her and that I'd been wrong.

As you know I had been in touch with Calder Race Track whilst I was in the Felon Cell. I was hoping they would have got their racetrack insurance companies attorney to bail me out. I would have at that point testified against Lily but after I'd spoken to Bob from the Race Track, he had phoned to Lily's attorney Mr. Harvey Roubencheck. Mr. Roubencheck told Bob that I'd been offered money for a statement supporting the racetrack that could only have come from Lily herself. I had never offered my testimony for money. Bob actually contacted me to tell me this, so Lily must have been very worried. I told Bob I would testify but I had no money so they would have to pay my expenses, I said I would take a polygraph test of necessary. They should ask Lily to take one as well. Bob said he would possibly send someone to where I lived and video my statement. I told Bob that between Lily and Donna I had lost everything. I did say that after the case was over if they offered me something for my help in saving them $2000000, then and only then would I be happy to except, but it was not necessary, I would have been just happy to give my statement at no cost to them. I just wanted Lily brought to justice.

So it was obvious Lily was phoning me in the hope of keeping me sweet until after her lawsuit. How devious.

I remembered a day when Lily took me to visit her ex, Mike to the bus he lived in. When she went to the toilet he told me that Lily was a perpetual liar and a dangerous woman. Oh how I found out the hard way.

Bob was very sympathetic, but I never heard from him again.

On 25th March Lily phoned me again. She was very quiet and said she knew I'd asked her not to call me again but she'd been thinking about the good times we'd had. She said they were very special and wonderful times.

"Remember Ricky when we set off just for a few days to visit my friends but didn't get back till 3 weeks later?"

"You're playing with my emotions, you destroyed all that we had because of the money."

I was starting to shake and I told her I was not well and was getting worse. I was starting to get really emotional on the phone and I had to put the phone down.

I told Taff I was going to bed, where I had a coughing fit and I could hardly breath. I don't know why I talked to her but

I felt I had to. I was taking notes in case one day I could use all this against her if ever I managed to get back to court.

The next day Lily phoned me again. Get this, to see how I was. She said she was worried about me and that she could not sleep the night before. This could have almost been a comedy script. She was asking about my son Craig. I told her all this was making me very ill and that I was trying to get my life back and that I was working really hard to try and get back singing. She told me I was a wonderful person.

"You're always wanting to help people Rick. I remember the show you did for my friends family to raise money to send them all to Disney.

"Stop saying all this to me, you are playing with my head. My doctor will not let me work and I'm having to see a therapist. I feel I'm losing my mind at times."

"I'll phone you tonight Ricky," she said.

I told her I was getting in touch with the courts to bring our case back to court and that I was asking for a jury trial and that I thought she would be going to jail and that my name would be cleared and it was as if she didn't hear a word. She just said she'd phone me again soon and that I had not to worry. She insisted that we stay in touch and that one day I would be glad we had. I asked her not to call again and she just said, "I'll call later sweetie."

SWEETIE!!!!??

I put the phone down and now had a really bad migraine. I was very tired. All these calls seemed to leave me exhausted and I had to go and lie down. When I told Taff and Janet, they had a really worried look as they could see how it was affecting me in such a bad way.

It was my 40th Birthday...wait for it...April 1st. Taff and Janet had set up a surprise birthday party for me and when I came back from shopping a huge banner was over a section of the house which said "Happy 40th Birthday Ricky."

When I went inside most of the family where there and my son Craig. It was all very emotional to say the least.

After being back from America for 16 weeks, I was entitled to get £45 a week rent allowance. It was back dated and as Taff and Janet had been kind enough to look after me and not take a penny from me, I spent it all on landscaping their garden which I was doing slowly over the weeks. It was difficult for me as I was not well with the dizzy spells I suffered sometimes meaning that I had to stop but slowly I carried on. I still had a lot to do but I was determined to do all that I had planned. I would finish it.

It was now 17th April. I decided to phone Mr. Kilpatrick and we talked again about my last day in court. David told me again that Mr. Rocque had not been in touch with him before my final day in court. David said it was absolutely vital that he did in order to prepare my case and Mr. Rocque should have told me the day of the court appearance so I could have been in court if it was necessary. David then went on to tell me again he had instructed Mr. Rocque not to take a deal and they could not deport me just like that. It would take from 6 months to a year to deport me. Mr. Rocque was very negligent in not phoning him, my immigration attorney. He said he would go to court against Mr. Rocque and that I should sue him for what he had done to me. Mr. Kilpatrick then said it was obvious Rocque had done a deal with the prosecutor. He said the prosecutor would assist Rocque in some other case and continued to say that by deporting me they would save the cost of a jury trial at the expense of justice being done. Therefore they committed perjury in open court before me, my witnesses and then the judge. The judge would not know I was still married and that Rocque had been told by my immigration attorney not to take a deal. He would simply carry out whatever deal Mr. Rocque had agreed to with the prosecutor so Mr. Rothschild would have been totally oblivious to the duress I was put under to get the no contest verdict. He continued.

"You, Mr. Dunphy, nor your witnesses were allowed to say a word in your defense. You need to write to the courts and tell them what happened."

I told him I'd been in touch with the probation people giving them all the information they needed and asked them to pass it on to Mr. Rothschild. David then asked me,

"What are they going to do? David asked me.

I said that I'd had no reply. Mr. Kilpatrick said that was absolutely horrific and said I should contact the Florida Barr Association and put in a complaint against Mr. Rocque.

"As long as your friends and witnesses are prepared to complain against Mr. Rocque

and come to court, Mr. Rocque will never appear in court again as an attorney," he said.

For his perjury in court he would have to go to jail and the prosecutor as they also had perverted the course of justice with their actions. These were very serious crimes for them to commit.

It was now June 11th and I still had had no reply to my second letter to the probation people. As for Mr. Birt Winkler, he took my money but had done nothing. He was supposed to get me out of jail. I told him I wanted to sue Mr. Rocque and the courts. He had done nothing and I was constantly told to be patient.

It was now 7 months and I have phone him many times but he was never in his office. When I did get chance to speak to him he said he wanted another $150 to get the court transcripts. I told him if he wasn't going to take my case to sue Mr. Rocque and the courts I wanted my money back. I had never heard anything from him so that was around $2000 lost, $1000 to Rocque , $1000 to Wrinkler and Donna a total of $1400 and Lily cleared our bank account. I was not even sure what was left in that.

12<sup>th</sup> June. Here we go. Lily was back on the phone. She got the dog, Poo Poo, to bark down the phone to say hello to her dad...ME. She wanted to know how I was and that I was in her thoughts. I told her I wanted her to send me my things and she said she didn't know what I was talking about. I was now trying to keep my cool and said the videos of the charity shows I'd done and videos of me on T.V etc and my copy write papers from when I copy righted my songs with the American Copyright of Congress and my tapes. She told me she sent them last Christmas and that I should have received it. I didn't believe a word she said.

I told some good friends of mine who were helping me go to Benidorm, Spain to help me recover from all this mess and I was to stay with a friend of a friend. He was an entertainer. So I was due to go in a couple of weeks. I was now nearly done in Taff and Janet's garden and I was so proud of myself. I was in the process of contacting agents and I went to an agent in Manchester. He had clubs where I didn't need my own sound system. I still had sheet music so this agent said I could do a 45-50 min show with maybe a three-piece band. I was going to do a charity concert for him as an audition. I just hoped I was OK and if he did give me some shows that I was OK to perform the shows anywhere near my best.

I was going to take some old cassettes to Spain with me in case I got the chance to sing. If I did it would be good practice for when I returned.

Chapter 21

# Fighting my Demons

*When health is absent, wisdom cannot reveal itself,*
*art cannot manifest, strength cannot fight, wealth*
*becomes useless, and intelligence cannot be applied*
Herophilus

I went to see my doctor again as I was still having a lot of problems with my emotions. I wasn't sleeping at all and my thoughts were constantly around my situations in the court room and the jails – constant flashbacks. I could be sat in a café, quietly having a coffee when I suddenly became tearful. Sometimes an onlooker would ask me if I was ok because they could see tears running down my face. Sometimes I was totally unaware that I was crying and would in my embarrassment quickly wipe the tears away, thank the person for their concern, finish my coffee and go home.

I used to be a triathlete, swimming, cycling, running. My old friends had been to see me to go running with them. I went but I was so weak and unfit I couldn't live with their pace. Some of these guys I used to leave for dead in a race.

Not long now, less than a week. I did the charity concert near Manchester and the agent was happy with me and said when I returned from Spain he would give me some shows over the weekend I got back. It would be Thursday when I got back and I would sing one show on the Saturday and if I was OK he would give me 2 shows on the Sunday. I told him I wasn't well and struggling to get over a very serious trauma

I'd had and as at the moment I was nowhere near the standard of cabaret entertainment I was when I left for America but I would get back to my best and even better.

I told Taff and Janet that if Lily called, although they didn't like what she had done to me, to humor her as I was now going to try and bring Lily, Rocque and the prosecutor to justice.

It made Lily look stupid after what I was supposed to have done and it would be clear to everyone why she was doing it, to try and keep me sweet so I didn't testify against her lawsuit. When you look back at all I had suffered, all because of her lawsuit. I should still have been in America, a happy married man.

I had now been told by my brother that while I was in jail that my mother had had a really terrible fall. When she fell she snapped her femur. My mom was seriously ill in intensive care and very nearly died. No one could tell me this. I would have gone insane. This was all so tragic, wasn't it?

Off I went to Spain. This friend of a friend I was staying with was a very good person and he was a very good act himself. Before the end of my holiday he actually trusted me to stay in his apartment as he had to return to England before I finished my holiday. So I was alone in his apartment for nearly a week.

I thought Benidorm was a really nice place, lots of entertainment places, beautiful beaches and mountains in the distance. I came across a really fabulous Cabaret Club called Carriages with lights on tables, a compare and a full show nonstop. One day I was sat outside Carriages and I heard the boss Steve talking to the compare Stevie. They had a problem. They were an act short for the night so I said I was a cabaret singer. They asked me to sing a few songs so I went to get my cassette tapes and as soon as I sang my first song I was told I was excellent. That night I did a full hour show. I had no idea how I would do, I really did struggle both with my show and my emotions. The place was packed with people and the boss asked if I could I do the next night and I said I could. All that night I couldn't sleep. I had no one. I was very much alone. I met some other people who lived in Benidorm but I was having a real problem being around people close up.

I was a nervous wreck before my show and I just knew my psychological problems were far from over. The owner of the club wanted me to stay but I had to come home. I wasn't ready yet to go and live in Benidorm. I knew, however, I would return as soon as I was well enough.

So I returned to England and the next day I went to see my doctor. I said I now had work with an agent and I wanted to come off the sick. He said I wasn't ready for that yet and that I should go and sing at weekends and stay on the sick and we would see how I went, so I did. I sang 2 shows on Saturdays and 2 shows on Sundays. I must admit I was still not a well man. My depression was still really bad and I wasn't sleeping and was in and out of emotional setbacks.

I found out that Lily had phoned while I was in Spain. Taff said he nearly told her to fuck off, but he respected what I'd asked of him.

It was Thursday, 2 days after my last show. I was in bed most of the day before. The shows over the weekend were a little much for me but I needed the money. I told my doctor I was preparing to leave England and start a new life in Spain and that I knew I could get work. he told me not to be silly that I wasn't ready for Spain yet, so I told him I would take a little while longer but I would be going in a very positive mood. On that Thursday morning I needed to go to the sand quarry for half a ton of sand. I just had a little bit more work to do on Taff's new patio and then it would be finished. Taff said to leave it and he would finish the last bit but I said no, I would complete what I had started.

I was on the way back from the quarry. I was towing a trailer and I was on a long straight road. I had just past the roadside café when there was a big bang and I was hit at force

222

from behind by a truck and jackknifed with the trailer hit first. Within seconds I was hit right at my driver's door by this truck and my car was badly smashed and the trailer badly damaged.

I sat in my car amongst all this wreckage with the indicator of the truck near as dam knit on my cheek. I was in a hell of a mess with shock and couldn't move. The police arrived and an ambulance. Eventually I was slowly taken out of my car from the passenger side as the driver's side was smashed into the car and I was taken to hospital. I had a rapid double whiplash injury. I was in agony however they let me out of hospital. I was told to stay in bed for a few days and I was now in an even worse condition. Just when I thought I was near to some sort of recovery some twat runs into the back of me and now my car was a write off. When my doctor found out he came to Taff's to see me in bed. I was still in shock and my mental state had now taken a serious setback and I had really bad problems with my neck. This accident would set me back months and I was to continue to have problems with my neck that turned out to be for the rest of my life. I can hear you all saying, what an unlucky bastard I am.

Just think if it hadn't been for Lily's lawsuit, I would have not been in England doing Taff's garden as a thank you for his kindness. When I say a lot of pain, I mean an awful lot of pain.

I just couldn't at this time put together my case against Lily, Rocque and the courts. It all had to take a back seat and so would going to Spain.

As I lay in bed, it was impossible for anyone to begin to understand my mental state and now my headaches were beyond words. The pain I was suffering with my neck was incredible.

At some point I was given a car by my insurance company with only 300 miles on the clock.

I was told I had to see a specialist in Manchester, privately. My insurance company was paying for this and I had a friend there who said I could stay the night. I took my son Craig with me and we stayed with my friend and his little girl.

About two weeks later I was driving this nice new car to Manchester. About 5 miles from my friend's house, I had just gone through the green light setting off at a junction when a woman jumped the red light and hit me on my right...yes hit me! I was in another accident on the way to see the specialist.

The police came and an ambulance. It wasn't a bad crash but my son was crying more because it frightened him. The lady in the other car admitted responsibility. My car could still be driven so I took it to my friend's house. The insurance company I was with sent someone with a new car to replace the one I was driving. I told the police I was ok and that Craig was fine but later I suffered sickness and diarrhea. Craig was fine but I was in shock with the upset of it all. My nerves were in a right mess with the shock of it all. I had to stay a few days at my friends then I went to see the specialist about my neck.

I had to wear a white collar all the time and when I got back I went to see my doctor he just put his head in his hands and said he felt so sorry for me. My neck injury was to prove to be a long lasting problem and I had to go back on the sick. I had to cancel all my shows for 2-3 weeks and I was having really bad vertigo. My agent said he couldn't believe all this shit could happen to someone. He said the response I had had from the clubs I had performed in for him was tremendous and that as soon as I was able to work he would book immediately. I needed to get back singing as soon as possible. I soon accepted shows even though I was in a tremendous amount of pain as I was putting money away to go to Spain.

One day I was told by my doctor to sign some papers and when I asked what they were for, he said he was sorting out papers to get payment for invalidity. I said that I wasn't an invalid and that I would return to Spain as soon as I could. He told me that without support the first thing that went wrong, I would be a mental wreck and in a foreign country.

Taff had to stop Lily from phoning. it was virtually impossible for me to continue to take that kind of psychological and emotional torture on top of all this. Chuck and Wendy are really worried now and so were all my family and friends. How was I going to come out of all this?

Within weeks I went against my doctor and my therapist as I started to accept shows. I was in terrible pain but slowly put the money together for fuel, my ferry from Plymouth and for the drive down to Benidorm with everything that I owned and a month's rent. I went to see my doctor to tell him to take me off the sick as I was going to Spain by ferry to Santander then driving to Benidorm. He told me not to be silly and told me I had an appointment for a medical. All I had to do was turn up. All the paperwork was done and invalidity was set up for me. I just had to attend this medical and it would all be sorted out.

The day before I was to have the medical, I went to the place it was being held and told the receptionist I would not be attending, she said

"Are you mad," she said, "you haven't applied for this your doctor has done it for you. To get the invalidity all you have to do is simply turn up."

I told her I was no invalid, that I wasn't going and that I was going to Spain to start a new life. My agent had got me a contract of work to sing in a club 6 nights a week and within a week I was ready. My car was my Ford Sierra. I had two, second hand doors and a wing and a second hand bonnet which were all different colours. The guy that hit me from behind was not accepting responsibility so the case at some point would go to court. I had some friends rebuild my car till it was all sorted out.

So, it was the morning. I was setting off to Spain the car is packed solid and the roof rack also packed solid. Off I went. There were lots of tears from family and friends. To say goodbye again was very difficult with my son in particular, but

I was only 2 hours away on a plane, so everyone was going to be visiting me on a regular basis in Spain.

I was on my way to the ferry, about 2 hours into my trip, when the roof rack flew off the roof and onto the side of the motorway. All the stuff on the roof rack was damaged, including my very expensive triathlon bike that was buckled. My bench and weights were all over the side of the motorway and the roof rack was completely smashed. I made a decision to throw everything into the field because I had to make the ferry and if I'd hung around I'd have been in trouble with the police. When I get to the ferry it was delayed up to 8 hours. I could have phoned someone to get me a new roof rack and bring it to me and I would still have had all my stuff. What could I say? My luck continued. What bloody luck?

As I was sat waiting for my ferry, I thought of how I was going to start to put my case together from Spain against Lily, Rocque and the courts. If you thought this was over, you've got another thing coming. This was far from over yet my good friends.

The ferry crossing turned out to be a particularly bad one across the Bay of Biscay and when I came to take my car off I had a puncture. It was all happening but I was on my way, driving down to the South East of Spain to Benidorm. It was a 10 hour drive over the Pyrenees Mountains, down to Zaragoza, then past Valencia and on to Benidorm.

It was November and it was cold and I was very tired. I had to meet with the agent's representatives and it was now 8pm. He would meet me in an hour then I will drive out of Benidorm 4 miles to La Calla where the agent had rented an apartment for me. Here he was, Danny, my agent, and we sat down.

"I'm sorry to tell you Ricky," he said "but the club you were to start at tomorrow will not be open for another 3 months."

I was gutted! You must think I am making this entire thing up! Sadly, no!

After I bought some food for my apartment and filled up the tank with petrol I had 45 euros to my total existence in life.

I went to see the boss of Carriages and he told me the job he had offered me months ago had been given to someone else but if he needed me he would contact me. Welcome to Spain Ricky!

Well I had a mountain to climb before I had even started. Why, why, why was this happening to me? I had to keep going round all the bars, until very slowly I picked up a show here and a show there.

I was still in touch with Chuck and Wendy and they knew I was going to try and sue Rocque and party. I was going to contact the Broward Barr Association to find out how to bring a complaint against Rocque day by day step by step.

I'm really sorry, I've had to tell you about all this but you really do need to know about all this so you can understand totally. The destruction of my life, simply because the police did not do their job and Rocque sold me out and of course my wonderful wife's part in all this.

Chapter 22

# Character References

*Only a man's character is the real criterion of worth*
Eleanor Roosevelt

I met a gentleman called Graham whilst he was on holiday in Benidorm. Both Graham and his wife became very dear friends to me. I was depressed one day and Graham asked me what was wrong. I then told him all about what happened to me in America. He was really taken back by all of it. I told him that I told the probation people in a letter what had happened to me in court. Graham asked if I had anything he could look at regarding what I had told him. I said I had written it all down and I had a file. I gave it to him and he kept it for many days. He said he was horrified. This man retired from the police force after 30 years exemplary service.

I'm writing this book, hoping I could still go back to the Florida Bar and Mr. Rocque be put into a court of law and suffer the consequences of siding with Lily Barron and doing the deal with the prosecutor instead of bringing Lily to justice with the assistance of my witnesses.

The letter written by Mr. Burton was sent with a lot of other papers to America.

I was sat here at my table in my living room. I was so confused I had so many letters. I would have liked to have been able to put them all in this book however because of the quality of the copies it has been impossible.

I was now in Benidorm and I had plenty of work. I ended up singing 7 nights a week in Carriages and I had developed a fan base. I got to know this family really well, Mum and Dad and their two daughters who were 9 and 7. We all became close friends. I used to pick the family up in the mornings and we would go off to places, down the beautiful coastline or up the mountains. We had a really wonderful time and the kids loved me.

"Ricky, tomorrow we have to leave our hotel room at 11am," they said to me one night, "but we don't fly till 5am the following morning. We have nowhere to shower and get changed.

"Don't worry," I said, "in the morning, I will come and pick you up with your cases and you can come to my home. I will give you a key and you can spend the day, then at night after a meal, I can take you down to Benidorm for your bus to the Airport."

The next day I went to the hotel at 11am and on our way to my home, some three miles away, I was stopped and surrounded by taxis. I was accused of taking these people to the Airport. This guy who was confronting me was like a Gorilla. I told him I was not going to the Airport and that they didn't fly until the next day and I was taking them to my home as they had to leave their hotel and they had nowhere to wait.

"No," he said, "you're a Pirate Taxi Driver."

The next thing I knew he punched me with a real solid hammer blow, breaking my nose instantly. He then hit me again. I was a mess with blood everywhere. The two little girls were horrified. My friend wanted to get out of the car but I told him no. We were surrounded by taxis and we wouldn't have a chance.

I then calmly told this guy, "You've just made a mistake you idiot. If they are going to the Airport then I have to get them there, but I'm not, you can follow me to my home. You will see they don't fly till tomorrow."

This story made the front page of the Costa Blanca News. I put in a complaint but nothing was ever done. I never said you could laugh did I? This is just the type of thing that happens to me.

When I first came to Spain I was really struggling for work, no money, the fridge in my apartment was empty apart from a bottle of milk and a loaf of bread and for days that was all I had. When I got a show I'd joke with my audience about how tomorrow I was going to the supermarket for some food, a little chicken and a cheap bottle of wine and I was going to have a banquette. I went to the supermarket and paid for my things. I'd put the lottery on so I checked my ticket and I'd won what I paid for the ticket, so I thought I'd buy another one. I thought I was on a roll. Performed a show, bought some food and even won the lottery. Then when I turned round to pick up my bag of food some bastard had stolen it. Now stop laughing!!! That's not nice!! I was starving for the best part of a week. Things happen around me that are not normal, don't you think?

In 1997 I contacted an attorney, Mr. Strickland. I sent him the complete file with everything in it, asking him to take on my case to sue Rocque and the courts, but mainly Rocque for starters. I spent a lot of time on the phone with this guy before I sent him the file and he appeared very upset with Rocque but ultimately he wrote me a pleasant letter but said he was unable to help me. He said there was nothing that could be done to vacate the plea of guilty, no legal remedy to right the wrongs, and because I had entered a guilty plea the matter was effectively closed. He wished me all the best and said goodbye!

What is it with all these attorneys? Are they saying that your own attorney can perjure himself in court and that's ok? Make no attempt to prepare your case and that's ok? Fail to provide proof that I was in fact divorced and that's okay? Refuse to allow my witnesses to speak and be aggressive with them, and that's okay? After being told a personal friend of my wife is in court to testify that she purged herself in a court of law to the judge and then was committing extortion against me, does nothing to bring this to the attention of the judge therefore obstructing justice and that's ok, because I took the plea of no contest under serious duress whilst I wasn't in a fit state physically or mentally to defend myself. I am told I cannot appeal against the ruling of the bar despite the fact I was put through all of that, still stating my innocence till they eventually get me to take the no contest plea.

I was sent a report by someone at the Florida Bar. They obviously wanted to help me, as it states the statute laws Rocque violated. This is without the charges of perjury in a court of law. How can all these people continue to do absolutely nothing?

I must say no way could I have gone back to jail for 6 months in the terrible mess I was in. Mr. Rocque could clearly see this; its why he pushed me till I broke, finally getting what he wanted. That simply cannot be legal or tolerated anywhere in a civilized world.

As time passes, I meet a gentleman, he's a fan and it turns out he's a judge, one day I met with him for a coffee. I tell him all about what happened to me, he was horrified and tells me I should send the file to the supreme courts of America, appealing my case and at the same time bring charges against Mr. Rocque, who in his opinion should never be allowed back in a court room (except as a criminal) he said Mr. Rocque violated everything he swore to do when he took the oath to become an attorney.

No one should be allowed to get away with the crimes Mr. Rocque committed when Mr. Rocque took my case he was obligated by law to meet, interview my witnesses and read all testimony supplied to him in his preparation of my case. It was vital for him to contact my immigration attorney Mr. David Kilpatrick. This gentleman Tom says the Supreme Courts have no choice but to send Mr. Rocque to jail because his crimes committed in a court of law were so serious. So in time with a little guidance from Tom, he says The Supreme Courts will have to deal with this and I would have to be compensated. Tom tells me, even if I'd over stayed my time in the states, I'm entitled to have a proper defense, it\s written in US law.

I sent a letter to the supreme courts in Tallahassee, Florida, as I am asking to bring a charge against Rocque and Broward County Courts, these are extremely serious crimes committed in a court of law. The Supreme Courts have to investigate these charges, Tom, a judge has put this together for me. Tom is more than confident justice will be done and I will have my name cleared and I would be able to go to America to visit my friends Chuck and Wendy, I simply can't wait!

I did receive a reply to this long, detailed and passionate appeal. It was woefully inadequate (seven lines of text) and nothing short of a disgrace stating quite clearly it would NOT investigate the complaint, I had no right of appeal and that was final. It sounded like a frustrated mother scolding her child, not what I would have expected from the land of the free.

What do I do now? How do I go about bringing these people to justice?

When I tell Chuck and Wendy they are deeply saddened and disgusted.

Rob Freeman is the guy I was putting a new production company together with in Miami. Rob was Number 1 producer in America, eight platinum albums. Read his letter, he mentions our new company. Everything was in the file sent to the Supreme Courts. I take enormous pride in all these character references. My life was destroyed, an innocent man, and at the same time real criminals are being allowed to walk free and given quite astonishing liberties under the Human Rights Charter. Something is clearly wrong Mr Obama, wouldn't you agree?

I won't give up, I will continue to try to find a way of getting justice. This is not a reflection of the American people, but even the American people must understand this kind of thing can happen to anyone of them.

Today is Feb 20 2010, yes after all these years it has to be clear to everyone how this has affected my life. I still cannot come to terms with all the terrible things that have been said about me. I'm finding papers and documents that when I read them leave me totally and utterly bewildered and in a very bad emotional state. Unfortunately because of all the letters and documentation, I feel I have to put a lot of them into this book, it's a lot of legal stuff, I'm having difficulty in how what and where to put some of this stuff. I can't believe I'm doing this but I feel I simply have to.

Chuck Wendy, John, Sari, Randy, Doug, my sister Maggie even my ex wife Sharon, mother to my son Craig have all be affected by Lily's devious desperate attempt to discredit me. Between her and Donna, they would succeed in disposing of me, getting me out of the country to protect Lily's lawsuit.

Lily herself told me she was shocked at what Donna was prepared to do for money.

What is obvious is that Randy Reynolds is afraid to upset Lily, he's known her for 10 years yet he was eventually up in court to testify against her about attempting to commit extortion against me. I read a letter Donna had sent to the immigration people.

I find this a particularly sad letter: she even mentions that on top of threatening to kill her and abusing her I suggested she take out a life insurance policy with me as the beneficiary. This is particularly heinous and the insinuation is obvious, that I was going to kill her! It doesn't get much more serious than that but again I am happy to take any form of polygraph test they care to throw at me

At first I wasn't aware that Donna had written this letter, I am very deeply hurt by this terrible line by line of total make believe, I've been very troubled by it.

This woman meets me and in a very short time tells me that I am to move in, announces to me that we are to be together forever. She makes out that I had nothing and that I have nothing worth offering to the American People.

I leave my beautiful home, give all my furniture away, sell my car, and leave all my family, my son. I had a full time agent, I was very respected, I did many charity shows. When I was with Donna, it was she that told me we were to get married sooner rather than later, I was working for a moving company and worked many many hours. I was very happy and very much in love, it was really hard work. I did this to prove to her that I am a really hard working man, I did everything I possibly could. Donna's son was stealing from me out of the safe, I now wonder if it was her son or it was actually her and she was just blaming her son for it. Everything was going ok until her ex started to phone.

Going back now to Donna's letter. I can tell you now there was never any push and shove or emotional abuse, bullying or irrational behavior and this taking out an insurance policy with me as the beneficiary and me getting hostile and irrational when she would not, how can I protect myself against this?

I would dearly love to take a polygraph test with me answering to all these allegations but Donna also has to do the same. She never told me she was going to divorce me ever, it was I that got my management attorney to pay the cost of the divorce. When I went to Donna's work I was in the reception and asked if Donna was there. Donna took me into an office and we had a very good talk, no problems at all and she agreed to pay me my money even though we were getting divorced and regards to the immigration, she was going to the marital fraud interview, It

was me that said if we're not going to be together then I did not want her to go to the meeting.

Another thing Donna said 'after throwing me out for the third time'. Donna never threw me out of the house. I left myself when her son who was on drugs got in my face, I went back the next day and they had packed my bags. I believe when I went to stay at Doug's house to calm the situation down that between them they had decided that she was going to give the ex another chance. Maybe give him another chance because he had money.

For a while we started to see each other, that's when I stayed with Donna and her son and her mom and dad at her apartment that remember I am supposed to have stalked her and harassed her in Lily's car to find out where she lived. I didn't even know Lily when I stayed with them for the weekend and may I say we had a really loving wonderful weekend, we even made love on a blow up mattress with her son asleep on the sofa right next to us, we actually made a puncture in the mattress and it went down, I dearly loved this woman and as for me threatening to kill her, what can I say? Can you imagine, she says I'm phoning for reconciliation and at the same time threatening to kill her, what a really stupid thing to say.

Now think about what she says next, I'm supposed to have called by her office with the divorce papers for her to sign, then gone to her home to collect them.

When she signed the papers surely I would have taken them with me? I only went to her office a couple of times and it was always very cordial. I did call by to see Donna at her home to ask about my money. If this woman had any fear at all why did she open the door and invite me in? When she did she made no attempt to tell me when I was to expect my money, the mood did change and yes she did ask me to leave. She forgot to tell you I asked for my ring back and I told her she didn't deserve to wear it by this time we are stood in the door way and she closed the door on me, yes I did have my foot in the door, I was still talking to her, our voices were raised and at that time her neighbour did come out with his dog, she then says that I became hostile and violent, raised voices, yes, hostile and violent, Ridiculous! Can someone please explain to me how we are talking by the door, I become hostile and violent with my foot in the door, how she can reach for a phone from the door with all this going on and call 911. I realised I wasn't getting anywhere and I left.

May I say Donna Van Buran is a very intelligent woman. She talks of being in fear of her life for a very long time, Donna knew I was living at Doug's home or Mario's another friend's house. She also had my beeper number. She also states in this letter and I quote in her very own words: 'I do know for a fact that he is working at Father and Sons Moving Company at 7950 Central Industrial Boulevard West Palm Beach, the phone number Is 970-9763. Donna had always known I worked for Father and Sons. She knew I'd been there ever since I was living with her.

Can someone please tell me why this woman fearing for her life didn't go to the police and had me arrested at Father and Sons? Why she didn't beep me and say I've got your money Ricky and when I went to collect it she could have had me arrested. The answer is a very simple one, she had no reason to fear me, I had never ever threatened her in anyway and as for threatening to kill her, I find it all very sad indeed, yes I was asking for my money and we did raise our voices. I must admit my lawyer Lori Hannah Anton was right when she said to me, we don't trust your wife Donna, especially when it came to money, yes they did say to me if you are not going to be together it's important that you divorce this woman because if you did become successful she would certainly come after you for money and another thing I did not need Donna to go to the Marital Fraud Interview. I had a partner in a management company Solomon King Inc. Our company could have sponsored me to stay in the country. Solomon King Incorporated was a Registered Company that could have been checked out.

The only reason I wanted Donna to go to the Martial Fraud Interview was if we were to be together, I loved Donna very much, I can't say any more than that.

The immigration office was in West Palm Beach where I was working for Father and Son, why didn't they come and arrest and deport me? I was literally just up the street

# Chapter 23

# More Lies

*The truth is rarely pure and never simple*
Oscar Wilde

The next thing we are going to talk about is Mr. Rocque's letter to Richard B Liss Assistance Staff Counsel, The Florida Bar. Our friend Mr. Rocque obviously has no fear as to who he lies to, this again perjuring himself as I will prove to you by using Mr. Rocque's letter to Mr. Richard B Liss. May I say all this talk of Donna and Lily being afraid for their lives is absolutely ridiculous.

Do you know how easy it would have been to have vengeance on both of them done by the guys in the felon cell, all I needed to do was in my hour of possible anger given these guys Donna and Lily's names and addresses, I know they would have gone missing, possibly as alligator food. When is someone going to see these two devious cunning and evil pair of bastards for what they are? And yet, even now I do not wish any harm to come to them. I remember one of the black guys telling me that Rocque was worse than a cockroach and told me I only had to say the word and he would be picked up, taken to the Everglades and fed to the Alligators. He laughed as he told me the 'gators would have probably spat him out because his meats so rotten.

"We hate bent attorneys Ricky." He said.

Can you imagine Alligator Rocque Handbags?

When Lily was constantly phoning me, I could have invited her to come to England, if I was this horrible man do you think she would have left the shores of England? I wonder how much money she got from the Calder Race Track, just think of all that cocaine she could stuff up her nose and champagne she could drink.

In Rocque's letter to the Florida Bar he states that he had set a date for a bond hearing to reduce my bond. He knew I had no money so it would be absolutely vital that he told Chuck and Wendy as they would have been the people who would have paid the bond. Mr. Rocque my own defense attorney did not contact my immigration attorney Mr. Kilpatrick, nor did he ever contact Mr. Kilpatrick right up to the day I was finally in court. It was only then when I demanded he phone Mr. Kilpatrick from the court that he actually spoke to him.

When Rocque visited me he was given Mr. Kilpatrick's Name and number and I told him he must call to speak to him regarding my status, but he failed to do so. Then after speaking to Mr. Kilpatrick from the courts, lied to me. Mr. Kilpatrick told him not to take any deals, married or not, they could not deport me just like that, so my own attorney perjured himself in a court of law when he told me and then my five witnesses in court that Mr. Kilpatrick told him to tell me I should go home. Then Rocque then tells the Bar that the state filed for pre trial detention based on the fact I was an illegal alien, but he never phoned to Mr. Kilpatrick so this could have been challenged, but clearly Rocque had no intention of challenging anything.

I was arrested on a battery charge not an immigration matter. Mr. Rocque was hired to defend me, an innocent man. Rocque had to contact Mr. Kilpatrick; Mr. Rocque was not a qualified immigration attorney by law. When he is representing a client he has to check that all information given to him is legally correct, he made no attempt to do so. Having Mr. Kilpatrick involved would have made things different. Mr.

Rocque tells the Bar that deportation proceedings were being initiated, what has that got to do with defending me?

My case should have been heard that day, my witnesses heard in court, but they were denied the right to speak, despite the fact Mr. Rocque knew the charges against my wife would have been perjury with witnesses attempting to commit extortion against me.

Mr. Rocque knows a friend of Lily's for 10 years is stood in court waiting to testify to this fact. Attempting to obstruct justice by asking Doug to lie in court and perjure himself. Say that I had confessed to him that I'd done what Lily had said, Mr. Rocque knew Doug was stood in court also to testify to this against Lily. Sari was in court to testify that Lily had told her in a bar, she was going to get me to fall in love with her, get me to marry her, so she would want for nothing when I made it big.

Mr. Rocque knew she was stood in the courtroom waiting to testify this, which means Lily Barron married me under a fraudulent circumstance. Chuck and Wendy were in court to testify that Lily had said in a three-way conversation on the phone that we slipped on the spaghetti on the stairs. Five witnesses!! Also Lily was attempting to de fraud the racetrack of $2000000. Also bringing in to court Donna Vanburan with me not even allowed to say a single word to defend myself against these serious and vile charges.

Mr. Rocque simply did nothing; by doing nothing he himself violates the laws by then himself obstructing justice. Allowing Lily Barron to walk free from court despite him knowing for a week what laws Lily had violated, what kind of an attorney do you call that?

Now the next part of Mr. Rocque's letter to the Bar puts Mr. Rocque in the most serious trouble an attorney could possibly put himself in, I quote from his letter:

I made arrangements for Mr. Dunphy's witnesses to meet me in person at my office, prior to the bond hearing to discuss their potential testimony. This was my Day of Arraignment when my witnesses were in court to testify on my behalf against Lily. The next part of Mr. Rocque's letter states, are you ready for this? I met with his witnesses and read their testimony and we proceeded to the courthouse. This man has now clearly perjured himself to the Bar that oversees the attorneys to make sure they don't violate their code of conduct, what a silly man!

Mr. Rocque fails to tell the Bar that he had at least 7 days to meet with my witnesses, each witness making many phone calls asking him when he was going to meet with them. He didn't say to the Bar he phones my witnesses, all five, the day before my hearing, to meet only one hour before the meeting itself and then arrives half an hour late! Mr. Rocque has told the Bar in this statement that he read their testimony, when in fact Mr. Rocque made no attempt what so ever, to first, interview each witness and he also made no attempt what so ever to read any witness statements, one of which alone was twenty pages, so Mr. Rocque in his own letter has now become a witness to himself in his own words to the Bar, committing a very very serious crime, Perjury!

All five of these witnesses later put in a complaint to the Bar that Mr. Rocque did not meet with them or read any testimony what so ever. Mr. Rocque has in fact violated many codes of conduct, yet wait for it, the Bar letter say Mr. Rocque has not violated any of the codes of conduct as an attorney representing his client. What does Mr. Rocque have to do in the eyes of the Bar for me and my witnesses to prove he totally failed to represent me, totally failing to make any attempt to prepare my case. Does this man have to shoot me in front of the judge before someone says hold on Mr. Rocque we don't think that's legal in a court of law; we'll have to discuss it at a meeting of the Bar.

Now. I'm supposed to be a criminal, yet no witnesses to any part of my so called attack on Lily, even the injuries do not confirm what she put in the statement, nor do they match the injuries the Police Officers put in the statement who were the first to see Lily.

Another one for you, I quote, 'Mr. Berchert informed me about the contents of a letter dated August 23 1995 written by Donna Vanburan to the Department of Immigration, again I'm not allowed to defend myself regarding this letter or its content. Mr. Kilpatrick should have been informed about this letter. Now it gets even worse for Mr. Rocque as Mr. Rocque did not tell me anything about Donna's letter. Mr. Rocque then writes, I then called Mr. Kilpatrick, Mr. Dunphy's immigration lawyer, Mr. Kilpatrick told me that Mr. Dunphy did have immigration problems. Again Mr. Rocque deliberately misleads the Bar by forgetting to tell them he only phoned Mr. Kilpatrick from the court room after I demand that he did so. Mr. Rocque would not let me talk to my attorney, saying the phone would not reach, so I had to take Mr. Rocque word for it that Mr. Kilpatrick said that I should go home.

As we've already established earlier, Mr. Rocque lied to me and all my witnesses by saying this as we now know Mr. Kilpatrick said not to take any deals what so ever. I still had rights, so we now know Mr. Rocque most certainly did commit perjury. Then having told me, my immigration attorney and all my witnesses in court that I was a divorced man, Mr. Rothschild had no idea about Mr. Rocque's illegal, unprofessional manor in his court, so how was he to know I hadn't signed my paper under incredible duress. My own attorneys lying to me, confusing me and mentally abusing me, when I was in a ridiculously bad state! How sad, how very sad! Is someone going to step forward and do something about this? Imagine after all these years I'm writing this still suffering mentally, my life could never be the same after all of what they did to me, when you think about it, how could it?

# The Florida Bar
## Inquiry/Complaint Form

Your Name _Wanda Niemiec (candy)_  What is the name and address of the attorney that is the subject of this inquiry/complaint?

Address _4330 NE Ter_  Attorney's Name _Michael Rocque, P.A._

City _Pompano Bch_ State _Fl_  Address _xxx SE x St Suite 5xx_

Telephone _xxx-xxxx_ Zip Code _33064_  City _Ft Lauderdale_ State _Fl_

Telephone _xxx-xxx3_ Zip Code _33301_

DESCRIBE YOUR COMPLAINT. PROVIDE DATES AND FACTS OF ALLEGED MISCONDUCT
(Use a separate sheet if necessary. Do not write on the back of this form)

I am a Friend and one of 5 witnesses for James
E. Dunphy.
I met Michael Rocque only once 9-21-1995
I, along with 4 other witnesses were scheduled
to meet with Michael Rocque and give our character
statements. He was 30 minutes late and rudely rushed
us through our statements. I doubt he was able
to comprehend half of what we told him. He offended
one witness. She threatened to leave the office.
After our hasty conversations with Michael Rocque
he rushed us out of his office and we all
ran most of the way to the courthouse. We were late!
We five witnesses were not allowed to speak on
Mr. Dunphy's behalf, nor was Mr. Dunphy.
Michael Rocque allowed the judge, court, US
and Mr Dunphy to believe that Mr Dunphy was
divorced, when in truth He was still married

Under penalty of perjury, I declare the foregoing facts...

---

ATTN: Florida Bar

I,ve been asked to write this letter in reference to the serious of event that took place regarding a Mr. James Dunphy and the case that is pending. On Sept 21st, 1995 Mr. Dunphy was to be in court for a hearing regarding the allegations his wife made of spousal abuse. A Mr. Michael Rocque was to be Mr. Dunphy's attorney and it is my belief that the actions of Mr. Rocque were extremely unprofessional and has caused Mr. Dunphy great harm. Prior to the hearing I was informed that Mr. Rocque would be contacting me in order to get a statement from me as a key witness in the case. Mr. Rocque never called me nor did he return my phone calls in order to meet before the hearing. On Sept. 21st. early morning I received a desperate call from Mr. Rocque's office stating that he needs to see me before the hearing in the afternoon. Our meeting was called for 1:30 and Mr. Rocque did not arrive until approximately 1:45pm. While waiting for Mr. Rocque it was brought to my attention that their were 4 other witnesses that were their at the same time all needing to speak with him before the 2:30 hearing. Mr. Rocque arrived and was extremely unprepared. He was scattered in his thoughts and at times extremely short and verbally abusive to me and the other witnesses as he hurried through trying to prepare for the upcoming hearing. None of the witnesses were able to inform Mr. Rocque of our testimonies that could have perhaps proven that the allegations against Mr. Dunphy were not only false but the malicious attack of a women who we all knew to have a very serious drug and alcohol problem. We had all at one time or another witnessed the abuse that Mr. Dunphy took from his wife, Lily, and were prepared to testify to that however we were never given the chance.

It is my belief that all the torment that Mr. Dunphy has gone through in the past 3 years is a direct result of the incompitence of Mr. Rocque and that this truly needs to be investigated into. I was also extremely stunned by Mr. Rocque's performance

*Samples from two of the four complaints from my witnesses against Roach*

What am I doing? Why am I writing this? Every word of what I have written is a totally honest account of what has happened to me.

In Mr. Rocque's letter to Mr. B Liss, he told Mr. B Liss that I would be held until deportation, under Immigration Hold. This again is not true, Mr. Rocque told me if I did agree to a no contest plea, I would be deported immediately within two days, so yet again he's perjured himself to the Florida Bar. Mr. Rocque also told all my witnesses in court, if I agreed to the no contest plea that I would be deported within two days. How does Mr. Rocque possibly think he could get away with this?

All Mr. B Liss has to do is go back and read the complaints from my witnesses against Mr. Rocque to the Florida Bar (Official Complaints) He will see for himself all my witnesses were told by Mr. Rocque that if I did take the no contest plea, I would be deported within two days. I had sent Mr. Rocque across to tell them what I had just been told. I was NOT deported within two days, but four days later I was put in a High Security Cell, you've read the rest! Mr. Rocque had also forgotten to tell Mr. Bliss that he told me Lily Barron had divorced me while I was in jail, so all had changed because of this. Mr. Rocque did not produce any legal document in court, to prove I was divorced. I've been told Mr. Rocque cannot tell me all has changed because of Lily Barron divorcing me without the actual final dissolution papers being produced in court. As your all reading this you know Mr. Rocque perjured himself in court because I was not divorced.

Mr. Rocque cannot take the word of Lily Barron or the prosecution on such an important declaration, if he did, then the prosecutor and Lily Barron or should we say Lily Dunphy are now both committing perjury and Mr. Rocque, incredibly incompetent at the very least. I believe Mr. Rocque and Mr. B Liss and also Lily, all knew we were still married.

Another thing is that Mr. Rocque did not tell Mr. B Liss in his letter that he also told me, because of my divorce, if I did wish for a jury trial and refuse the no contest plea that apparently the Judge Mr. Rothschild had told him to tell me I would have to go back to jail for at least 6 months before they would give me a jury trial and because I was now divorced, win or lose my jury trial, I would be deported immediately. How could he possibly leave all this information out of the letter to Mr. B Liss? I was in a very bad psychical and mental state. I was totally incapable of withstanding anymore. Mr. Rocque also forgot to tell Mr. B Liss in his letter that I was not deported and when I phoned Mr. Rocque from the Felon Cell he asked me what the weather was like in England, he was so incompetent, he never made sure my immediate deportation had been carried out. So he didn't know I was in the Felon Cell!

I think it's very possible that Mr. Rothschild was never told by Trip or Rocque that I was divorced or not divorced. I think it's very possible they made the whole story up to put me under incredible pressure to take the no contest plea. I think it's also very possible the judge Mr. Rothschild never said anything at all about me being sent back to jail for 6 months at least before I would be given my jury trial. If this was to be true, what monstrous behaviour this is in a court of law! Also Mr. Rocque forgot to mention to Mr. B Liss that he did absolutely nothing to get me out of the felon cell. I'm now going to remind you all again just who Mr. Rocque had sent this letter to:

> March 2 1998 *(This is staggering tenacity from Rocque)*
> Mr. B Liss
> Assistant Staff Council
> The Florida Bar
> Fort Lauderdale Office
> Cypress Financial Center
> 5900 North Andrews Ave
> Fort Lauderdale Florida 33309
> Re: Complaint of Mr. James Dunphy
> Florida Bar File no: 98-51-123(17F)

Again Mr. Rocque sent this to the Florida Bar, who make sure attorneys are seen to do nothing unethical.

How about this for a possibility, could Mr. Rocque now after all this time be a judge? Imagine each member of that bar that sat and read all my witnesses statements against Mr. Rocque, then ruled he'd done nothing to violate his code of conduct as an attorney and did not rule that he had totally failed to prepare my case, again violating the rules of the Bar. Each person that sat on the Bar that day, should be made to account for why they did not bring Mr. Rocque to justice and have had him brought before Mr. Rothschild, the same judge he purged himself before in court of law.

I'm going to have to stop now, I've had to take a couple of days off from writing this, it's been very difficult for me to bring myself back to this table to continue with this, I feel very drained.

RESPONDENT VIOLATED DISCIPLINARY RULES 6-101 (A) (2) AND 6-101 (A) (3) OF THE CODE OF PROFESSIONAL RESPONSIBILITY WHICH PROVIDE THAT A LAWYER SHALL NOT HANDLE A LEGAL MATTER WITHOUT PREPARATION ADEQUATE IN THE CIRCUMSTABCES AND SHALL NOT NEGLECT A LEGAL MATTER ENTRUSTED TO HIM.

How can the Bar sit and deliberate Mr. Rocque's behavior and not rule that he violated 6-101 (A) (2) 6-101 (A) (3). Above?

# Chapter 24

# Words from HSFC

*Once he is motivated no one can change more completely than the man who has been at the bottom*
Malcolm X

Over a period of time I received two letters from Frank in 9.0. Remember I told Frank to go to school whilst in jail and get the Diplomas now that he didn't get when he was young. Also I told him to put himself through the Turning Point Program, to clean himself of his drug problems. Also I told him to work out as I did and it would help him deal with the stress he would suffer trying to clean himself up.

He calls me 'his dear friend' and says how pleased he is that I have escaped this hellhole, but goes on to say how he misses me.

The letter dated Friday 8th December 1995 is for me a joy, and in it he tells me how I was able to help Frank change his ways.

The second letter dated April 28th 1996, and I was so, so happy to see how well Frank had done. I'm very proud I was able to influence people whilst in custody in a good way.

I simply must introduce this photograph directly into the book, in it you can see me and Lily, whitewater rafting, this at the time when she's suing the Race Track for $2,000,000 for neck, spinal and pelvic injuries.

This photo was taken in the middle of Lily's law suit. Lily actually complained that the water was not rough enough but as you can see, she seems to be enjoying the experience and clearly not in any pain or discomfort. The photo was taken by the company that organized the day. Lily paid for it with her own credit card, it has the stamp of the company on the back, this photo was stuck between some papers that Lily had sent in the package she has sent to my brother John. She obviously doesn't know she accidently sent it, The Dumb Shit!

I found the photo some years later myself by accident. You can imagine what would have happened if I'd have turned up in court to testify against Lily's case, then produced this photo. I'll say it again; all of this happened because of Lily's Law suit, she wanted me out of the way.

I said earlier that Lily reminded me of when we set off to visit some friends for 3 or 4 days then came back 3 weeks later.

We set off to go to Ocala, which incidentally is where Chuck and Wendy have moved too. It's beautiful racehorse breeding country, green pastures, white wooden picket fences. Lily told me she was going to buy some land of her friends and we'd have a place built. I told her thanks ok, but if she didn't treat me with more respect she would live there alone with her two million dollars.

From there we headed to Hershey where they make the chocolate, another place where her friends had horses but this time they trained their horses for racing. Lily said she had ridden in races for them when she was a jockey. Everywhere we went people would say, has Lily calmed down now? I'd just say, I hope so.

Whenever we got to one friends house, she wanted to go to visit the next friend and I kept saying, you said just a few more days. I was working for Father and Sons but now I was in charge of a truck and two black lads. Lily then talked me into driving further North to Eire on the great lakes, not far from Canada. I ended up doing all the driving, this is where I met the family that had been in the fire, 3 little boys, 2 of them escaped ok, 1 of them sadly didn't, he suffered brain damage, all very sad. This is when Lily asked if I would do a big charity show, to raise money for the family to go to Disney, which I did.

We had to drive back some time later, I met Lily's brother who was a real knob, took me across a lake on a flat bottomed boat at high speed with his friends, they tried to frighten the shit out of me. I just asked if it could go any faster, they were a pair of pissheads, they just got drunk and said I was a boring old bastard because I wouldn't get drunk. This is where I met Lily's mom; I stayed at the house. Lily's mom was an alcoholic and yet Lily's mom warned me to be careful as Lily had problems, can you imagine that?

After a few days she wanted to go to West Virginia, she said we'd go white water rafting, I said I didn't know about doing that and she said I'd got no balls, so we went. I must admit I'm glad we did, things were going very well on the trip so far. Lily was really good to be around, we were actually happy, no arguments, no drugs. Then she said lets go to visit my other friends in Vinton Louisiana, near the Texas border. Doug was now asking me when we were heading back and Jerry the owner of Father and Sons were saying they had some big jobs coming up. Before going to Vinton we called off at New Orleans.

We stayed at the top Hotel, Monty Leone. I said where are you getting this money from? She said it was none of my business, I'm paying you to drive, I want to do this Ricky. We stayed one night at the Monty Leone and one night at the Château Hotel in the French section, then onto her friends from in the middle of nowhere, Vinton, just off the border of Texas. Here they had a cock fighting arena like a big tweet cage with wooden benches in a circle.

Really wealthy Texans flew in by helicopters, small planes, stretched limos to gamble, they had an old night club that they hadn't used in years, so I went to have a look inside and found an old sound system, so I told Lily, I wanted to do something for the hell of it. She said what's that? I said I'll put the sound system up by the tweety cage, I want to sing inside the tweety cage before they start cockfighting. She said I was mad and that no one had ever done anything like that before, I said that's why I wanted to do it, to be the first person ever to sing cabaret in a cockfighting tweety cage.

Her friends said if Ricky is brave enough to do it, we can't promise that the people gambling will take to it. So I did it, the floor was straw, the sound system sounded like an old Railway Station. If you squeeze your nose and started to talk, it was a little like that, it sounded terrible.

I was going to sing just three songs, Drove All Night, Roy Orbison, Dancing In The Dark, Bruce Springsteen and then a song I wrote myself called Sitting in a Corner, I sang this to the guys in the Felon Cell it's a blues rock track. My first song they simply look at each other as if to say what the fuck. The second song, no reaction but when I sang my own song it was amazing, they were bopping and started to stand up gigging. It was a real site, some of these guys had no teeth, they cheered me, hooted and hollered, Lily was proud of me and happy.

Oh I didn't tell you whilst in New Orleans we went to the house of blues and introduced myself to the owner, he invited me to sing with the live band. But Lily said no, she wanted to go to her aunties in Dallas, I said come on this is a great opportunity for me but she insisted we had to go. So off we went, what a long drive.

When we got there Lily's aunt said we'd have to stay in a hotel, they didn't seem over friendly, the next day Lily wasn't very happy and said we'll go back to Vinton, I said what a lot of driving for nothing, I felt really sorry for Lily they didn't seem that over happy to see her, we stayed in Vinton another night then set off to drive back, but then she wanted to drive right the way back to Pennsylvania again, another friend with horses. She was very happy now, so things were good between us.

I really did like these people. The next day we took two incredible horses out, right up the mountains, we were gone nearly all day, she had us riding up very steep ridges, coming back down the horses were nearly sliding on their backsides it was so steep and very dangerous. At the top of this very high ridge it was so, so beautiful, it was like being in heaven. She really became very romantic and passionate, we got off our horses and ripped our clothes off and made love. I'd never known her to be like this, she told me how much she loved me. It was very emotional, we then raced down the mountain, I let her win J Okay, maybe I didn't.

The next day we set off to drive back home, 3 weeks later, 3500 miles I'd driven, but it turned out to be just what the doctor ordered, but once we were back it wasn't long before she was acting strange again and having different personalities again.

One day she had really upset me by saying sex was nothing and that she knew some really wealthy ladies that she said would pay me hundreds of dollars to have sex with them, this came right out of the blue. I thought she was joking but she got a little nasty when I said stop talking stupid, she said I wasn't a man, that she was okay with it as long as I was and we'd make a lot of money FAST.

She made me feel sick, it really shook me up what she was suggesting. I thought what a wonderful loving time we'd had, but sadly it was back to reality. I was really upset by this and life continued.

Well back to Spain, my relationship was very good with my now Spanish fiancé. The only problem was she lived in Madrid, 200 miles away with her very old mom and dad. I started to learn a little Spanish; I would see Maria every 3 to 4 weeks just for the weekend. I was still in touch with Chuck and Wendy very often. They wanted me to visit them but the deal in court that I could return after 1 year became 5 years then I was told 10 years, so I set about contacting the American Embassy in Madrid.

They sent me loads of papers to fill out, I had to pay for these papers, Mr. Graham Burton, the retired Police Sergeant helped me fill out the forms for a visa to travel to the USA and Chuck and Wendy filled out papers to say they would sponsor me. I went on the train to Madrid, stayed the night with Maria and her parents.

We went to the Embassy, Maria could not come into the building, even thought she was a Spanish citizen. I was in this place for over 2 hours, I could not phone Maria and she was sat in a café all that time. When I finally got to see someone I had to speak through a thick glass panel, this guy was a real serious asshole, nasty and cold. He took my papers, came back to me some time later, simply told me because of my crimes I'd committed, I wasn't going to be allowed to visit my friends.

Ten years later and in fact they were putting a lifetime ban on me ever going to the states. I was mortified; I told him I was not a criminal, that I was innocent. I told him it was all because of Lily's lawsuit that she was committing a 2 million dollar fraud against the Race Track. I said I didn't know how her case had gone; I showed him the photo when we white water rafting. I said he should inform the FBI and allow me back to America and I would testify against her. He wasn't interested and walked off. I then had to leave; my dreams of visiting my friends Chuck and Wendy were totally shattered. Can someone please tell me how they can get away with that?

As time passes, seven years, Maria and I split up. I waited for her to come and live in Benidorm, but it never happened and she continued to look after her mom and dad and I got on with my life.

I was on a mission, I needed to try and find someone who would take my case. I made many phone calls to different attorneys but no one would agree to take on Rocque and the courts. One day I was given the name of a Mr. John Connes, and I telephoned him. I was on the phone well over an hour, and he was flabbergasted at what I had to say. He said if I could prove half of what I was saying it was serious and I would be looking at a $20 million lawsuit.

"That bad," I said.

"Monstrous." He said.

I sent him everything. Mr Connes is a retired judge practicing part time.

Three weeks later I phoned to speak to him and his secretary said he would not take my case. I needed to know why, and phoned him many times till one day he eventually took my call.

"Is there something wrong with my case?" I said. "No," he told me, and in fact you haven't proved half of it, you proved all of it.

He said the lawsuit would be in excess of $20 million and I told him to write a contract that if he won I would get 5 million and he would get the rest. There was a slight pause and I half expected to hear something positive but he sighed and said he was sorry but he still wouldn't take the case. What do you make of that? He also told me if I did make it to court I would almost certainly win.

So where does that leave me now? What can I do to find someone to take my case?

It's almost impossible for me to get a grip of the fact that Lily and her now dear friend Donna married me in very fraudulent circumstances; between them they have broken just about every law in the book, along with Mr. Rocque and the prosecutor in the highest court in the land.

The Bar Association was put in place to protect people from attorneys such as Mr. Rocque who swore an oath when becoming attorneys to protect the rights of people.

Innocent until proven guilty it should be but instead, as the Police Officer sadly put it at the when I was first arrested, **"Guilty until you prove yourself innocent. Welcome to America."**

What happened to the constitution, what happened to The Human Rights Bill?

Where were the Florida Bar and why didn't they bring Mr. Rocque to justice? How sad for the American people is this!

My very dear and wonderful friends Chuck and Wendy lost a young nephew in the Iraq War fighting for Liberty and Justice thousand's of miles away in a foreign country. Chuck and Wendy shed tears when they told me of their loss and at the same time expressed their anger and shame at the unbelievable injustice of what happened to me, someone they loved as a member of their family. How much pain do you think it caused them?

I was told by the prison psychologist that because of what I'd suffered during the course of my life that I had become dependent on Lily and Donna in my own desperate attempt to find love and happiness. He said I was very vulnerable to such a degree that I would put up with almost anything from these two in the hopes of being happy. I had given everything up because I was in love with first Donna and then Lily. I did not enter America to marry two people fraudulently, as they put it.

My efforts to bring Donna, Lily and Rocque, the prosecutors and the Florida Bar to justice have been frustrating to say the least. The supreme court in Tallahassee said I can't appeal the decision of the Bar Association, yet the Supreme Courts of America some thirty years after the incident had the film producer (Roman Polanski) extradited to face charges of having sex with a 13 year old girl but appear to show no interest bringing to justice or investigating what I had sent them. It's all clearly a case of double standards and they appear to be saying that it's okay for Mr Rocque to perjure himself in a court of law, clearly obstructing justice and failing to prepare my case and represent me correctly in accordance with the law, breaking the code of conduct as an attorney and not allowing my five witnesses to testify.

Now I would like to think after reading this book you must come to the conclusion that I did not enter America fraudulently. Donna swore to me on many occasions she would love me and make me happy and told many friends and family the same but then simply dropped me when she thought I wasn't going to make the showbiz big time as fast as she obviously wanted me to. Donna was the fraudulent person, not me, but the truth didn't sink in until sometime after our divorce. I should have left America there and then. Yes I stayed longer than I should have, but that was all I did wrong, even then I was working hard to find a sponsor.

I received a document my immigration attorney Mr. David Kilpatrick sent me after I'd actually been deported! It states I'm granted to stay in the USA till September 30th 1994, then I would have to leave voluntarily. It states if I fail to leave then specified proceedings will be initiated to enforce my departure, but it then says if those proceedings were initiated I could renew my application for status as a permanent resident during such proceedings.

So I say it again, my case should have been heard, the five witnesses heard, and it would have been done and dusted and Lily sent to jail. Then my immigration situation could have been dealt with and at least if I had been deported it would have been as an innocent man and I would have been allowed back to America to visit my friends, even if it had been five years later. I could have been back to the States and not wrongly branded a serious, violent criminal, something that hangs around my neck like a millstone to this very day.

Chuck and Wendy visited me in England some years later and then came to see me in Spain. That's how much they think of me and it breaks my heart that I am unable to visit them in America. Lily's lies and deceit hasn't only affected me, she has also traumatised these wonderful, loving people.

# Chapter 25

# Worth Waiting For

*Every heart sings a song, incomplete, until another heart whispers back. Those who wish to sing always find a song. At the touch of a lover, everyone becomes a poet*

Plato

Some years have passed, I now have a son called Brandon, he is six years of age and I am 57 years old.

My car accident claim took five years to come through. The money from the accident a mere £15,000 went on the deposit on our home we now live in. My fiancé is called Cheryle a beautiful and talented woman and a wonderful mother. Cheryle, once herself a Police Officer and has a degree in Law. Cheryle laughs when she tells me if Mr. Rocque had been the village idiot he could not have possibly lost the case against Lily Baron. This, remember from someone with a law degree.

Cheryle is a presenter on a Radio Station in Benidorm as well as performing cabaret. She is an excellent singer and entertainer, I am proud to call her a fellow professional.

My mother has passed away and I've lost two of my dear sisters, one 54 and the other 53, the years have bought me much pain and sadness. My sisters never saw our beautiful Brandon, but I have found happiness with my new family although I do struggle terribly with depression due to my experiences at the hands of the American Justice System. A day never passes that I don't think back to my horrific experiences in America. I still intend to continue to fight in the hope that one day my case will be overturned and my name cleared and therefore be allowed to travel to America with my family, no longer branded a menace to society. That is all I ask for.

I have a dream, in that I hope my wonderful friends Chuck and Wendy both live to see the day I walk up to them and embrace them on American soil. I'm now in tears as I write this and I can't stop thinking of them.

During my time in America I wrote some poems. I'm going to put these poems in this book, you will feel my emotion and you'll see the disturbed mind I had whilst writing them.

It saddens me deeply that the title of this book came from the mouth of an American Police Officer. He was an embarrassment to every decent law abiding citizen of America. I sincerely believe he was a sour apple in an altogether big barrel, and that the majority of American people are good hardworking, honest people. I was proud to be associated with the majority of the people I knew and worked with and the words and actions of a handful of officials will never alter my mind.

# A Gift

A long time ago I was given a gift and from that day many problems through I did sift.

Yes from that day, a woman strong and bold, went through many pains of life which I'm sure to this day I may never have been told.

She took a seed, planted it deep in my heart.

The seed of love. I was given right from the start.

Love can be painful, love can seem unkind, but to be quiet honest, I really do not mind, for it's others that loose not me, fools to themselves unfortunately. One day they will see.

For I am special, my mother told me.

So a fine teacher I had, the very best, she knew life's bitter twists, would provide me with tremendous tests.

Now I walk my path, I grow stronger each day, as long as I can love, I thank god and prey this gift of love he never takes away. Thank you mother this is all I can possibly say.

I love and miss my mom

Written by James Dunphy

# A Grieving Father

It's impossible to explain the deepest hurt deep down that I feel.

Many wasted years without frights to yield.

I was given a wonder of the world in a child, my son, blessed he is though he suffers from Down syndrome. Side by side my son and I worked as a team.

Only to learn how this world could turn so mean.

An angel as a wife turns Devils daughter it seems as life twists and turns to extremes.

But god must have a plan, though I stagger to see how my son benefits not being with me.

I love my son

Written by James Dunphy

# Take my Heart

Excuse me but may I ask

What in my life has become, what seems an impossible task.

But before I tell you, I must explain.

I walk this path not really wishing to find fortune or gain.

Not looking to inflict upon anyone the horrors or sorrow or pain.

My mother told me, be a good boy, peoples feelings are not to be used and played with like toys.

Ok, I'm sorry I'm not telling you what I wish to ask,

What in my life has become an impossible task.

Please take this heart, put it in a safe place

For I really do fear if broken once more, will be shattered forever without a trace.

My fear of being hurt again horrifies me, I think I may end up in a mental institution J

Always look on the Brightside of life as the song goes.

Written by James Dunphy

# A Limit

Life can be so unkind you know,

We've loved so much but forgotten how to show it.

Feelings driven back, now locked deep inside,

The love we had, appears to have died.

Cried oceans of tears, it makes no difference, we are both ready to face the circumstances of all that we've treasured, all that we've built, may we find our lives full of guilt.

Did we try hard enough? Did we try to agree? To compromise we must if we are to succeed.

So much to lose yet so much to gain, disagreement, we find, seems all that remains.

We've been through so much, oh so much pain and anguish together.

Maybe we'll never be clear of the stories to be weathered.

I held your hand through the pain of having a child,

Can we both compromise? Isn't our future worthwhile?

I will love you in some way for all ways but you must understand there is a limit to what I can withstand.

A very sad day today for me.

James Dunphy

# Like Me Looking At Me

We've lived apart for many years

But must have cried the same tears

Not unhappy, yet still sad

For what we really needed, we thought never could be had.

A quiet loneliness, we both shared.

To think of such happiness, we did not dare.

I look at you what do I see?

Someone needing to be loved and cherished and made feel important and understood desperately.

I wait each day, I can only prey, someone will take my hand and lead the way.

I got it wrong again, I always do....How twisted is this, I'm talking to myself.

James Dunphy

# Sleep

A silence so deafening and a whisper so loud,

Echoing beyond are our thoughts, monsters of darkness, or angels so bright.

Fears that we hide, come out in the night.

Deep in our minds, we're anything we choose

From a king in his palace to a beggar without shoes

But we have no control over who we might be, so all we can do is, hope, wait and see.

Oh so foolish this nonsense, I cannot explain.

The thoughts of a mad man but yet I am sane

Rolling around like the wheels in a mill

Are my memories of this call it what you will.

Dancing are jesters on coffins in a line

What's the significance of this? Oh yes the end of time

But what has all this to do with me?

Before I can answer, I'm awake and set free.

I must be loosing the plot

James Dunphy

# Thoughts

From the depths of nowhere lies the answer to all

Down glistening passages of time

Deep out of reach in the far regions of time

Deep out of reach, in the far regions of our mind,

Echoing around and around as if lost in endless rhythm.

Say nothing of this to the unsuspecting eye's.

For the eyes of darkness are all they are

As the man with his long white stick

Stalking along , but they never see him.

Written off he disappears like invisible ink

Out of their thoughts, the problems not theirs it's his,

But that's all they ever think.

But don't let them hear you, or they'll say you're mad

But if this is madness then hell in this case is sanity.

Stop, Don't try working it out, for it may hurt your brain

And if damage occurs, you'll be left like them.

Left without light and without light

You'll never see deep in the depths of nowhere

Where lies the answer to it all.

*Am I mad? I always cry when I read this. I feel no one understands me. Your possible answer. No wonder if you write poems like this.*

# Wrong Again

You took the strength from my body
Then threw my soul away
But I still loved you
And now I'm lost astray.

Though my diamond still shines
She sends no light to me
And in my sheer amazement
I really do wonder what I did to thee.

Your promises to me of no more pain
Meant nothing to you, when sunshine turned to rain
I remember it well; you said I'm not like the rest
All though we're all in Gods image, maybe yes.

I can only dream of the family we'd share
Of the house we'd live, it didn't matter where.
Again I got it wrong, maybe I should write another
song
Sleep well and god bless for I am still strong.

Sadly this book is living proof that in America, someone can simply pick up the phone, make the most serious accusations about you, you can then be arrested without even being asked what your version of events is. You're then photographed like some terrible criminal, locked away for three weeks without being given a public defender. Then put before a judge for a bond hearing without being told, so no one can bond you out. Your accusers are allowed to speak against you but you're not allowed to defend yourself. You can then hire an attorney, give this person five vital witnesses to testify against your accusers for committing a long list of crimes against you.

Your own attorney can, in front of your five witnesses, the public and the judge, commit perjury in a court of law along with the prosecutor on behalf of the state. Your own attorney obstructs justice by not demanding that your witnesses be heard in court. Then the prosecutor and the attorney you hired whilst you're under extreme pressure, co hearse you into a deal you desperately don't want. Then totally fail to make sure the deal is carried out. You and your witnesses can put a complaint into the Bar Association, against the attorney representing you for mal practice, but rule him having done nothing un ethical. You then complain to the supreme courts, they then fail to investigate. You're branded a criminal for the rest of you life...HOW'S THAT?


It's now the 4th of June 2011. I'm still in touch with Chuck and Wendy. Wendy is in ill health and needs oxygen to breath.

The USA now has a black president, Barack Obama. I actually believe this man to be very proud and have deep determination and to do what he believes in his peoples and countries best interests. He's clearly a devoted family man and has a very good 1st Lady and they look really good together. They have just visited the UK, I was impressed by the way they treat people equal, whether they are wealthy or poor. I'm

267

very impressed with this guy and his wife, I've seen him now many times on TV giving speeches, he dislikes corruption and people who purge themselves.

It's going to take some time but I think I will write to Mr Obama and ask him to personally have my case investigated... Yes I can hear you...Do you think the President of the United States of America, in the middle of many world crises and national disasters will actually want to help you Mr Dunphy? My answer is YES, if he is the man he has led the world and his people to believe he is then that's exactly what I do believe he will do as all the wars around the world he is fighting for people's freedom of speech, human rights and justice.

I really do believe if Mr Obama knew of the injustice that I have suffered, he would want to bring these criminals to book, so justice can be done, my good name cleared and some compensation awarded to me, my ban from visiting my wonderful friends in America lifted. So one day I will take Brandon Craig and Cheryle to Disney World Orlando, Yes this will happen. I think Mr Obama would want me to stay determined in my fight for justice and maybe through my case being investigated, things could be changed. So people in the future will not have to suffer what I've endured.

The whole world seems to be in turmoil, Japans Earth Quake, Australia's Earth Quake, wild fires and flooding throughout the world, tsunami's, tornados hitting the USA, volcanoes erupting and not forgetting the chaos in the financial world.

I think it would make a very good ending for my book, that Mr Obama puts everything to rights. I can hear you say, but what if Mr Obama does nothing? I suppose it will still make an ending to my book. If he does nothing, he would be seen to be a hypocrite, but I don't think for one moment that will happen and I think this book will help people that have suffered the way I have and it may guide them as to how they can go about finding their own justice and hopefully will help them find strength in the years ahead.

Regarding this book, I believe, that Mr Obama has given me the strength to come back to my book. The last few nights I have been up until 4am writing, It's been very emotional especially late at night.


I'm now going to tell you something that makes a total mockery of their attempts to try and discredit me by saying I married fraudulently for a green card. As you know I am an Entertainer and every entertainer dreams of working in Las Vegas, now listen to this. Doug who was like a brother to me used to go to Las Vegas on gambling trips and invited me to one such trip. I told him I didn't have that sort of money and he told me not to worry as Caesar's Palace were paying for our flights, picking us up at the airport in a stretch limo and putting us up in the Penthouse Suite.

Doug explained he had a Caesar's Palace gold card and we would use this card to pay for everything. Doug said he was given the gold card because him and his friends were regular visitors to Caesar's Palace and gambled fairly heavily. He smiled as he said "I'll add you to our party, Ricky, it won't cost you a dime."

Doug said he wanted me to bring my singing videos and other promotional stuff as he knew people at the hotel. We flew from Fort Lauderdale to Tampa then on to Las Vegas, it was absolutely out of this world. Doug introduced me to the manager of Caesar's *Palace* Group World Wide and he took the promo package from me and promised to look at it. A couple of days later Doug told me the entertainment manager was very impressed with my videos and wanted to have a breakfast meeting with me the following morning to discuss putting a band behind me and working for the group.

"How about that Ricky?" Doug said.

I said. "But we fly home tomorrow Doug, at 8am."

He said, "No you stay here for a few days and then fly back."

I explained that I had to fly back tomorrow because I'd promised to sing at a dear friend of Lily's, wedding.

Doug said. "Are you completely mad Ricky? This is a massive opportunity for you; this guy leaves in two days. The money will be huge, do the bloody deal, sign whatever you need to, stuff Lily and this wedding this guy thinks you're superb."

I told him no, I have to keep my word as my word means a lot to me and I wasn't going to let Lily and her friend down.

So I flew back.

What was I doing flying back to be with Lily if I just married her for a Green Card?

When I got back and told Lily, she was really pissed off with me as she screamed. "I could have flown out to Vegas and we could have rented an apartment, have you lost your mind, you idiot?"

"But what about the big wedding," I said

"Fuck the wedding." She said

To be honest Doug actually said screw Lily and stay in Vegas, this is where you belong and that I'd soon find someone else.

But no... I flew home to be with Lily. Oooouch I can hear all of you saying. Hindsight is a wonderful thing, the way things turned out maybe I should have stayed in Vegas but then again fate takes a hand and now I have my beautiful Cheryle and my miracle Brandon.

Regardless, I should have been given justice.

Well, as you know when Rocque met with me I gave him notes for Mike, notes for Donna and me and notes for Lily and Me. We wanted to photocopy the lot and put it in the book but my writing is so bad and tiny that when we tried to downsize it you couldn't read it. So Cheryle has put the lot into typed form, so you can actually read what Rocque was given to prepare my case. I have all the originals, so if we ever get back to court I have everything available. There are also the four actual complaint forms filled out by my witnesses, these are extremely serious complaints against Rocque.

## The Florida Bar Inquiry Complaint Form

After reading these, plus my own complaints against Rocque they ruled him as having done nothing unethical at the Bar Association Hearing. If this hearing looked at all the evidence against Rocque it should have been impossible for them to have done anything but disbar this man and bring him to justice, and now I remind you, the ultimate court, the Supreme Court ruled the bar cannot be appealed. It's beyond belief they reached that conclusion after reading everything I sent them, that's if they did?

Surely the Bar should have been able to clear this up by bringing all the witnesses into the Bar Hearing? But anyway how could the bar have had a just and fair hearing in the first place without all parties present, how can that be real justice?

I have a letter from the Bar saying I had no proof against Mr Rocque, just bare allegations that Mr Rocque provided me with an ineffective assistance of counsel. They said. 'We cannot conclude that the level of representation fell below the standard of care.'

They could not have possibly read the serious complaints against Rocque by my witnesses, so how can they have sat at his bar counsel? Maybe they didn't.

The notes given to Mike at the jail by me, entitled Donna and Me, Lily and Me and Notes for Mike and also copies of the actual complaints. When you read them you will think – How could they have possibly come to the conclusion that Rocque didn't act unethically?

I'm going to be very honest now. I've been telling you about Mr Rocque's letter to Mr B Liss, Assistant Staff Council, The Florida Bar, and his rebuff to the allegations against him. I thought I had lost this letter, but found it by accident today. This is the letter in which he says, 'I made arrangements with Mr. Dunphy's witnesses to meet me in person at my office prior to the bond hearing, to discuss their potential testimony.'

He fails to tell Mr. Liss that this was literally half an hour before going to court ??? and as you know he made no attempt to interview any of the five witnesses in detail or read any documents given to him.

Mr Rocque completely and utterly fails to tell Mr. Liss that his first words to me in court were, 'everything has changed Mr Dunphy because you are now divorced and because of this you no longer have legal status.'

Remember, he told all my witnesses in court the same thing. He tells Mr Liss that I had an immigration problem, but he fails to tell him despite the fact that I told him it was vital to contact Mr Kilpatrick, my immigration attorney.

I'm sure Mr. Liss would have agreed to contact Mr David Kilpatrick, which was vital to my case.

Mr Kilpatrick told me I should sue Mr Rocque and was prepared to testify against Mr Rocque on my behalf. In Mr Rocque's letter to Mr B Liss he doesn't mention a word of Lily's attempt to claim two million dollars from the Calder Race Track.

Mr Rocque's ridiculous quote to me in court 'Why would Lily lie, Mr Dunphy'?

My reply, "Two million dollars Mr Rocque, you idiot."

Sorry to remind you but this is what Rocque had lined up in court to testify against Lily.

- Mr Randy Reynolds was in court to testify that he witnessed in court Lily telling the judge that she had sent all my things to England, yet after the court hearing she asked Randy to visit me at the Stockade asking him to tell me she had my things and she wanted 3000 dollars or she was going to destroy my things, therefore committing extortion against me plus perjuring herself to the judge himself, plus he was going to tell the judge that Lily had told him it had took the police three days before they actually caught me when I was arrested the night of the so called attack.

- Mr Doug Santi was in court to testify that Lily had phoned him asking him to say in court that I had confessed to him that I had done what Lily had said in her statement to the police. He was also there to testify that Lily had told Doug that we slipped on the spaghetti on the stairs. Asking Doug to lie in court is a very serious crime, attempted perjury, bringing false witnesses to court.

- Mr and Mrs Norman were in court to testify that Lily had visited them a matter of weeks before the incident, telling them I'm, glad Ricky has you because he will be needing you soon. Also that Lily in a three way conversation on the phone also said that we slipped on the spaghetti. Now remember she says as you can read in her statement to the police nothing about slipping on spaghetti. Mr and Mrs Norman were also with us on the night of the incident.

- Sari Mitchell was in court to testify that Lily had told her one night in a bar that she was going to get me to fall in love with her, marry me, then when I made it as a star she would want for nothing for the rest of her life, therefore married me under false pretenses. This is a serious crime in America.

- Mr Rocque had a 20 page letter from my brother in England, a police officer. Telling Mr Rocque Lily had sent parcels to the UK after the date in court when she told Rothschild she had sent all my things to England, but she'd sent old papers and work clothes, she told John in a phone call that she still had my things and wanted 3000 dollars and also in her conversation to my brother John states that we slipped on the spaghetti. Plus John had sent the Air Lingus receipt proving the date she posted the parcel and the cost. She also told my brother John that she had broken ribs and a broken collarbone. Mr Rocque knew of this letter but did nothing; Lily had broken neither her rib or collarbone.

- If I had done what Lily said I'd done, dragging her up the stairs and throwing her down 3 times, her injuries would have been ridiculously worse than they were. Any idiot doctor or police officer would say the same after reading her statement and simply looking at her on the night.

So Mr Rocque, with all his witnesses and written testimony puts me under serious duress and was agitated with me as I still wanted to fight my case, after he had lied to me in court by telling me everything had changed because I was now divorced and had no legal status.

I was in no psychical or mental state to take Mr Rocque's abuse and mental torture in the way he co harassed me into taking the no contest plea, putting me under tremendous pressure. Then he tells Mr Liss I took the plea freely of my own will. What an evil animal! Surely if Mr Judge Rothschild knew how Mr Rocque had got me to take this plea he would put Rocque away for a long time, never to practice again. I still have all letters and documents provided to Mr Rocque for the day when we go back to court. Throughout my ordeal in court Mr Rocque refused to let me speak to any of my witnesses.

This is the letter from Mr Rocque to Mr Liss, assistant Staff Council, the Florida Bar.

*Dear Mr Liss:*

*Mr Dunphy was charged with Domestic Battery for beating his wife at that time Lily Baron. The Assistant State Attorney was seeking a sentence of one year in the Broward County Jail based on the evidence and the injuries Lily Baron suffered.*

*The Defendant was arrested on August 12 1995 for Domestic Battery. The magistrate judge set Mr. Dunphys bond at $25.000 twenty five thousand dollars for the offence charged. A defence motion to have Mr. Dunphy released on his own recognizance was filed and then denied on August 29 1995 prior to me being retained. Upon being retained, on September 8 1995, I had met with Mr Dunphy at the jail and I obtained any information he could provide me. Mr Dunphy wanted to get out of jail as soon as possible so I set a hearing to reduce bond. Prior to the bond hearing the State filed a Motion for Pre-Trial Detention of Mr. Dunphy based on the fact that Mr Dunphy was an illegal alien and deportation proceedings were being initiated as well as the fact that the Assistant State Attorney, Tripp Beckert had the evidence that Mr Dunphy was a substantial risk to both the victim and his previous wife.*

*I made arrangements for Mr. Dunphy's witnesses to meet me in person at my office prior to the bond hearing to discuss their potential testimony. I met* with his witnesses and read their letters concerning Mr. Dunphy and we proceeded to the courthouse for the bond hearing. On September 21 1995 the date of the bond hearing, I spoke with the Assistant State Attorney. He told me that he was prepared to call Lily Baron, the victim and also Mr. Dunphys first wife Donna Van Buran and that both of them were going to testify in detail how Mr Dunphy was a dangerous threat to them and why both feared for their lives. Mr. Beckert also informed me about the contents of a letter dates August 23 1995, written by Donna Van Buran to the department of Immigration and Naturalization Services which detailed why she feared Mr. Dunphy and the letter also informed the Department of Immigration that if it had not already been done that she wanted to withdraw her petition for legal status for Mr. Dunphy. Additionally Mr. Beckert informed me about the contents of a letter dated August 31, 1994 from the Department of Immigration and Naturalization Services allowing Mr. Dunphy to voluntarily stay in the United States only until September 30, 1994. Additionally Mr. Beckert told me that Mr. Dunphy had an IMMIGRATION HOLD on him because he was in the United States illegally and that he was being deported. I also spoke with Lily Baron and Donna Van Buran and they told me in detail everything that the prosecutor told me.

Then I spoke to Mr. Dunphy and after telling him all of this information I then called Mr Kilpatrick, My. Dunphy's immigration lawyer. Mr. Kilpatrick told me that Mr. Dunphy did have immigration problems.

Then I informed Mr. Dunphy of all his options: proceed with the bond hearing and then go to trial, or resolve the case by way of a plea. I advised him

*that the state was seeking one year in the Broward
County Jail if he were convicted to trial. Furthermore
I explained to Mr. Dunphy that the case could be
resolved by a plea the witnesses would not get to testify
on that day. I explained to Mr. Dunphy that the state
offered him a plea and the plea was this: If he wished
to resolve the case and he was leaving the country he
could plead to probation and report by mail from his
home in England and that the state wouldn't request
any further jail sentence but that he would be held
until his deportation under the immigration hold.*

*Mr. Dunphy freely and voluntarily entered a
plea to the charge as evidence by his plea sheet and
the judge's plea colloquy. The defendant pled, was
sentenced and subsequently deported by INS.*

*Very truly yours
Michael J. Rocque*
(I have the original letter, signed by Rocque)
*CC: James Dunphy*

IN THE CIRCUIT COURT OF THE
17TH JUDICIAL CIRCUIT IN AND
FOR BROWARD COUNTY, FLORIDA

CASE NO. 95-11684 (42)
FLORIDA BAR NO. 164907

IN RE: THE MARRIAGE OF
LILLY BARON,

    Petitioner/Wife,

vs.

JAMES E. DUNPHY,

    Respondent/Husband.

**FINAL JUDGMENT
OF DISSOLUTION OF MARRIAGE**

THIS CAUSE having come on to be heard upon Final Hearing on the Petition for Dissolution of Marriage, and the Court having heard and considered the testimony of the Petitioner, LILLY BARON and being otherwise fully advised in the premises, it is thereupon

ORDERED and ADJUDGED as follows:

1. That the Court has jurisdiction over the parties hereto and the subject matter hereof.

2. That the Court finds that the marriage is irretrievably broken and therefore, the marriage is hereby dissolved, _a vinculo matrimonii_.

3. That the Court finds that the parties have no children and that there are no assets, whether real or personal property, to be divided and there are no debts of the parties to be adjudicated.

4. That the Court hereby retains jurisdiction over the parties hereto and the subject matter hereof for the purpose of entering such further orders in connection with the enforcement of this Final Judgment as may be just and proper.

DONE and ORDERED in Chambers at Fort Lauderdale, Broward County, Florida, this _____ day of October, 1995.

J. LEONARD FLEET
A TRUE COPY   OCT 0 5 1995

CIRCUIT COURT JUDGE

Copies Furnished:

Harvey L. Rubinchik, Esquire
James Dunphy, pro se

_The final dissolution of marriage proving roach lied in court when he said I was divorced_

278

# Supreme Court of Florida

Office of the Clerk
500 South Duval Street
Tallahassee, Florida 32399-1927

DEBBIE CAUSSEAUX
ACTING CLERK

PHONE (850) 488

May 26, 1999

Mr. James Edward Dunphy
1-37 Cala Norena
Mont Benidorm
La Cala 03500
Spain

Re: Complaint against Mr. Michael Rocque

Dear Mr. Dunphy:

In response to your letter filed May 25, 1999 , you are advised that the Supreme Court of Florida will not investigate a complaint concerning the failure of the Florida Bar to find probable cause.

Pursuant to the Rules Regulating The Florida Bar, a complaining witness is not a party to the disciplinary proceedings and does not have the right of appeal. In the absence of a recommendation of discipline by the Bar, the case is final and no investigation will be ordered by the Court.

I regret that we are unable to assist you.

Sincerely,

Debbie Causseaux

Debbie Causseaux

DC/kb

*Letter from Supreme Court ruling that the pursuant does not have the right to appeal.*

# Further Papers

Here are transcripts of papers given to Mr Rocque when I was at the stockade, originally six handwritten notes written by me, headed '*notes for Mike.*'

Lily told Wendy one morning that she had sent my clothes to the UK and then the same day phoned and told Wendy she had not, then said she had sent my clothes to England but not my master tapes and anything to do with my music, stage wear etc.

Lily told Randy my friend and boss that she had sent my clothes to the UK. She told Randy that I ran off on the night and it took the police 3 days to get me. She told Randy when he wanted to collect my car that my car was being reposed by a finance company. The car was worth less than 600 dollars, Doug bought it, and the car was paid for in cash. The car was in my name, everything was in my name. On the day I was in court the Judge Mr Rothschild ordered Lily to hand over all my things. I had told Mr Rothschild she had all my masters, photos, stage clothes etc all priceless to me, 17 years of my life. Lily told Mr Rothschild that she has sent everything to England. That same day Randy came to visit me at the jail. He said he had a message from Lily. She still had all my stuff and that she wanted 3000 dollars or she would destroy it all. She had my phone book plus all my ID, drivers licence etc. Also Randy told me she had smashed my beeper. I was buying a TV from Randy but I had not paid for it, it was still Randy's. When Randy went to collect the TV, she told him it had gone but she had no idea where. Randy is a good man but he told me he feared what she would do to his property etc if she found out he had told the judge all of this. Lily had a three way phone call to Wendy and Doug. Wendy and Chuck did not know Doug till all this happened. Lily mentioned in this three way phone call that we slipped on the stairs together. Lily phoned Doug and asked Doug to testify against me and tell lies about me but Doug will go to court for me.

Lily told my brother in England that I had no friends at all and that all her friends that knew me wanted me out of the country. I have lots of friends.

Lily said in her statement to the police. A written statement she made, that she had phoned my ex wife in the UK and that my ex wife told her that I had beat her three time and her father. This is not true, I have letters from the UK, from my ex wife, her father and my brother. She has also phoned other members of my family, we are a very close family and she has put my family through hell.

Lily in her statement to the police told them I slapped her, then in court said I punched her 2 times, but this is not in her statement. I did not punch my wife, I did not drag her up and down the stairs, I did not kick her in the ribs. I did not tell her I would kill her when I got out. I loved my wife. I think she is a very troubled woman, I feel very sad for her. I am not a perfect person, I'm normal. I feel she needs help with drugs. My life will never be the same again after this, I worry how this will affect me. I have lost everything.

[Redacted]

My son is in the UK, he's 11 years old and he's handicapped he has downs syndrome. The last time Lily spoke to my ex wife in the UK, she asked her what did my son think to his dad being in jail. That finally did it for my ex wife with Lily...How Sick!!!

The two boxes Lily sent to the UK contained all my old work clothes old T Shirts, she'd thrown old papers, some flyers from the agents I used to work for. Lily sent this stuff COD it cost my brother £350 when he collected the boxes.

When I saw Mr Rothschild in court I thought Lily had sent 2 boxes of my clothes, but Lily still had all my really good clothes, my master tapes, my photo's, all my private papers for tax etc. My phone book, my wallet with my ID, my sheet music. I have nothing but my shorts and a vest, no shoes. When I get out I cannot do any shows, singing telegrams or auditions for future work. I can not promote myself or anything. Some of the masters Lily has belong to other writer from the UK, they are in my care, this stuff is priceless, can not be replaced. Some of my promo photos are one in a million shots, Lily wants $3000. Lily also has my PO Box key, she took the key off my car keys key ring. She has my post ever since I have been in jail, all my bank mail goes to Lily's PO Box.

I still have some furniture at the apartment and my workout bench etc. Randy tells me he believes Lily to be moving from the apartment. Lily told Randy only last week, she has now moved all my things from the apartment.

When I went to court I was not told I had two hearings. I was told late at night when I was in bed that I had court the next day. I knew I had court at 10am but I did not know I had a bond hearing so I was unable to have my friends and witnesses there. I saw a lady for five minutes before the bond hearing. For the second court I had no attorney at all. My friend Chuck and Wendy were very nervous, Wendy could hardly talk with a sore throat. Lily smiled when Wendy tried to talk. Wendy could not talk so Chuck had a go, he was not correct in part of his statement, he was so shook up. In court they said I was a dangerous man and a flight risk, my passport is with my immigration ATT Mr Kilpatrick.

Lily wants me to be deported because she fears I may testify against her two million law case against Calder Race Track, her accident was the day after Hurricane Andrew so she's nearly to the end. Me and Lily went white water rafting, mountain horseback riding, she told me after her accident that she rode Exercise for Shaun Musgrave at the track, but when she started her case against the track, she stopped.

We went rafting etc, last summer one year ago, this would look really bad for Lilys case if the tracks insurance were to find out. I also think because of the amount of money Lily stands to gain, that my safety, possible life is in danger when I come out. Randy fears what Lily will do to him if he goes to court against her, Randy has known Lily for ten years. I believe Lily has been doing drugs a lot, she slept a lot and did not eat hardly, her moods were extreme, no interest in sex, constantly sniffing, making horrendous noises, then spitting all the time, constantly complaining about money. Since I have been in jail I have not been well, dizzy spells, head aches, stiff neck, not sleeping, waking up with losing the feelings in my arms and total loss of feeling in some fingers. I failed TB test but I've been told by the doctor, I don't have TB but I've been in contact with it, so I'm on medication for 6 months to build my body back up against TB. I'd often asked Lily to go to church, but she never would. Oh Lily took my plate off my car, all my documents out of the car to do with the car, I don't know how Lily sleeps at night. I'm a good man always did my best and worked hard. If I became a star she would have wanted for nothing. I was very much in love with my wife.

Notes given to Mike when at the stockade headed *Donna and me.*

Donna's son was stealing from me and his mom and school. He was doing drugs. I sat and talked with him as a friend, went to football with him. Donna sent Eric to Savannah Hospital in Port St Luise. He spent four weeks in hospital. I went home to the UK, we spent three months. Donna wrote to me nearly every day, cards, gifts etc. After three months apart Donna came to the UK to meet my family, Donna came back to the USA after two weeks. I had to rent my house, sell my furniture, car, I give away. I came back to the USA to be with Donna and Eric. Eric had been in hospital but was home when I arrived in the USA. But he was still stealing, he stole from school and was still doing drugs and being very untidy around the house, Donna had me talk to him. I had to check his jobs around his bedroom and bathroom from a list Donna gave me.

Donna then wanted to go out with ex husband Scott down to Miami to have dinner and send the afternoon with him. I said no, but she could invite him to our home, we would cook him dinner and he could stay the night, until I have met with him and built some kind of relationship with him, then maybe if his intentions were honourable towards Donna, she may then in the future spend time with him alone. Donna had been divorced only 12 months, she told me he was still in love with her. Scott is a cruise director on the ships, a fellow entertainer, me and him would have a lot in common, but no attempt was made by him or Donna for us to meet. I was Donna's husband struggling for work. Scott could have helped me with work if he wished or at least help with some connections but he did not. So I questioned his intentions towards Donna, but he was still welcome to visit us. Donna also wanted to have dinner with an ex lover now and then. I told her he could come to dinner, get to meet me, try to develop a friendship the three of us, Donna was not happy with this. Eric, Donna's son became more and more of a problem. One night Donna and I were having words when Eric came out of his bedroom in a very threatening manner. I told him to go to bed that me and his mom were having a disagreement, that it had nothing to do with him, but he was still making threatening movements towards me. I then thought it better if I leave for the night. I put some clothes together just for the night to cool things down but Donna took my door key from my key ring. The next day I came home from work to find she had packed my bags, I had to sleep in my car for one night. Donna moved house to Sample Road West Coral Springs, after maybe a week, she invited me to her home. I stayed a few times, then I stayed the whole weekend with her parents, we went sea fishing off the pier, we had a wonderful weekend, her mom and dad went home. I had been to her mom and dad's house in Ocala. They are very nice people; we got on very well together. When they left we spent the last night together. I was to go to work and stay with my roommate for a few days. That night in bed I spoke with Donna about Scott and her ex-lover. I told her again very nicely, if she wished to be going out with other men without me first meeting them then she needed to be with someone else. I told her I loved her, that we had a wonderful weekend, but I had to be honest, she said she would never wish to do that in the future, that I could meet her ex´s, she told me she loved me and we made love. The next morning I got up for work at 4am, she made me a coffee then off to work I went. This very same weekend, Donna had a phone call from the town house she rented in Kendle, Miami. The AC had broken down again, she had a lot of problems with the AC but this time it was completely broken. I gave Donna a cheque for $1000 as a loan to be paid back because she did not have the money for the AC. The gentleman renting her house had a wife and children and he was very upset because of the heat, I was to see Donna later in the week, we were slowly putting out marriage back together. I phoned Donna but she told me she was not happy about not being able to meet with her ex's and she had changed her mind about the whole situation, so we had words on the phone and decided not to meet for a little while, we had a meeting with the immigration people about my work authorisation. We met in the parking lot, I told her she didn't have to go in the building unless she wanted to. I told her I loved her and still wanted us to work things out, but I still meant what I said about the ex's. She told me she was not going to the next meeting, which was about four months later. Later that week or so, I moved to WPB to be with my manager and his wife after about three weeks me and Donna did not get back. My manager was worried about me being married to Donna but not living together, we had a possible record deal pending, but Mr King my manager would not go ahead with nothing while I was still married to Donna because she could cause me problems over money if I was successful. So I met with Donna at her office at work, it was all very nice, we talked and we agreed we were not getting back together again. So I told her about my manager, I told her he would not go ahead with anything unless we were divorced. So my manager paid for the divorce. I told Donna I would still need my $1000 back, she told me ok but she never had the money at that time. After the divorce some weeks later I had an accident in my car, my car was totaled I needed some money so I phoned Donna at work, she told me she would send me a cheque for $39.00 that was all she could pay. Some weeks later I phoned again to hopefully get some money, I was driving a car smashed down one side, having to climb out the passenger side, she told me again she had no money. Weeks later my car finally blew up, so I had no car so I needed my money. Me and my manager had gone our separate ways, I was now seeing Lily. I phoned Donna at work to ask for my money but she was out, I phoned again but she was out. So I phoned Pam a friend to me and Donna, when we were together Pam married me and Donna,

Pam is a notary. I asked Pam to let Donna know I had lost my car and I had no money to buy one, I really needed my money please and could she phone me but Donna did not phone me. Lily helped me with her car till Doug a friend of mine bought a car for me $600. Sometime later I needed money to send to the UK, I was renting my house, the girl renting my house did not pay the rent for some time and my house was going to be taken away from me. I phoned Donna at work, they said she was not in the office, so I left her a message could she phone me it was very important, every time I phoned her office I was a gentleman. Donna did not call, so I called Pam, I told Pam I could lose my house if I could not find some money, could she please talk to Donna , tell her about the house, this was a good 14 months after I last spoke to Donna in person, or by phone, but I still heard nothing from Donna. Whenever I phoned Pam I was always very nice to Pam as she is a friend of mine too. Donna said she would always be my friend but this was not to be.

Before Donna and I got divorced with her permission I went to her house to collect her wedding ring, she was giving the ring back to me. I got to the house and she had put the ring under the door mat. I knocked on the door, she let me in and gave me a glass of wine, it was all very nice until I asked about my $1000. She said she was unable to pay me anything. I said what has happened to this honest woman I was supposed to have married, she then stood up shouting get out of my house, so I left. I told Lily all about Donna, Lily was not happy with Donna. Me and Lily were just going out, not married yet and I was living and working in WPB. Lily told me to call by Donnas office, take the number from her car and Lily would talk to a friend of hers who was a private detective, George from Shoppers Broward, he had computers that could run numbers to find out Donna new phone number as Donna had gone private, I did this but I lost the number so Lily could not do anything. Sometime later Lily and I got married. I thought

I saw Donna in WPB one day in a different car, I told Lily I had seen Donna in a different car at this time Lily had a job at the Corel Springs Diner, my car was broken down so I was taking Lily to work, as I took Lily to work we drive past Donnas apartment complex, I told Lily that's where Donna lives, so Lily told me to on my way home go to Donna and see if her new car was outside her apartment, it was so I took the number and gave it to Lily. Lily had George check the number but she said I did not have enough numbers from the car to run the check. I never went again. Donnas boyfriend beeped me one day to ask why I was phoning Donna, I told him the whole story and he said he would talk to Donna, he beeped me again and said she was not going to pay me, that we were divorced, that I was not entitled to my money. I told him, she still promised to pay me, the divorce was done quick for both of us but she still owed me the $1000. He said forget it, I told him I would go to court when I had the money to do so and I will get the $1000 back, but I hoped Donna would pay me without going to court. I told Lily about this, Lily asked me for the two numbers off my beeper, the numbers that Donnas boyfriend had called me on. I asked why did she want the two numbers? She said George would run the number through his computer, George came up with a pay phone and a business number, both in the Corel Spring Area. I phoned the private number but nobody knew a Donna Vanburan, so I said I was sorry to have bothered them, the man said that's ok, that was the end of that. The next time I saw Donna was in court, I had not personally spoken to her or seen her for 18 months. She says she fears for her life, if so why had she not had a restraining order on me, not to call her work, or Pam, or go near her work or her home? But she didn't! Lily stood up in court and told the judge that I was harassing Donna, that she was fearful for Donnas life. Lily told the court I used her car to follow Donna home from work to find out where she lived. Why would I need Lily's car to do that when I already knew where Donna lived months before?

Before Donna and I divorced we had stayed together at her home in Corel Springs, even with Donna's parents and her son Eric. Donna and I slept on the floor for two nights, Eric on the sofa while her mom and dad slept in Donna's bed. The day her mom and dad went home we slept in her bed, that was the last night we ever stayed together. Donna and Lily did this to me together, Donna to save $1000, Lily to help me get out of the USA. Donna also said she had gone to get a permit for a gun.

Papers given to Mr Rocque when I was at the stockade. Originally 22 hand written notes written by me headed *Lily and me.*

I met Lily at the Village 200 Grand Opening Night. She was with Randy. Randy is my friend and boss. He was at first a friend to Lily. She told me about her last husband Mick Pollock. She told me that Mick Pollock and her lived in a bus. When they split up, she at first had the bus, Lily told me that Mick had the bus stolen by a Mr John Manning, they stole the bus, took everything from the bus and set fire to it. Lily lost everything, she had no clothes and lived in a garage next door to Randy, the roof let water in. Lily had a terrible hatred for Mick and John Manning. She told me someone called Jimmy drove the bus fir John and Mick. For many months Lily was trying get her money back, always phoning detectives in Texas and other parts of the USA. She wanted to get back at John Manning and Mick. John Manning went to jail on other charges. Lily did everything she could to keep John Manning in jail. Lily has a 40.000 dollar law suit a claim on Mr Manning. Lily told me Mick said he would kill her if she pressed charges against him. Lily told me that her and Mick did a lot of cocaine and it had become a problem. Mick she told me was very sexually perverted. On his birthday to show him how much she loved him, she has sex with a call girl while Mick looked on, then he joined them. Lily told me she did not enjoy doing it but she wanted to show him how much she loved him. I believed Lily when she said she didn't enjoy it and that she would never do it again. The hatred towards Mick and John was a big concern to me. She never stopped talking about it and she would sometimes sit up all night rocking in her chair. On the night of her wedding to Mick he took her to a sex motel with movies, drugs and changing partners. Lily was very upset with him, she told me that Mick was gay, that he would look at gay videos with a male friend of his. Lily used to drink a lot I was told by Brian Smeak. Brian is a friend of mine too, he's a trainer at Calder Race Track. Lily and I started to date, Lily was very private with her phone number. I had to beep her because she did not give me her home phone number for some time. This I thought was wrong; I could never just call to her house without beeping her first. In all the time I've been with Lily her moods would change all the time sometimes to extreme. Lily had a big lawsuit against the Calder Race Track. Lily was a rough and tumble kind of girl, she would often thump me in the arm and chest, I always told her to not do that as it hurt and left marks on my arm. Lily and me became very close, we spoke of marriage. One day she told me she wanted 15% of my Gross to be paid to her for five years. I was very upset with her, I said I will marry you only if you love me. I said that marriage should have nothing to do with money. Lily told me marriage was like a business and it would make her feel part of me. I said no, she bartered me down half I said no way, she wanted protection from me, if I became ill nobody could go after Lily and her 2 million law suit against the Calder Race Track, so I had Acello Pedrosse, a friend of mine write up a prenup'. Acello said all his entertainers had one and that this would protect her and me at the same time, I have never heard of such a thing in my life before.

Lily was always happiest with me when I was entertaining. She always enjoyed the attention we had from people at my shows, then Lily would have a drink, then change and become loud, often using the F word even if family were close by, I often had to say something to her. Lily used to be a jockey and worked for years at racetracks. Lily had a very hard up bringing, when I first met Lily she danced and danced the night away, she used to walk in the dark every morning at about 7am, sometimes I would walk with her, she was so fast I couldn't keep up with her. Then one day she told me, no more walking or dancing or anything stressful because her attorney with her case against the Calder Race Track told her to stop as the Race Track may be having her followed and videoed, she became very frustrated. Lily always did a lot of spitting and sniffing, made horrible noises when doing this, it often made me feel sick when hearing her do this. Lily spent half her life asleep, she did not work; her attorney said no work as it would not help her case if she worked at that time. Lily was a very strong woman; she used to like flowers and plants and spent a lot of time in her garden she cut back on, so I ended up doing most the gardening for her. When we set out to get married Lily would not tell her friends even her close friends that we were to marry and this hurt me. I said are you not proud to be marrying me? I could never get Lily to look me in the eyes and tell me she loved me, this hurt me, she said that she loved me in a special way, I didn't understand what she meant by that. I would ask her if she loved me and she would mutter the words fast saying I love you, never clear. I thought she had a problem showing love because of her past. Even if we had sex we never made love, it was always just sex, I like candles and soft music, Lily would say just get on with it stick it in. She was not romantic, only a couple of times in all the time I knew her did she become passionate at all. She told me to give her time and that she used to be passionate and romantic and she will again one day. In her closet she had 5 or 6 sexy garments, teddies etc, she never wore one for me. She said she used to wear them for ex's, so I said throw them away, it upset me to see them but she didn't. She told me all the time every week how she used to love her ex husbands and boyfriends, that they will never be loved or have sex like they did with her, this upset me because I was never shown by her what she told me she gave all the ex's in her life. She said give her time, it would come back. Lily always had everything her own way all the time. Lily could be very kind to me but then through her own stupidity spoil all that she did. All the people I knew told me not to marry her, that she would only hurt me. Doug a friend of mine told me if I married her I would end up in jail one day. Lily wanted to marry me but then she would tell me she was helping me by marrying me, I told her if she married me it had to be for love not help or %'s off me. I really loved Lily, we spent a lot of time together, I thought she really needed me, that I was a good man for her, not like her ex's, I really thought we would be happy, we both had hurt from our past. One night I was on the phone with Lily with one of her friends. In the phone call her friend asked Lily how she was doing with the drugs now, Lily passed it off. When I asked her if she had a problem with drugs once in her past, she said no. I know nothing about drugs at all, I come from a very small village North of England, all this was new to me and I'm very proud to say I've never done drugs or smoked in my life. I come from a good family, 5 sisters, 2 brothers.

Lily was still very private with her beeper even Doug noticed when at his house.

Lily's daughters both told me that they loved their mom, but what was I doing with Lily? I thought it was sad and some of Lily's friends told me I was a brave man, that they liked Lily but she was crazy. One of Lily's friends told me that all the men in Lily's life, that she had made them crazy, his name Bob, his wife Chris.

Lily did a wonderful thing for me for my wedding Christmas surprise, Lily brought my brother John and son Craig out from England to be my best men at my wedding, but still she would not tell her friends when we were to wed. Lily embarrassed me in front of my brother, getting herself drunk, I asked her not to but she said don't be a kill joy, but I knew what was coming. She taunted my brother with drinks, saying an American man would drink another. If ever me and Lily set off to the beach or for a night out, I'd say just one or two drinks, no more, she'd say ok, but then when we were out she always got that extra drink and pushed one extra on me. Lily did not have to get really drunk to change; just two or three all night would make her a different person. On the day we got married me and Lily had words in the park, she would not invite all her friends to the wedding that night, I was upset with her. The same day of the wedding her attorney had my attorney on the phone saying Lily would go ahead with the prenup, but if the marriage was over after six months, what alimony would Lily have? I told my attorney Acello to tell them the wedding was off, I was very offended, at this time I was broke, how could they talk of such a thing? I think now that they thought I was going to become a star.

Sometimes Lily would drink a bottle of Tots Sparkling wine by herself, even sometimes in the day if I was at work and sometimes on the odd occasion she would drink 2 bottles. I've seen Lily go out in her car often after drinking shots. Lily and I often went out and had a good night but she would spoil things by the end of the night.

When we got out apartment together I did a lot of work on the outside to make Lily happy, but no matter how hard I worked sometimes at night I would want to get romantic but still she would show no interest.

Lily was still perusing John Manning and Mick, Mick had now had the bus fixed up and was using it again. Lily was now talking about setting fire to the bus because Mick was helping John Manning when John came out of jail I saw a side to Lily that disturbed me. Lily was often very untidy around the apartment, I did the house work, I even used to bath Lily's dog poo poo...Yes! I took the dog for walks etc. Lily's case against the Race Track was still running, Lily was trying to get into the pain centre South Beach Miami, she said it would do her case a lot of good if she got in the centre. Lily told me to never tell anyone to do with the doctors that she had ever done drugs or it would stop her going. I thought at this time Lily needed this hospital not for her neck and back but for the whole course because she would see many different doctors. I had a couple of meetings with her psychologist at the centre and I told them all about my problems with Lily, I did not mention the drugs, Lily was in the hospital for 4 weeks, I missed just 3 days, I did a show at the hospital for Lily whilst she was in. The doctors told Lily the main part of the treatment started when she got out, that she must exercise for one hour a day every day and she had videos books and cassettes on the workouts she must do, I went to the hospital and they showed me how to work on Lily. When she came out she did not do anything they told her, I told her I would do everything with her but she did not. The doctors told Lily if she did not do everything they told her to do when she got out that the month in hospital would be for nothing, I now believe it was all done just for her lawsuit. I was doing as many different things as possible to make money, singing telegrams, dig ditches, shows, I was paying my own way, half the rent, water, my own car insurance etc. my phone, I paid all my own bills but money was hard. Lily was ok, she got 1000 dollars a month from her settlement plus what from her part time job, but the more money I made, Lily would ask me to pay more of the bills. Lily paid all the deposits on the apartment then when I sold my house I would pay half the deposited to her. My home is in the UK. Lily was becoming more and more a bitch but she also told me to get used to it. Lily would go off to her friends for the weekend sometimes and not take me, she in one month left me three weekends. Some weeks later she left me on the beach one day, took off for the weekend, I was very worried, I phoned hospitals, police, after two days and nights she phoned me from a call box, she said she was going to hit the road, give me everything and just go. She told me she had spent two days with another man. I told her to come home, I wasn't bothered if she had been with ten men, that I loved her and that things would be ok, I was devastated. When she came home, her nose was very swollen; her nostrils pink and as I started to talk to her, her nose started to bleed. She told me she had done cocaine over the two days that she had played with a double-headed vibrator that this man had. She was wearing a black t shirt belonging to this man, I put my arms around her and told her everything would be ok and said lets live life just the two of us, forget about John, Mick and all the past. She told me how much she really did love me and that she was sorry. I asked why she did what she did, she said she had to get something out of her system but it was all past her now. She told me that she would never need to see or speak to Mick again and that she didn't want the money from John, she just wanted us to workout. This I had waited to hear, I found it all very difficult to handle but I loved her, this last for two days when Lily suddenly said she wanted me and her to go to see Mick at the bus, so she could tell him she was not bothered what he'd done or John and that she had found herself, she wanted to give him a cassette of me singing. I said I was shocked to hear this, that she had made a promise not to have anything to do with any of the guys again, why must she even this of this after all the hurt they had caused her but she thought I was wrong, I felt sick, I told her I thought she still had feelings for Mick, but she said no I was wrong. Even though we were married Lily had still not told many of her friends that we were married, I was getting used to this now. Lily was still very untidy around the apartment, but she had rules for her and rules for me. Like my car keys, my phone book and my beeper, I had to keep them In the bookshelf, if I left any of these out she would thump me on the arm saying where does the book live? Then hit me on the head and say where does the book live? As I said on the bookshelf she would continue to hit my arm, where does the book live, over the head, where does the book live? I would tell her to stop, if I backed away into the kitchen she would follow me, still doing the same till she stopped, she found this funny. If I left my pen out of my address book the same would happen again, this would also happen in the car if I could not remember my beeper number or our home zip code she would do this. Lily would always tease me with sex, on the night she would wear nothing lay on the sofa and show me her breasts, then lick her lips saying do you like my tits, then she would walk past me to the bathroom bend over and show me her pussy opening so I could see inside, then say you may get it tonight, but I'm not going to promise, she would sometimes pull my shorts down to give me oral sex then when I was hard, she would stop and say I'm just teasing you but I may finish it off later but she never did, we would just go to bed and she would say not now maybe in the night, but apart from maybe two times did she ever. I sometimes slept in the other room as I could not stand laying alongside her without making love to her. Lily started to say I was not a man; I could not look after her. The more I tried she would never give me any credit, she told me one day we would live in Ocala, but I told her unless she started showing me love and respect it was only a matter of time before we split up. I told her when she got her two million unless we were happy that she should take her two million and go and live in Ocala, I cannot live with someone who does not love me and show it. All the time I worked I was promoting my singing and my songs. Chuck and Wendy two very good friends to me and Lily were helping me with my singing they did flyers, ran a hot line for me, they were wonderful people to us both, but Lily backed off from their kindness. Lily was not used to the attention and affection people often showed me, she did not seem to like it. When I told her how close I was to my family it seemed to intimidate her, she would sometimes say why don't you go home to your family if you're so close and miss them, I felt very sad for Lily, she had not known the love of a family but I told Lily she had a family in England now she was married to me and one day we would go to the UK to see them, things seemed to get slowly better for me, I was working with Randy, Randy is a friend of Lily's, I was working part time but hoping to go full time soon, still promoting my songs and doing the odd singing telegram. Lily was now working for Extra at the flower department. When Lily bought my son and brother to the USA she helped me to take Craig to see Pluto in Orlando, she also helped me with my immigration by telling Mr David Kilpatrick she would pay him, I told Lily I would pay the money back to her for David Kilpatrick when I sold my house. She paid him $350 then two days before the final meeting with David and the immigration she told me she was not going to pay the rest, so I went to see Mr Kilpatrick at his office, I told him what Lily had said, I told him I would pay him from the house I had to sell, he told me no to worry he would wait. I also had a long talk to David about Lily's problems and mine; he was becoming a friend now. I was becoming happier with my life in general except for Lily just not seeming to be trying, Lily said she was having problems with her money that she had a lot of payments, but she always had the same payments, by me paying half she had to have been better off, but if I questioned her with what she was doing with her money she would show me a list of payments and say it was none of my business. Going back some time we were in Key West for a few days. Lily and I had words one night, she had been on the phone at 11pm to someone, it was a friend of mine, she was always upset when people phoned her late at night so I told her, what was she doing bothering people late at night? Lily said she was talking to Doug my friend about us. Lily never let me talk to her friends about us, she said that it was our business, no one else's. So I said once again a rule for her and a rule for me. We got into bed, at the hotel we had two beds in the room, she was in one I was in the other. I was really giving her a piece of my mind, she didn't like what I was saying, she told me to shut up but I told her to hear me out. When I continued to tell her she jumped off the bed and started hitting me, I told her to stop but she did not, I slapped her in my defence and the hope she would stop, I slapped her once, she did stop and then went back to her bed and to sleep. The next day we went on with our few days away. Lily can have a tantrum, shout, say nasty things, then twenty minutes later be all sweet and wonderful as if nothing had happened. Many months after we were married Lily was on the phone to someone, she asked me to sing a song to them over the phone, I did and we had a nice talk to those people. Her friends were telling us that some of Lily's friends had married. I asked Lily with my hand over the phone if they knew if we were married, Lily said no, but don't tell her because she had problems, she said she would tell me after the call. It was this friend that asked Lily how she was doing with the drugs. When the call was over I asked Lily why we could not tell her we were married and what were the problems her friend had, but Lily would not tell me. We then started to have words, Lily stood up started to unplug the TV with a big smile on her face, she said I'm going to show you something, she took the TV into the bedroom. I said Lily please don't do anything silly, don't do anything to hurt me. She took the TV into the bedroom and then locked the door, she would not put the TV back and would not open the door, I told her that I would kick the door if she would not open it, she found the whole thing funny and was laughing at me, so I told her I would count to three then I would kick the door in. I kicked the door, we had a small boom box that we kept the door open with, I was putting the boom box by the door when I turned it on by accident, she was stood shouting at me to turn it off because it came on loud straight away and in my frustration I dropped the boom box and it broke on the floor. She said look what you've done now, she then said she was going for a walk with the dog. When she came home she had the police with her. I could not believe what she had done. I talked to the police, they left, Lily thought it was funny and I was horrified, I thought what a sick thing to do. For the first time I became a little worried as to what Lily was capable of if she gets mad at you. I remember one day when she lived off USI she was walking her dog when someone's dog ran out barking. When she got home, she phoned a friend of hers, this friend's husband had something to do with the dog patrol. Lily told me to get in the car we went just round the corner as we passed the house she told me to take the number of the car where the dog ran from. She then phoned George with the number. He ran the numbers the next day, he told her the gentleman that owns the car has a record with drugs, he was an Alien to this country, she said I wonder if the immigration knows about his record. I said Lily, their dog only ran out barking, as long as they stop the dog doing that then leave them alone. Lily has a vindictive manner to her. Tell me what do you do, what can you say when you know deep inside this woman you love very dearly does not love you and you realise she married you for all the wrong reasons, but you really love this person, what do you do?

Lily and I did meet with Mick one day, we went to see him at the bus, the three of us sat in the car. Mick was high as we spoke to him, he told me she still loved him but it could never work. He said she was a perpetual liar and she was a dangerous woman. He also told me while I was married to her that Lily had phoned Mick saying that she wanted to maintain a relationship with him, she told him she would go down to see him, do cocaine and have sex, I was deeply hurt. When we left Micks bus Lily told me she had phoned Mick, but she was thinking of going to see him, do some cocaine and plant some on the bus, then she said she was going to leave and not have sex, then she was going to phone the police not saying who she was and that drugs were on the bus. For days I did not know what to think, once again my love for her pulled me through, how stupid I must have been! She also told me she had paid to have John Manning made a woman in jail by a black man. (Raped) I just thought she was making this up, she also said she was looking for someone to do John Manning harm when he got out, but I did not believe her, I thought she was just saying these things because they had hurt her. I now believe if you hurt Lily she is capable of anything to get back at you, I fear for my safety when I come out of jail.

Well things stayed the same for some time, one day up, the next we were down. I found myself crying some nights just wishing she would cuddle me, so many things happened with Lily I've not even put on this paper. On the night of my arrest we invited Chuck and Wendy to go out with us, they came to our home. I had a long phone call from my mother and some of my sisters. Lily was wanting to go out. I spoke to my mother and sisters for 45-50mins. Lily seemed a little on edge, Lily also talked to my family. We then watched a video of me, Chuck and Wendy had never seen this video nor had Lily. It was a song I wrote, me as a puppet with children, I love kids, Lily really was not too bothered. We then left to go to a pub, I was to sing a couple of songs for the owner as an audition, maybe I could sing for money sometimes for the owner. Lily kept pushing me, telling me to go sing, I had to tell her to calm down, I would get up and sing when the time was right. She was complaining about how cold it was while we had our food, so we all moved. Lily was in a strange mood, she was starting to get a little loud, Chuck and Wendy noticed more than me, I was thinking about the show I was soon to do, I went to talk to the band. Chuck and Wendy told me Lily seemed in a funny mood. When I had sang we left to go down to the 21000 Club Hotel. We loved this place, people got up and sang to Marria on the keyboards and piano, it was very popular here, Lily loved the attention we had. By this time Lily had been drinking, she wasn´t drunk but she was tipsy at the Mark 21000 she had two more drinks. I got up to sing, it went very well, Lily had during the night hinted to me that I was going to get lucky that night with sex Chuck and Wendy were with us, when we left we said goodbye to Chuck and Wendy outside. We then walked to our car, Lily pulled her sundress down showing me her breasts, I told her to stop it that we were outside and someone may see her. Lily found this funny and did it again and then again in the car smiling at me, I drove us home. Lily had had too much to drink, as we got near the apartment Lily woke up from her sleep and told me not to not even think about sex, I told her I didn´t want sex, I wanted to make love to my wife, light a candle, soft music. She said forget it. I told her here we go again, we've had a good night, and she had given me the come on all night. She even told Chuck and Wendy outside the 21000 Club Ricky was going to get laid. I told her maybe if I was Mick or one of her other boyfriends she would want to. We got out of the car; we were now really having words at the back of the car. I told Lily maybe if I was perverted, did cocaine, robbed and set fire to a bus, maybe if I had a gun to her head like one of her ex´s had done in the past. I told her everyone she had ever loved had treated her like dirt, that even her own family did not phone her or visit her. The back of the car was open and I was taking my double cassette player out of the car while I was saying all this. What I was saying was not nice but unfortunately it was all the truth. Lily took hold of my tape deck and threw it on the floor, as I tried to stop it hitting the floor she was coming down on me to hit me, the tape deck hit the floor and in my defence I slapped Lily on the face, this happened very quickly, Lily stood back as I took hold of my tape machine under one arm I had a black bag in the other hand, Lily hit me a few times, I just ducked her, she locked the car, she had a doggy bag with food in it. As we walked to the apartment shouting at each other she hit me, as we walked up the stairs she was hitting me over the back of

301

my head and neck with the doggy bag, the bag burst, she then took some spaghetti and was throwing it at me from behind as I walked up the stairs. At the top of the stairs I put the tape machine down and the bag, I walked down to her I picked up some spaghetti off the floor and put it in her face, I then turned around and walked up the stairs, before I got to the top, I slipped on the spaghetti, I fell on my right thigh but I grabbed the rail with my right hand, this stopped me falling down the stairs, Lily was coming up the stairs to my left but a step or two behind me, Lily also slipped on some spaghetti but Lily had no rail her side so she fell down the stairs and hit the rail at the bottom but she jumped up straight away and we were still shouting. I told her to go back to her perverted cocaine-sniffing husband so she could stuff her nose with cocaine with him, that they belonged together. Lily walked off down the street; I took the tape machine and black bag to my bedroom. I then looked through our living room window to see where she was, I thought she was just outside, but she was walking the street. I thought my god, she had no shoes on her feet and just a sundress on, she could be walking the street at that time of night like that in the area we lived. I was worried for her despite what happened between us over the months, I still loved her. So I went down the street to her, I told her to come home, that it wasn't safe for her to walk the street with nothing on her feet with just a sun dress on at that time of night but she would not come home, so I took her arm and started pulling her home but Lil is very strong, she was hitting me, so I tried to put her over my shoulder, like a fireman, but I could not hold her, she was shouting at me and trying to hit me. I told her to stop being stupid that she couldn't walk the streets like that and to come home, but no she was crazy, trying to hit me. I took hold of her hair, I held her at arms length so she could not hit me. I then led her home, she was still shouting and jumping around trying to hit me. I told her again stop being silly, that she was going home to bed. When I got her to the apartment, I took her to the bedroom, I told her to go to bed and sleep it off, I told her she could do whatever she wanted in the morning, that we were finished, I could no longer stand the way she was. I walked to the door, I told her I would sleep in the other room, she came at me shouting she was going to kill me. I push one hand on each of her shoulders and pushed her on the bed again telling her to sleep it off. I left the bedroom closing the door, I could hear her on the phone, so I walked back to the bedroom as I walked towards her she jumped on the bed shouting get away, leave me alone. I couldn´t understand why she did this, I was nowhere near her, I didn´t know she had put the recorder on the phone, I took the phone into the kitchen, I didn´t want her bothering people with our problems at that time of night. When I was in the kitchen I could hear her on the phone again, we have a phone you can still use like an intercom, by this time I walked into the bedroom she had called the police. The police were talking to her, Lily was making quiet a thing of the whole thing, so I just said out loud she could leave, I think I even said she could take a taxi. Lily left the apartment. I walked outside, she was walking down the street. I saw her shoes at the bottom of the stairs. I picked them up and brought them inside. On the way up the stairs, I picked up some of the spaghetti with my fingers. Within a short time the police came. They asked me what had happened; I told them we had a bust up. They asked me where she was; I said she had left the house. I changed my clothes to a vest and shorts. I phoned my friends Chuck and Wendy. I spoke with Chuck, I told him we had had a bust up and that I thought the police might be back, I told him some of what happened and that it was very heated. The police came back I was arrested. Each time the police came to the house it was all very gentlemanly. The police officer told me if he was in plain clothes he would have beat the shit out of me, I asked why, he said my wife had bruises on her, at that time I could not understand how, I had forgotten we had slipped on the stairs

303

with Lily jumping up straight away and walking off down the street, I did not know she was hurt. Even when I brought her home, because she was jumping about hitting me and shouting.

When I was in jail I met a young guy, his name Rich. He told me he was a vet at the Calder Race Track. I told him my wife used to be a jockey at that track. That me and Lily knew Shaun Musgrave a trainer and Brian Smeak, a trainer. He said that he knew them both and that he would be seeing Shaun the next morning. Rich was getting out, I told him to say hi to Shaun for me, he told me he would phone Lily to tell her how bad it was in the jail. Rich phoned her from the jail he spoke with Lily and asked me if I wished to speak to her. It was then Lily told me she was hurt, but she told me she loved me. I told her it was over between us, that I loved her but I could stand no more, she told me, we'd be friends. Lily asked me to phone her back in 10-15 mins because she'd got a call coming in. When I phoned back she was joking what a great spaghetti fight we had. I was very shocked to hear her making light, I said it's not funny, I was in jail. She told me she was going to drop the charges but she was taking an order out for me to stay away from her. I told her she did not need to do that, that I did not want to see her again. She told me she would send my things to England, I told her no I was staying in Florida, that she was not to touch my things, that someone would collect them. I had an order to stay away given to me in jail. Wendy the next day had a phone call from Lily, Lily was upset saying what was I doing calling Calder Race Track, Rich must have said hi to Shaun, Shaun had phoned Lily, but Lily thought I had called the track. Lily became different from then on.

# Acknowledgements

I would like to take this opportunity to thank Mr and Mrs Norman, Chuck and Wendy. From day one of meeting these wonderful and loving people and their beautiful family, I experienced love, devotion and honesty at a level that would be extremely hard to come across anywhere in the world.

They supported me though my trauma and were a crucial link to my brother John in the UK. They visited me in jail and put funds in a kitty for me while I was in custody, they came to court to be my witnesses and they both came to visit me in the UK because I was banned from travelling the USA. Years later they even came to Spain to visit me with their daughter. I love them both dearly and it's my dream to visit them in the USA with my beautiful family, my name cleared, an innocent and respected man.

I would like to thank Randy Reynolds for his hard work throughout and his devoted friendship and despite the fact he was a friend of my Lily's, came to court to testify on my behalf. Randy did this despite being afraid Lily may damage his property. He's an absolute gentleman and a true friend, thank you Randy.

Another thank you goes to another wonderful friend Doug Santi, who gave me a room in his home when Donna kicked me out onto the street. Doug treated me like a brother, I love him dearly. Doug was also in court to support me and testify against Lily Barron, I hope very much to meet Doug once again when I finally make it to the USA.

Sari Mitchell is another person, a wonderful loving lady, a dear friend to me, she also came to court to support me and testify against Lilly Barron. Sari was a brilliant kid's entertainer and a wonderful human being. It never failed to upset me what all these people had to witness.

I would like to thank the author Ken Scott, who is an absolute gentleman and helped me through what was an immense achievement for me. He's met with me on many occasions, and constantly supported and encouraged me to continue to write this book and to finally bring it to a conclusion. I think its fair to say the book would never have been finished if it wasn't for Ken as every time I read it back I wanted to add and change things. He taught me so much, and helped me with finding a publisher too, thank you so much Ken!

One of his books, "Do The Birds Still Sing in Hell?" is a must read, one of the best I've ever read and is being turned into a movie next year, please check out Kens website and his other books.

www.kentheghost.com

Now another thank you, to Hayley, who had the near impossible job of editing everything that my partner Cheryle has typed up. I had the pleasure of meeting up with Hayley on many occasions to discuss my book. Hayley made me feel so comfortable and totally at ease. Slowly but surely Hayley ground through every page, thank you Hayley for your hard work.

I would also like to thank Big Steve as he was responsible for making my flyers, a really nice guy, very helpful and I am very happy with the flyers, if you need flyers contact what's going on Benidorm at bigstevecat@ntlworld.co.uk

So can you imagine the huge thank you, I owe to my beautiful partner Cheryle? Words cannot describe how much I am in her debt. Initially I wrote by hand page after page of this horrendous story and shared it with the love of my life, even when, I suppose she'd had enough of it and had more important things to do. I took her through all the traumas I had been subjected to; she was my crutch and my shoulder to cry on. I'm not a writer, I know that, the hand written volume was badly written, messy, poor spelling and grammatically woeful but slowly over a three year period she typed up what was essential for this book to ever make it to this stage. I love her dearly along with Brandon and also my other son Craig in the UK. Between them all they have carried me over the finishing line.

If you read my book and it impacts upon you please leave an Amazon review and mention it on your Facebook and Twitter pages. If you feel very strongly about what I have been through, contact the American Embassy, protest, tell them this should not have happened and remind them by law you are in fact innocent until proven guilty and not the other way round.

I'll never forget the police officers face as he made that statement to me. He was smiling; a wicked grin etched across his face and the image comes to me again and again in my nightmares. He was shaking his head as he spat it out. "Guilty until you prove yourself innocent, welcome to America."


# And Finally...


The world is a more dangerous place these days, but still we fight for what we believe is right. In recent years we have witnessed the slaying of the Libyan leader Colonel Gaddaffi, after an uprising by his own people, Bin laden is dead as is Saddam Hussein, collaboration between their own countrymen and the USA. I never thought I´d live to see these things.

More recently Syria and Iran are now ticking time bombs and North Korea have joined in the sabre rattling almost daring the Superpowers to take action against them.

Just recently a young solider was hacked to death in London street, the photographs and video footage available via the internet for all to see. Everyone I speak to have been very moved by the unprovoked slaughter of Drummer Lee Rigby, our hearts go out to his family, how does a family come to terms with such an event?

Almost daily, there are hundreds and thousands of soldiers and civilians killed throughout the world by suicide bombers, terrorists, extremists, dictators and militia and dare I say it, so called civilised governments.

There are more than a dozen conflicts being fought world wide as we speak, some justified to liberate downtrodden people, giving them the chance to live in freedom. There are other battles going on too, battles for justice, wars to protect human rights and freedom, the right to a fair trial.

What happened to me in the courts of America is an insult to every single person who has been killed or seriously wounded believing they were fighting for a just cause. To some my case may seem like a none event and to many it will be but at the end of the day my fight is no less significant than the US Marine fighting in a foreign land for what he believes is right, no less significant to the undercover operative infiltrating a corrupt African regime or the weapon inspectors in Syria who believes that he is standing up for what is right in trying to prevent a despot carrying out genocide against his own people.

To me, my fight for justice is just as important because it's about what is right and wrong and it's about liberty and justice in the so called 'Land of the Free.'

The American Legal Judicial System failed me and attorneys such as Mr. Roque got fat and rich betraying the very foundation to which they swore an oath.

In an ideal world I would like Mr. Obama (I have written to him.) to have a public enquiry, assign someone to investigate my case and bring these criminals to justice on behalf of not only the American people but show the world no matter who you are you are innocent until proven guilty.

In closing I finish on an interesting point. I have asked a personal friend in America to look up my criminal record there and he found nothing registered against me on both the criminal and immigration records.

And yet still I am branded, even to this day a menace to society and a dangerous man, and yet... no public record against me. The US Embassy in Madrid has told me categorically that I can never return to the United States.

I am haunted by my traumatic time in the hands of the Criminal Judicial System in the USA and still, on occasion I break down in tears when I'm alone, for no particular reason than I know I have been wronged and hung out to dry, ignored in the hope that I may somehow simply disappear and stop fighting. But I won't rest until something is done, until I get closure on this particular part of my life.

I will stay strong and keep fighting and believe me this book is just the start. I've started to hand out thousands of flyers relating to the book and have radio and TV interviews lined up after the launch party.


I sing most evenings and at the end of my act tell my audience about the book and my experience in America. They are more than a little sympathetic. I will get justice, believe me I will, wouldn't you if you'd been lied to, swindled, coned, cheated on, robbed, beaten up, had your career destroyed and mentally scarred for life?

The only reason why I hang around is to see what happens next!

# Last But Not Least

A few words from the girl who knows me best of all.

I know my fiancé better than anyone after living with him for over 11 years. I know the heartache he has been through and yet you will never meet a more committed man in every sense of the word, he has been the driving force and the rock I have needed through our life together especially in the hard times and he has been the greatest Dad our beautiful son could ever have wished for

I know the price he still pays today after meeting and marrying the wrong women. He struggles on a day to day basis with the psychological effects of being locked up for a crime he did not commit. Lily clearly set him up, it´s plain as day to see, and yet the US Legal system couldn't see it and failed him in every sense of the word. They treated him appallingly, and kept him locked up for weeks on end with no communication, no help from anyone, stuck in a prison with child sex offenders and murderers, drug dealers and rapists. It's enough to destroy a decent human being for the rest of his life and believe me it has all taken its toll on poor Ricky.

The American Legal System cannot be allowed to get away with such a crime; no innocent human being should be treated in such a terrible way. Ricky still cries when he thinks back to the inhumane way he was treated and forgotten about and the awful memories haunt him every single day. In the 11 years we´ve been together, of course we´ve had our arguments, that's normal, but I´ve never seen any violence, not even a hint of it. Ricky is the most gentle human being on the planet and would go out of his way to help anyone. He is certainly not a menace to society, which he has been labeled. He is the most dedicated partner and father anyone could wish for. It has been very difficult for me to see him go through all of this as he wrote

310

this book but I am also incredibly proud of him for doing so, (Well done Love!!) All he needs now is some closure, the closure he deserves by getting the justice he should have had in the first place! Until that day comes we will be thankful that we are simply happy together as a family and will get on with our lives with our son Brandon. I pray daily that Ricky will get the justice he deserves and perhaps when that day finally arrives he will finally be able to enjoy a thoroughly deserved uninterrupted nights sleep.

*Cheryle Louise Hipkiss*

CPSIA information can be obtained at www.ICGtesting.com
Printed in the USA
LVOW06s1523110914

403633LV00016B/757/P

9 781783 334292